SAYING WHAT YOU MEAN

BOOKS BY ROBERT CLAIBORNE

TIME (1967)
DRUGS (1969)
CLIMATE, MAN AND HISTORY (1970)
ON EVERY SIDE THE SEA (1971)
THE FIRST AMERICANS (1973)
GOD OR BEAST: Evolution and Human Nature (1974)
THE BIRTH OF WRITING (1975)
THE SUMMER STARGAZER: Astronomy for Absolute Beginners (1975)
MYSTERIES OF THE PAST, with Lionel Casson and Brian Fagen (1977)
OUR MARVELOUS NATIVE TONGUE: The Life and Times of
the English Language (1983)
SAYING WHAT YOU MEAN: A Commonsense Guide to American Usage

TEXTS

MEDICAL GENETICS, with Victor McKusick, M.D. (1973)
CELL MEMBRANES, with Gerald Weissmann, M.D. (1974)

SAYING WHAT YOU MEAN

A Commonsense Guide to American Usage

ROBERT CLAIBORNE

W· W· NORTON & COMPANY
New York   *London*

Published simultaneously in Canada by Penguin Books Canada Ltd,
2801 John Street, Markham, Ontario L3R 1B4
Printed in the United States of America.

The text of this book is composed in Baskerville. Composition and
manufacturing by The Haddon Craftsmen, Inc.
Book design by Jacques Chazaud.

Library of Congress Cataloging-in-Publication Data

Claiborne, Robert.
Saying what you mean.

Bibliography: p.
Includes index.
1. English language—United States—Usage—Diction-
aries. 2. English language—Usage—Dictionaries.
I. Title
PE2835.C58 1986   428′.00973   86-5334

ISBN 0-393-02312-5

W. W. Norton & Company, Inc., 500 Fifth Avenue, New York, N. Y. 10110
W. W. Norton & Company Ltd., 37 Great Russell Street, London WC1B 3NU

CONTENTS

ACKNOWLEDGMENTS

Many people helped in the writing of this book. Pride of place goes to my daughter, Amanda Claiborne Schulman, who with Mark Sherman, of Columbia University, carried out the laborious job of collating and indexing the source materials I have drawn on. Without their work, the writing would have taken months longer than it did. No less helpful was my sister, Clara Claiborne Park, Professor of English at Williams College, who read the entire manuscript and made many useful comments and suggestions. Thanks are also due my editor, Starling Lawrence, my agent, Peter Skolnick, and especially my copy editor, Otto Sonntag, who labored hard and long to ensure that the text contained only those "grammatical errors" that I wanted.

Here seems an appropriate place to express my gratitude to some of the many people, living and dead, who over the years, in person or through their writings, have stimulated and encouraged my interest in language and helped me sharpen my skills in using it: my mother, Virginia McKenney Claiborne; Frederick Dixon, former Principal of Charlotte Amalie High School, Virgin Islands; Frederick V. Fassett, Jr., former Professor of English at Massachusetts Institute of Technology, and Eda Lou Walton, Edwin Berry Burgum and Margaret Schlauch, former Professors of English at Washington Square College, New York University.

Later aid or comfort came from Gerard Piel, former publisher (and editor in all but name) of *Scientific American,* and, most of all, from Eric Partridge, author of *A Dictionary of Slang and Unconventional English* and many other invaluable works on our native tongue, whose friendship is warmly remembered and sorely missed. Special thanks are due, as always, to Sybil, my wife.

The manuscript for this book was written on a Kaypro 4 microcomputer, using the Perfect Writer (Version 1.20) word-processing program, with Plu*Perfect and Smartkey II enhancements; spelling was checked with Perfect Speller and The Word Plus. The printout was made on a Silver-Reed EXP 550, linked to the computer through a Quadram Microfazer 64K buffer.

New York and Truro, 1983–85

SAYING WHAT YOU MEAN

INTRODUCTION

What Is "Good English"—and Who Says So?

Writing is the making of meaning, first, last and always:
it is other things only because it is this.

—C. H. KNOBLAUCH AND LIL BRANNON

Walk into any large bookstore and you can pick up half a dozen books on English usage. All of them deal with the same subject —"good English"—and all of them identify certain words, word usages or grammatical constructions as "good" and others as "bad."

Curiously, however, few of them will tell you much (if anything) about *why* a given word or construction is good or bad. For some, the meaning of "good English," like the proposition that all men are created equal, is self-evident. Other authors (those of an authoritarian temperament) describe usages they dislike as **SUBSTANDARD,*** **ILLITERATE*** or worse—which are, of course, merely different words for "bad." Still others dodge the question by collecting a panel of usage experts (some of whom are real experts, but all of whom have "name recognition") and polling them: if a majority says it's good, it's good; if not, not. (For examples of these different approaches to usage, consult the Bibliography.)

*Words in **BOLDFACE CAPITALS** refer to entries in the body of the text, which can be consulted for further information.

This is O.K. if you're willing to take the author's (or the panel's) word for it. It is not so O.K. when you discover (as you will, if you dig a little deeper into the subject) that the authors of different books don't always agree. As for usage panels—is the majority always right? (It certainly isn't in politics!) What about a bare majority? In short, just whose word are you supposed to take?

It is even less O.K. if you happen to encounter an authority such as Prof. Robert A. Hall of Cornell University, who will tell you that "there is no such thing as good and bad (or correct and incorrect, grammatical and ungrammatical, right and wrong) in language." If *he*'s right, then all the authors who've been trying to define "good English" have been hunting the Snark—and reading them has been a waste of time.

I believe—for reasons we'll get to shortly—that Hall is wrong: there *is* such a thing as good English. This view is certainly not original, nor is it—to me, anyway—of much interest in itself. The really interesting questions are what good English is, and who says so, and on what grounds.

Many of us, asked to define "good English," would say "grammatical English"; others would say "educated" or "Standard" English, which to most people means about the same thing. Both these statements are true, but they are only half-truths. And even to the extent they're true, they don't really tell you very much, since they raise as many questions as they answer. If good English is grammatical English, what is "grammatical" and who defines it? If it's Standard English, who sets the standard?

To take the first question first, the commonest meaning of "grammatical" English is English that conforms to the rules set forth by grammarians in their books. But what if the grammarians disagree—as they sometimes do? And what about the time, only a few centuries ago, when English grammars didn't exist: did Shakespeare and his contemporaries, with no grammars to tell them what was right, all speak and write bad (or at least inferior) English?

Curiously, a few writers (notably the critic John Simon) say just about that. Simon holds that our grammar is "better" than that of Shakespeare and the other Elizabethans; indeed, he believes that English, over the centuries, evolved from "chaos" to a state of near-perfection. It achieved this happy condition (so far as one can judge from his writings) around the time of World War II—oddly enough, just about the time Simon himself was learning English (his native tongue is Serbo-Croatian, though he speaks several others). Since then, it's been downhill all the way: "verbal pollution, linguistic corruption, cultural erosion."

Anyone having even a nodding acquaintance with scientific linguistics—which deals with (among other things) how languages develop and change—knows that the idea of English or any other grammar evolving from chaos to perfection is, quite simply, nonsense. Neither English nor any other language was ever chaotic (meaning without rules), because without rules nobody could have learned it. And these rules, which collectively we call grammar, existed long before grammarians began writing books about them, just as the law of gravity existed long before Newton wrote his *Principia Mathematica.*

Grammar—the rules by which languages are constructed—is, like Caesar's Gaul, divided into three parts. **Phonetics** specifies which sounds and groups of sounds can be used to make words, and where in the word (beginning, middle, end) they can be used. The human vocal apparatus can produce well over a hundred distinguishable sounds, but no language uses as many as fifty of them (English uses about forty).

Phonetic limitations are even more stringent when it comes to *combinations* of sounds. Thus English consonants can, in theory, be paired in some five hundred different ways, but only fifty of these pairs are actually used to begin English words.

Even leaving out the "forbidden" sounds and sound sequences in a given language, we are still left with hundreds of millions of phonetically possible combinations. Of these, however, only a small fraction are real words (in English, something like half a million; in other languages, a good deal less than that). **Semantics** or **vocabulary** specifies which of the "permitted" sound sequences in a language actually mean something, and what they mean.

Just as most sound sequences aren't meaningful words, so most word sequences aren't meaningful statements. **Syntax** specifies how words (and other linguistic elements, such as **INFLEC-TIONS**, prefixes and suffixes) can be combined to actually say something.

At each step, therefore, the rules of grammar sharply reduce the number of possibilities; indeed, a major function of these rules is to reduce the almost limitless possibilities of the human vocal apparatus to a number small enough for the human brain to use in communication. Without such limitations, language could not exist: if any combination of sounds could mean anything, we'd end up saying nothing.

A central fact about grammatical rules is that they are in no way "logical" or "reasonable." For example, there is nothing about the word "cat" that either looks or sounds like the furry animal that is rubbing against my legs as I write this, and the same goes for its equivalents, such as the Spanish *gato* and the German *Katze.* Likewise, there is no rational explanation of why, in an English sentence, the verb normally follows its subject as closely as possible, while in German the verb often at the end of the sentence falls. Neither of these arrangements (nor any of the hundreds of other ways in which sentences are constructed) is any more "logical" than the other; they just exist.

Grammars are illogical because they were devised by people, not grammarians. That is, they evolved, over thousands or tens of thousands of years, among different groups who "agreed"— quite unconsciously, of course—to use sounds in certain ways to say certain things. Very few of us are aware of the complicated rules that govern our native tongue, or could specify them if asked: we pick them up automatically in childhood, in much the same way as we learn to walk. (Could you describe the intricate series of muscular movements that occurs every time you take a step?) But the fact that we aren't consciously aware of the rules doesn't prevent us from using them to communicate with our fellows—provided that *they* are using the same set of rules.

Often, they aren't—*even though they are speaking the "same" language as we are.* In fact, if you think about it for a moment, you'll realize that the phrase "English grammar" is something of an abstraction: different groups of English speakers use somewhat different sets of rules—that is, different grammars.

Anyone who's ever seen a British movie or TV program knows that British phonetics are not the same as ours—that is, Britishers don't pronounce most words as we do. Indeed, pronunciation differs even from one group of Britishers to another. Such differences form the main plot element in the musical comedy *My Fair Lady* and Shaw's play, *Pygmalion,* from which it was adapted: Eliza Doolittle and her disgraceful parent clearly spoke a very different kind of English from that of Professor Higgins and Colonel Pickering. Similar phonetic differences, of course, occur within the United States: a Texan doesn't sound like a Californian, and neither one sounds like a a New Yorker or a Cape Codder.

As with phonetics, so with vocabulary and syntax. The British put their bags in the *boot* of a car and use a *spanner* when they have to change a tire; we put ours in the *trunk* and use a *wrench.* Likewise, the British often say that American English is different *to* British English; we say that the two are different *from* one another (see **DIFFERENT FROM**). And, just as with phonetics, we find variations in syntax and vocabulary within both countries as well as between them.

All these varieties of English, defined by somewhat different grammars, are known as dialects. To many people, "dialect" means a regional variety of a language, especially if it differs from the "standard" version of that language. In fact, the term also applies to the varieties spoken by different social or ethnic groups within a region—as with Eliza and the Professor. American social dialects include "educated" or Standard English (roughly, the dialect of Americans with a college education), "uneducated" or blue-collar English, and Black English (the dialect of some but by no means all American blacks). And all of these also vary from one region to another.

English grammar doesn't just change from one region or social group to another; it also changes from one time to another. Six hundred years ago, for instance, such words as "know" and "gnaw" were pronounced as spelled; today the K and G are silent —indeed, the consonant pairs KN and GN are "forbidden" in modern English. New words come into the vocabulary and old ones drop out or change their meaning: "nice" originally meant "silly," "deer" meant an animal of any kind, and "soluble"—I'm not making this up—meant "not subject to constipation." Anyone who's read Shakespeare knows that his syntax is not identical with ours; for example, when Polonius asks Hamlet "What do you read . . . ?" we'd say "What are you reading?"—or perhaps "Whacha readin?"

Thus English grammar, whether we examine it in space or in time, is not one set of rules but many sets. And from the scientific standpoint, any set of rules that is used (or was used) by a substantial number of native English speakers is (or was) just as "grammatical"—if the term means anything here—as the others. The only people who truly speak ungrammatical English are those foreigners who, having learned the grammar of their own tongue in childhood, have trouble adjusting to the rather different grammar of ours.

With these facts in hand—and let me stress that they *are* facts, not my or anyone else's opinion—let us take another look at some of the ideas we've already discussed. First, "grammatical" in the scientific sense evidently means something much broader and more diverse than "grammatical" in the schoolteacher's or usage expert's sense. But—the fact that English grammar varies from place to place and from time to time does *not* mean that 'there ain't no such animal," as Professor Hall seems to be saying.

(People vary a good deal too—but that doesn't mean that there's no such thing as a human being.) If, for example, we recast Polonius's question "What do you read?" not as "What are you reading?" but as "You what reading?" we have constructed a sentence that no native English speaker would use, or would ever have used. The sentence follows the rules of *no* English grammar, present or past; that is, it's "ungrammatical" by definition.

Many people, of course, use "grammatical" in a much narrower sense. In their view, the question "Whacha readin?" is ungrammatical, even though it is used normally and naturally by tens of millions of native English speakers. To such people, there is only one kind of grammatical English: the kind that is taught in some schools and enshrined in some textbooks—which usually turns out to be the kind they use themselves.

Most of these people are merely using the word "grammatical" in the popular rather than the scientific sense, but some are out-and-out snobs: that is, they are saying or implying that the only "good" English is the English they and their friends use. Such language snobbery is an old story: it existed in Shakespeare's day, when one critic advised writers to "take the usuall speach of the Court," which he defined as the upper-class "speach" of London and the surrounding region. Elsewhere in England, he declared, even gentlemen "condescend" (lower) their speech to that of "the common people." Shaw, who had such fun satirizing linguistic snobbery in *Pygmalion,* once remarked acidly: "It is impossible for an Englishman to open his mouth without making some other Englishman hate or despise him."

He was not exaggerating: in Shaw's England (and to a considerable extent even today), the dialect of the English upper classes was seen as the only "proper" English; all other dialects—regional as well as social—were "low." People talked of "off-white" (not-quite-upper-class) accents in much the same terms as they talked of "half-caste" (not-quite-white) people. And this view was not (as you might think) limited to the upper classes themselves;

it was shared by many Britishers of other classes—witness Eliza's desire to "learn to talk proper."

Nor is linguistic snobbery unknown in our own country. People speaking certain regional dialects are often expected to fit regional stereotypes; thus many Americans will assume that a man speaking "Texian" must be a macho wheeler-dealer, though he may in fact be a university professor who writes poetry. And educated people in any region often consider the use of "ungrammatical" (i.e., uneducated or blue-collar) English as a mark of intellectual or even moral inferiority—apparently on the assumption that people speaking such dialects are either too stupid or too lazy to learn to talk properly.

In recent years, this sort of snobbism has begotten a reaction, often called "linguistic populism." The populists—many of them academics and educators—claim that all dialects (i.e., grammars), including blue-collar English and Black English, are equally "good." Their conclusion: schools should not teach Standard English at all.

A few of them go even further. Inspired by what I'd call half-assed and quarter-understood Marxism, they portray attempts to teach the grammar of Standard English as some sort of ruling-class conspiracy. Grammatical rules (in the words of two such "Marxists") are "the property of a once privileged minority class imposing its order on a willing majority." The statement is, of course, nonsensical on its face (how, for instance, do you "impose" something on "willing" people?). More important, the grammar of Standard English, whatever else it may be, is not anybody's property, any more than French grammar is the property of the French; both "belong" to anyone willing and able to learn them.

Yet the linguistic populists, apart from their tiny lunatic fringe, are addressing themselves to real problems—though not, I think, very thoughtfully. They say, for example, that "children have a right to their own language" (i.e., dialect)—hence should not be forced (in school) to learn another "language." The first statement is reasonable enough, but also, I think, trivial: children have always exercised the "right" to use their own dialects among themselves, and always will, regardless of what teacher says. But this fact tells us nothing about whether, *in their own interest,* they need to learn a second dialect—specifically, Standard English.

The linguistic populists are also saying something rather more important: that people should not be considered inferior simply because they don't speak educated or Standard English— a view both humane and sensible, and one that I certainly can't quarrel with. Common decency and common sense alike demand that we judge what people say by whether it makes sense, not by whether it is phrased in certain prescribed ("grammatical") ways. People who speak "ungrammatical" English do so for the same reason that Chinese people speak Chinese: they learned it at their mother's (and father's) knee, and from their playmates. Speaking the language or dialect you grew up with doesn't make you good or bad—just human.

To be sure, there are a fair number of people in this country —and elsewhere—who sneer at foreigners because they talk "funny." Most of us, however, are a bit more sophisticated, especially if we've traveled abroad: we know that if foreigners sound funny to us, we sound just as funny to them when we're grappling with *their* language. Obviously it's no less silly to sneer at people because their *dialects* differ from ours.

Again, however, the linguistic populists have moved from a reasonable premise to an irrelevant conclusion: the fact that *people* are equally good (or equally bad), whatever dialect they speak, does *not* mean that the dialects themselves are equally "good." Before making any such judgment, we must first ask: good for what? The only sensible answer is: good for communication, because communication—the giving and getting of information —is what language is about.

If you've ever been unlucky enough to find yourself among people whose language you couldn't speak, and who didn't speak yours, you'll know immediately what I'm talking about: you couldn't tell them what you needed or wanted—or understand what they needed or wanted from you. It is our ability, through language, to share our needs, ideas, plans and feelings with our fellows that makes human cooperation and human societies possible; in a very real sense, it is what makes us human.

If communication is the test—or anyway *a* test—of good English, then evidently all dialects of English are *not* created equal. Some are more useful for communication than others—and (to complicate things even more) different ones communicate better in different circumstances.

Communication, whether we're talking about the sound waves of speech, the light waves bouncing off a printed page or the radio waves of broadcast speech, always involves at least two people: a sender and a receiver. And unless the sender and receiver are "tuned in" to one another, communication will be blocked. That is, if A is trying to convey information to B, his (or her) success will depend, not just on what he says and how he says it, but on how well B can understand what he's saying.

The extreme case, of course, is when A and B speak different languages. But the same principle applies, though to a lesser degree, if they speak different dialects of the same language. Here *some* communication will probably take place—but how much will depend on how different the dialects are. A may be saying, in his dialect, precisely what he means—yet B, speaking a different dialect, may receive only a blurred notion of what A is getting at.

Or sometimes a completely clear but wholly mistaken notion, as in the old story of the American woman in London who was shocked when a young Englishman told her "I'll come over and knock you up when I get my screw." (American translation: "I'll come around and call on you when I get my pay.")

Then there was the professor of linguistics who worked in a shipyard during World War II, and found (as he reported later) that "Would you please hand me that wrench?" was much less effective, as communication, then "Hey, gimme the fuckin wrench." As I myself learned at the same time and in much the same way, there are times and places where "nonstandard" English is standard—and if you want to communicate effectively, you'd better learn it.

Evidently, then, what constitutes "good" (clear) English depends on who (or whom) you're talking to (see **WHO/WHOM**). But does this mean we must master the diverse dialects of *all* the different kinds of people we may have occasion to talk to or (even worse) write to or for? Not quite.

When it comes to communication—especially written communication—with a broad variety of Americans, one American dialect is quite definitely better than the rest: the one generally called Standard American English (SAE). It is better, not because a majority of American speak it (they don't) or because using it is a mark of intellectual or moral superiority (it isn't), but because *nearly all Americans, if they understand written English at all, understand it.* No other American dialect is anything like this widely known.

American books, magazines and newspapers are written (apart from dialogue passages) in SAE. The governmental and corporate bureaucracies we must all deal with from time to time communicate in SAE (though often confusingly—see **BUREAU-CRATESE**). And the directions and manuals that come with the innumerable products and gadgets that enrich or complicate our lives are written in SAE (though often ineptly).

In short, SAE is "better" than other varieties of American English because—and only because—with it we can get information from and give information to far more of our fellow countrymen and -women than we can with any other American dialect. If communication's the game, SAE's the name.

So far, so good. But precisely what *is* Standard English—and who sets the standard? This problem has exercised the minds of scholars and critics for at least five hundred years, and they still don't completely agree.

The first person to deal with the question (though he didn't use the term "Standard English") was England's first printer, William Caxton. Like several generations of printers after him, Caxton doubled as editor, publisher, bookseller and, where necessary, translator. It was under the last of these hats that he confronted the question of what kind of English would be both clear and acceptable to his readers. In the preface to his translation of Virgil's Latin epic *The Aeneid,* he described the problem in a witty passage that is worth quoting at some length. (I've modernized his spelling, punctuation and, in a few places, his syntax.)

Having translated a few pages of the poem, says Caxton, he then "oversaw" what he had written in order to correct it.

> But when I saw the fair and strange terms therein, I doubted that it would please some gentlemen who late[ly] blamed me, saying that in translations I have [used] overcurious terms which could not be understood by common people, and desired me to use old and homely terms in my translations. And fain would I satisfy every man, and to do so took an old book and read therein, and certainly the English was so rude and broad that I could not well understand it. . . . Certainly our language now used varies far from that which was used and spoken when I was born.

Moreover, he notes, the English in common use varies from one part of England to another. As an example, he tells a tale of a London merchant who found himself in Kent—less than a hundred miles from his home—and asked at a farmhouse for eggs. The farmer's wife replied that "she could speak no French"—which considerably annoyed the merchant, since he too knew no French; he was speaking perfectly good London English, but "she understood him not." Eventually it occurred to one of his companions to ask for "eyren" (the Kentish term)—and immediately the lady understood what was wanted. "Lo, what should a man in these days now write," Caxton enquires quizzically, " 'eggs' or 'eyren'?"

Certainly [he continues] it is hard to please every man, by reason of diversity and change of language. For in these days every man that is [of] any reputation . . . will utter his communications and matters in such manners and terms that few men shall understand them. And some honest and great clerks [i.e., scholars] have been with me, and desired me to write the most curious terms that I could find. And thus, between plain, rude and curious, I stand abashed. But in my judgment the common terms that are daily used are lighter [i.e., easier] to be understood than the old and ancient English.

It is no coincidence that Caxton was a printer, for it was printing that had made the question of standardizing English really urgent. In earlier times, books were of course copied by hand, meaning that they were few and expensive—nor could most people read them anyway. Thus nearly all communication was by word of mouth, meaning that the "communicators" were likely to be using the same dialect—and even if they weren't, misunderstandings (as with the merchant and the eggs) could be cleared up quickly, if not always amicably.

Printers, however, were producing books for hundreds—eventually, thousands—of readers, quite possibly speaking different dialects, *whom they would seldom if ever meet face to face.* If the language of a book was unclear, that was just too bad for the reader—and worse for the printer, since he stood a good chance of losing a customer. Caxton, the very first printer in England, was shrewd enough to see the problem—and, even more remarkably, to diagnose its causes: "diversity and change of language."

By "diversity" he meant what we call dialects, both regional —for example, London "eggs" vs. Kentish "eyren"—and social —the "homely terms" proposed by some of his readers vs. the "curious" words favored by the scholars, "which could not be understood by common people." (Some scholars clearly haven't changed much since the fifteenth century.) He was no less aware of linguistic change—the fact that the English of his day differed considerably from the "rude and broad" language of some old books and, indeed, had altered noticeably even during his own lifetime. (We now know that in his day English was changing very rapidly, though nobody knows why.)

Ever since Caxton, printers, editors and critics, faced with the continuing "diversity and change of language," have been trying to define "good English"—to decide, in effect, whether they (and we) should say "eggs" or "eyren." All in all, they have made a fairly good job of it. English spelling, though unquestionably confusing in many ways, has been standardized, apart from a few differences between Great Britain and the United States (our "color" and "theater" vs. their "colour" and "theatre," for instance). So, to a considerable extent, have vocabulary and syntax, though here too (as we've seen) Standard American English differs in minor ways from Standard British English.

Yet the critics still don't wholly agree on what is Standard and what isn't. One reason is the continuing influence (conscious or otherwise) of social snobbery, a subject we've already examined briefly and will hear more about later. Even more important, perhaps, is that most of them have started with a false assumption (again, conscious or otherwise): that definitions of "good usage" can be permanent.

The fallacy is an old one, dating from at least the early eighteenth century, when the well-known writer and critic Jonathan Swift declared that he could "see no absolute necessity why any language should be perpetually changing." Since change was not only unnecessary but also (as he saw it) distinctly undesirable, he concluded that it should be halted. To that end, he proposed the formation of a royal academy, along the lines of the recently formed Académie Française, whose declared aim was "to give definite rules to [the French] language"—and permanent ones. (The Académie never succeeded, though it's still trying.)

Now, Swift, one of the best-read men of his time (ca. 1700), knew perfectly well that his English was not the English of Shakespeare (ca. 1600), which in turn was not the English of Caxton (ca. 1500) or—even less—of Chaucer (ca. 1400). How on earth could he have supposed that a language which had been "perpetually changing" in the past could be prevented from doing so in the future?

The most likely explanation is that the wish was father to the thought. Swift was deeply **CONSERVATIVE** in politics and, like most true conservatives at any period (as distinguished from today's "radical conservatives"), resisted change of any sort, feeling that it would almost certainly be for the worse. In addition, like later conservatives, he looked back to the Good Old Days when life was supposedly better and language had not been "corrupted" from its original, supposedly "pure," state.

A detailed critique of the "Good Old Days" theory (or illusion) would take us beyond the scope of this book. Worth noting, however, is that in language, at least, the location in time of those wonderful days keeps changing. The critic Ben Jonson, writing in the early 1600s, felt that the best English was that of Chaucer (d. 1400); a century later, Swift believed that the purest English was that of Jonson and his contemporaries, and in another century the ideal had become the English of Swift and *his* contemporaries. John Simon, as we've seen, apparently believes that the English he learned in the 1930s was better than any of them—and *much* better than that of the 1970s.

The truth is that nobody has ever offered any evidence that English was "better" at any time in the past, or that changes in its grammar have in any way "corrupted" or otherwise damaged it. Shakespeare was surely the greatest writer the English language (some would say, any language) has ever produced. But he was great not because he wrote better English than we do but because he wrote English better—a distinction that is important enough to think about for a minute. Equally, if many modern Americans fail to communicate effectively in speech or writing, the reason is not that modern American English is bad or "corrupt" but that they use it badly.

Swift's proposal for an academy was debated pro and con for several decades; some more liberal men of letters called the idea "unworthy of the genius of a free people" (neither then nor later did most Englishmen take kindly to self-appointed authorities, in language or anything else). But the coup de grace, in 1755, came not from any liberal but from Dr. Samuel Johnson, as conservative as Swift and his successor as a sort of one-man supreme court of English letters.

In the preface to his famous dictionary, Johnson noted that he had begun the work in the expectation that it "should fix our language, and put a stop to those alterations which time and chance have hitherto been suffered to make in it." Experience, however, had taught him better: "We laugh at the elixir that promises to prolong life for a thousand years; and with equal justice may the lexicographer be derided, who being able to produce no example of a nation that has preserved their words and phrases from mutability, shall imagine that his dictionary can embalm his language, and secure it from corruption and decay."

Johnson, as I've already noted, was every bit as conservative as Swift, as witness his intimation that change in language was equivalent to "corruption and decay." But he was far more realistic. Linguistic change might be a Bad Thing, but he recognized that neither he nor anyone else could prevent it: "sounds are too volatile and subtile [*sic*] for legal restraints; to enchain syllables, and to lash the wind, are equally the undertakings of pride, unwilling to measure its desires by its strength."

One might think that Johnson's magisterial judgment would have permanently scuttled the notion of "fixing" the English language, but it continued to crop up. John Adams (later our second President) proposed the formation of a society that would "correct, enrich and refine" American English until "perfection at last stops their progress and ends their labor." His proposal sank without a trace—as anyone with any sense of the American temperament, even more distrustful of authority than the English, could have predicted. Most recently, Simon, whose politics are no less conservative than Swift's, has proposed the formation of an "Academy of the Anglo-American Language." Personally, I'm not holding my breath.

Resistance to linguistic change has always shown up most frequently and conspicuously in denunciations of new words. As early as the fifteenth century, a somewhat flaky bishop, one Reginald Pecock, proposed that English be "purified" by eliminating the thousands of words it had borrowed from French and Latin. Instead of "impenetrable," for example, he proposed the "pure English" term "ungothroughsome." His fellow countrymen deemed his proposal not worth thinking about—or, as he himself might have put it, "not-to-be-thought-uponable."

New words continued to draw fire during the sixteenth century. Critics denounced the "inkhorn terms" that scholars were borrowing from Latin and Greek, the "oversea language" imported by English travelers who had visited France and Italy, and "Chaucerisms"—obsolete terms that had been deliberately revived by some writers. Thus the scholar Sir John Cheke declared himself "of the opinione that our own tung sholde be written cleane and pure, unmixt and unmangled with borowing of other tungs." Ironically, his own words demonstrated the futility of locking the stable door, since the horse was already long gone: "opinione," "pure," "mixt" and "mangled" had all been brought into English by earlier "borowing."

To be fair, many of the critics were not simply objecting to new words. They pointed out, quite correctly, that the novelties were often introduced simply as a way of overawing the reader, who was supposed to conclude that impressive language meant impressive ideas: that (as the writer Thomas Wilson put it) the author was speaking "by some revelation." (As in Caxton's day, men of "reputation" evidently still wrote "in such manners and terms that few men shall understand them.") Here the critics were clearly on firm ground: new or unfamilar words used self-consciously to impress rather than inform—today we'd call them pompous or trendy—were (and are) legitimate targets.

Wilson also made the further, and equally sensible, point that the obsessive use of new and unfamiliar terms made for obscurity, not clarity. He urged his readers to "speake as is commonly received: neither seeking to be over fine, nor yet living over-carlesse, using our speeche as most men do"—advice that rings as true today as it did four centuries ago.

In emphasizing the importance of clear, straightforward communication, then, the critics were making perfect sense. Regrettably, however, they—like not a few modern critics—failed to grasp that the obscurity and pomposity they complained of were the result, not so much of the words that writers were using, new or otherwise, as of the way they were using—or overusing—those words. Indeed, some of their contemporaries recognized what nearly everyone concedes today: the words themselves, far from being bad for English, were good for it.

Some of the new words had come into English for the most practical reasons: they described things and concepts for which the language had no words, and had therefore been borrowed (as the educator Richard Mulcaster put it in 1582) "out of pure necessitie in new matters." But Mulcaster went further: English, he declared, acquired new words not simply from "necessitie" but also out of mere "bravery to garnish itself withal." As another critic, George Pettie, pointed out, borrowing was "the ready way to inrich our tongue and make it copious."

And this was the crucial point. Looking backward, we can see that Mulcaster and Pettie were describing the phenomenon that has "inriched" English far beyond any other language. For over a thousand years, English speakers have been "garnishing" their language with words they didn't really need, whether by borrowing from other tongues or by coining new words from their own tongue—or simply from their own fancy, as the poet Edmund Spenser coined "braggadocio," and Lewis Carroll, "chortle." The result? Where the largest English dictionaries include close to half a million entries, those of French have a mere 150,000, while Russians must make do with some 130,000. This enormous vocabulary gives us words for almost every shade of meaning that the human mind can contrive—and enough left over to let our best writers play with the sounds and rhythms of words as well as their meaning.

Some writers unquestionably employ Mulcaster's "garnish" overlavishly, to the point where the ornamentation obscures the sense—and are, quite properly, criticized for it. But their problem, it cannot be too often stressed, has little to do with the words themselves (unless these are intrinsically obscure) and a great deal to do with how those words are deployed.

Worth noting also is that any "threat" posed by new words is often temporary, since many of them won't last. For example, of the roughly ten thousand words that entered English during the sixteenth and seventeenth centuries, only half are still in use. On past performance, then, something like half the energy spent by critics in denouncing allegedly obnoxious novelties is wasted; any given new word is as likely as not to simply drop out of the language as mysteriously as it came in. Of course if one could tell *beforehand* which new words will survive and which won't . . . but nobody has yet managed that trick.

Neither history nor common sense, however, has stopped critics from attacking new words. Often their criticisms clearly reflect their personal feelings about the sort of people who use (or are thought to use) such words: people with bad characters obviously use bad English.

Swift, for example, attacked the "corruption" of the English vocabulary by radical religious groups (roughly equivalent to modern counterculturists) and by "licentious" courtiers. He objected to such (then) slang terms as "mob" and "crony" because they had been coined by "some pretty fellows" (foppish young men of fashion).

A century or so later, it was the Americans who had bad characters and were therefore (as most English writers saw it) doing the language in. Americans were, of course, uncultivated, didn't talk like upper-class Britishers and—even worse—showed no inclination to apologize for their uncouth ways. No less irritating was the fact that the United States had, in 1776, told Great Britain to drop dead—and made it stick. For some time afterward, therefore, many Britishers felt toward America as many Americans today feel about Cuba: it was a small, uppity, subversive country whose opinions on language or anything else should be spurned by respectable people.

As one outraged British writer summed it up, the Americans "make it a point of conscience to have no aristocratical distinctions—even in their vocabulary." That is, they considered "one word as good as another, provided its meaning be as clear." And the notion that a society—or a language—could get along very well without aristocratical distinctions obviously threatened the very foundations of social order.

Thus additions to the English vocabulary on our side of the Atlantic—which eventually numbered in the thousands—were inevitably seen as "corrupt," "barbarous" and (of course) threats to the "purity" of the language. The same writer who had bemoaned our lack of aristocratical distinctions called the new Americanisms "as utterly foreign as if they had been adopted from Chinese and Hebrew"—indicating that, whatever his knowledge of Chinese or Hebrew, he knew very little about English. In truth, the vast majority of the objectionable terms were English through and through. Some were words that had passed out of use in English ("fall" for "autumn," "I guess" for "I suppose"); others were old words given new meanings, such as "gap" (in a mountain range) or "clearing" (in the forest).

Around 1825, the American Noah Webster, like Samuel Johnson a famous dictionary maker, tried to inject some common sense into the controversy. In a conversation with a British visitor, Captain Basil Hall, he pointed out, first, that Americans had "not only a right to adopt new words, but were obliged to modify the language to suit the novelty of [their] circumstances" (as Mulcaster had put it over two centuries earlier, "out of pure necessitie in new matters").

No less trenchantly, Webster compared changes in a language

to "the course of the Mississippi, the motion of which, at times, is scarcely perceptible, yet even then it possesses a momentum quite irresistible. *Words and expressions will be forced into use, in spite of all the exertions of all the writers in the world*" (emphasis added).

"But surely," said the rather shocked Hall, "such innovations are to be deprecated?"

"I don't know that," Webster retorted. "If a word becomes universally current in America, where English is spoken, why should not it take its station in the language?"

"Because," said Hall, "there are words enough already." Happily, Hall's was a minority view: most English speakers, on both sides of the Atlantic, have always operated on the principle that when it comes to words, there's no such thing as "enough."

Webster's nineteenth-century common sense had little more impact than Johnson's eighteenth-century variety: English literati (eventually joined by some Americans) continued to denounce the appearance of new words—and the words themselves (as Webster had predicted) continued to spread, despite all the critics' exertions. The invariable sequel was a weeping and a gnashing of teeth over the decline and approaching fall of English.

As far back as 1908, the eminent American grammarian Thomas R. Lounsbury noted "the prevalence of complaints about the corruption which is overtaking our own speech," and described sardonically the "very many worthy persons" who saw English as "in the condition approaching collapse." These "foretellers of calamity we have always had with us," he remarked dryly; "it is in every way possible that we shall always have them." He was right; we still do.

So whenever you read a jeremiad by one of these foretellers of calamity declaring that the English tongue is bound for hell in a hand basket, remind yourself that the author is telling you not a twice- or even thrice-told tale but one that has been going the rounds, in one version or another, since the days of Good Queen Bess. Each generation produces its own crop of doom merchants announcing that English is "in the condition approaching collapse." And generation after generation English, like the Missis-sippi, just keeps rolling along.

Equally persistent from generation to generation is the lin-guistic "principle" that bad character equals bad English. Thus John Simon ascribes today's alleged corruption of English to the influence of such undesirables as "underprivileged minorities, especially if these happened to be black, Hispanic, . . . female or homosexual." Other low types often blamed (and almost always wrongly) for the supposed decline of English include turn-of-the-century immigrants (see **PREMODIFICATION**), student rebels of the 1960s (see **MEANINGFUL**) and people from the worlds of business and advertising (see **CONTACT** and **CRAFT**). The Watergate tapes evoked an absolute chorus of critics deploring the language used by Richard Nixon and his crew of political pirates—and they didn't mean the (deleted) expletives (see **WATERGATE ENGLISH**).

There is simply no way to describe this view as anything but self-deluding twaddle. Often enough it is also self-serving twad-dle: to say or imply that people whose opinions differ from yours have bad characters is a cheap and easy way to "win" an argu-ment. The plain fact is that usage has nothing whatever to do with character or morality: bad men don't necessarily use bad English, nor good men, good English. Personally, I can think of at least a dozen of today's public figures (names on request) whose use of English would satisfy the most puristical stylist, yet whose actions—in my judgment, anyway—have often been very bad indeed.

English, like every other language, has been and will be *abused* —sometimes very skillfully—for purposes of deceit, profit, self-puffery and the like (I'll have more to say about this later). Tricky Dick and his henchmen were an outstanding case in point, but they certainly weren't the first—nor, unfortunately, will they be the last. Such abuse is indeed deplorable, but it would be even more deplorable if it led us to confuse abuse with bad usage.

To carry the argument to its conclusion: the fact that critic A or editor B or columnist C, or all of them put together, happen to dislike a particular expression is in itself evidence of nothing but their personal opinions; it is we who must decide for ourselves whether these opinions are sensible or silly. And if we want to decide wisely, we must evidently rely on something more than *our* personal opinions.

There are in fact four fundamental principles of scientific linguistics that are central to any rational, commonsense discussion of usage. Understanding these principles won't enable us to resolve *all* the disputes in this area, because, as I've pointed out earlier, no language is constructed scientifically. Nor will it make our judgments completely "objective"; personal taste and experience will always play their part. What it can do is make our judgments *more* objective, by giving them a scientific, factual foundation.

1. **Ultimately, usage determines usage.** That is, what words mean at any given time depends on what people use them to mean. "Nice" to us means "pleasant," "agreeable" or "attractive," and the fact that four centuries ago it meant "foolish" (ultimately, from the Latin *nescius,* ignorant) has, like the flowers of spring in *The Mikado,* nothing to do with the case. The same principle applies to syntax—what words to use in what contexts or constructions. For years, purists insisted (as some still do) that **CONTACT** was a noun, not a verb, meaning that to speak of "contacting" someone was ungrammatical or worse. The plain fact is that if enough people use it as a verb (as tens of millions of British and Americans now do), then by God it *is* a verb, all the critics in the world notwithstanding. Only when we recognize that fact can we move on to the real question: should we or shouldn't we use the verb, and if so why—or why not?

2. **Usage changes**—a point I've already touched on repeatedly. The English language, like every other language, has changed in the past (even during my own lifetime—and I'm not *that* old!). It is changing today, and there is not the faintest reason to suppose that it won't change in the future—as Webster put it,

in spite of all the exertions of all the writers in the world. Attempts to stop it from changing are, as Dr. Johnson declared, as futile as trying to stop the wind from blowing. Of course change, in usage or anything else, brings problems—in this case, often problems of clarity (see the next paragraph). But only after we have accepted the fact of change can we think constructively about how to cope with those problems.

3. **Change can hamper communication.** That is, if the meaning of a word is changing, there will be a period, more or less prolonged, when it will sometimes be used in the old sense, sometimes in the new. As a result, people reading it may well be uncertain about which meaning is intended in a given case. There is nothing novel about problems of this sort: in Chaucer's day, for example, "wyf" meant both "wife" and "woman" (its original meaning), and only the context could tell you which was meant. The poet's "Wyf of Bath" was no man's wife but five times a widow—and a woman in every sense! Yet his scandalous young "carpenteris wyf" was indeed the carpenter's wife—poor fellow! When we use modern words of this sort, then, we must do so in a context that makes completely clear which meaning we intend (see **UNIQUE**), or not use them at all (see **BIMONTHLY**).

4. **Communication involves more than meaning.** The words we use, and how we use them, can convey more than the information we have in mind: they may also communicate to our hearers or readers what sort of people we are—in their eyes if not our own. It is no doubt regrettable that some people insist on seeing certain usages as evidence of illiteracy, stupidity or bad morals. But such people exist—and communication with them must take their views, wrongheaded though these may be, into account.

If, then, you know that certain usages will lead some people to judge (or misjudge) you in ways you dislike, you evidently need to do some thinking about how important these folks' opinions are to you. If they're important enough, your obvious move is to adjust your usage to suit, even though in your heart you know they're wrong. Usage questions of this sort are seldom more important than knowing which fork to use at a formal dinner—but that can be pretty important if you like formal dinners and hope to get invited to more of them.

If certain usages will label you, rightly or wrongly, as "low class" (defined any way you like), others will make you sound like a stuffed shirt (see **BE ABLE TO** and **WHO/WHOM**), or a bureaucrat, which comes to much the same thing (see **-IZE**), or self-consciously trendy (see **HIGH-TECH LANGUAGE**). You yourself may feel that the label is unfair, but unless you avoid these usages it will stick. Of course if you don't mind sounding pompous, or *want* to sound trendy (as some people do), then O.K. for you.

Three more principles of usage are not, so far as I know, "recognized" by scientific linguistics—though I think most linguisticians would agree with them. Rather, they reflect the almost unanimous consensus of professional editors and writers, which my own thirty years' experience in the writing business has amply confirmed.

5. **Clarity is not the only test of good usage—but it is the most important one.** A word or phrase or sentence may be "grammatical" enough to meet the standards of the most finicky purist, but if its meaning isn't clear, it's still bad English. Equally, if it's clear, even though "ungrammatical" by some people's standards, then I for one am willing to at least stop and think a moment before denouncing it.

Unclarity comes in all degrees. A very minor example shows up in the work of a well-known science writer. Discussing the prehistoric origin of monster legends, he described mammoths, sabertooths and cave bears as "fearful"; I would have said "fearsome" (see **FEARFUL/FEARSOME**). This particular usage, however, will at worst merely check the flow of our thoughts for a moment, since the writer clearly meant to say that these creatures were frightening—though they were, just possibly, frightened as well. Yet even such brief checks are worth avoiding.

At the other end of the spectrum we have sentences like "The microscope has an uncertain origin lost in improbable legends of the Middle Ages which, if true, could have been the ancestor of the first magnifying glass." Here the writer has not merely failed to say clearly what (s)he meant; (s)he has managed to say nothing whatever that anyone can decipher.

6. **Clear English is likely to be "grammatical" (Standard) English—but grammatical English is not necessarily clear.** Or, as Ben Jonson put it nearly four hundred years ago, "To speake, and to speake well, are two [different] things."

Some examples will show what I mean. The first is from a magazine article on the early history of Edenton, North Carolina: "Located at a considerable distance from the coast, Edenton's commercial importance was unrivaled within the colony." Now, this sentence is ungrammatical, by the rules of Standard English, because it contains a **MISPLACED MODIFIER:** if you read it carefully, you realize that "located" refers to "commercial importance," though it was obviously meant to refer to "Edenton." This is a minor error, since nobody is likely to be confused as to what was located where—that is, it didn't really obscure what the writer meant to say.

But correcting this error, along the lines of "Located at a considerable distance from the coast, Edenton had a commercial importance . . . ," leaves us with a much more serious problem that has nothing to do with formal grammar. By bringing together into one sentence Edenton's location and its commercial importance, the author is implying that the two were somehow connected. Yet neither the sentence nor its context gives us a clue to the nature of that connection.

Indeed, the context makes matters even murkier: the author has already told us that Edenton, far from being located "at a considerable distance from the coast" was right *on* the coast— was, in fact, a leading colonial seaport. Conceivably, what he was trying to say was that Edenton was located *far from the open sea,* which it is, but what (if anything) that had to do with its commercial importance is something you must guess at. And if you have to guess, then don't bother checking out the grammar—it's bad English!

A second example is from a recent book on international terrorism: "But his sex life would be loudly revealed when he turned up a phonograph to recordings of gunfire and martial music." This sentence, too, is ungrammatical, by any standard: you don't turn up a phonograph *to* recordings, you turn up recordings *on* a phonograph. But again, correcting the grammar does little to clarify the meaning. Maybe turning up those recordings revealed something—loudly or otherwise—about the man's sex life, but the author doesn't really explain what. Bad English! (It is also, I suspect, *deliberately* bad English: that is, the author, by intimating that the man was turned on by turned-up martial recordings, was trying to create a sinister impression without saying anything specific enough to be contradicted.)

Both these examples combine both bad grammar and bad usage—and *the bad (unclear) usage has little if anything to do with the bad grammar*. Our third example, by contrast, is grammatically impeccable—but no less unclear. Professor Hall, immediately after assuring us that there is no such thing as bad English, declares "There is no such thing as 'written language.'"

The sentence is grammatical, simple—and about as obscure as you can find. Its apparent sense—that there is no such thing as language that is written down—clearly can't be what the author had in mind, since he wrote it and we're reading it. Conceivably he was trying to say that there is no difference between "written language" and "spoken language" (which is arguable), or that spoken language is more important than written language (also arguable), or something else entirely. The sentence is bad English, not because it's ungrammatical (it isn't) or because it's nonsense (though I suspect it may be) but because it fails to make clear what kind of nonsense—or sense—it is.

A really spectacular example of grammatical bad English comes from a recent thriller by two professional journalists. At the very beginning of their first chapter, the writers confront us with a hotel lobby "carved in time," in which a carpet "crawled like a stain toward the horizon." The furniture is of "indeterminate proportion," while the walls are cluttered with waist-high counters, "each chockablock with white-coated workers."

What "carved in time" means I can't even guess; likewise with that furniture of "indeterminate proportion" (furniture can have good proportion*s* or bad ones—but indeterminate?). The carpet crawling toward the horizon conjures up a lobby at least the size of a stadium, and appropriately enough: the counters chockablock with workers sound like rows of bleacher seats. I don't think I've ever read a worse paragraph; I never finished the next one.

Which brings us to our final principle:

7. **The fewer words (or even syllables) you use, the better.** Redundancy—using more words than you need to make your meaning clear—is like using too much water when you brew coffee: it dilutes the flavor, and discourages people from consuming it (see **BE ABLE TO**).

* * *

So much for the principles and reasoning that underlie the judgments I make in this book—judgments of the sort I hope *you* will learn to make on your own. Now let me say a little about the book itself: why I've written it, and how you can best use it.

To begin with, you may quite reasonably ask what my qualifications are for writing a book of this sort. One is that I've been fascinated by the meaning and use of words since I was in my teens, and in pursuit of that interest have done a fair amount of reading about linguistics. When it comes to the English language, I've read a good deal more than a fair amount—enough to write a book about its history (see the Bibliography).

My most important qualification, however, is that for nearly thirty years I have made my living with words, as an editor and writer. Moreover, and unlike the great majority of American writers, I have made a pretty good living. How did I manage to succeed where so many others have not? Luck—being in the right place at the right time—certainly played a major part. But as I look back, I think that even more important than luck was my concern with clarity: with putting words—my own and other people's—together in ways that would tell the reader what I or they meant, with no ifs, buts or ambiguities. I know how to say what I mean and to help others say what *they* mean; being a thoughtful person, I have naturally thought a good deal about how it's done. The results of that thinking are summed up in these pages.

Let me emphasize, however, that I haven't tried to write "the last word" on American usage. No such book will ever be written, unless American English becomes a dead language like Latin or ancient Egyptian. Our native tongue will continue to change, meaning that some of my judgments about it will be out of date fifty years from now—as many of the judgments I criticize herein are out of date today. It is not even the next-to-the-last word; I have not tried to deal with all—or even most—disputed questions of usage.

In particular, I have completely ignored the area of phonetics —that is, how words "should" be pronounced. I don't think anyone will ever standardize American pronunciation, and doubt it would be worth the trouble anyway. Pronunciation is important for communication mainly in face-to-face (or phone-to-phone) situations, in which misunderstandings can normally be cleared up immediately. If you're concerned about how to pronounce an unfamiliar word, my best advice is to consult any up-to-date dictionary. And if, as sometimes happens, the dictionary gives more than one pronunciation—listen to the people around you.

Second, I have left out most usage problems that concern merely the differences in meaning between similar words. The only exceptions are cases where the experts disagree over which word means what, or where use of the "wrong" word can label you in one way or another (see, e.g., **FORCED**). When it comes to meaning, there's no substitute for a good dictionary, and I certainly haven't aimed to write one.

Finally, I have said almost nothing about differences between American and British usage, which though a fascinating subject is not really relevant to this book.

What I've written is precisely what my subtitle says: a *guide* to usage—a book that, by examining some selected usage problems, will guide you in solving the many problems I haven't had the space to tackle. Which is to say that I've focused on the questions you need to ask when you're confronted by a problem in usage, and on where you should look for the answers.

From everything I've said up to now, you can guess that the most important of these questions is **Is it clear?** As the Roman writer and orator Cicero put it long ago, the aim of writing is not simply to be understood, but to make oneself impossible to be *mis*understood. Ask yourself, then: is there *any* way in which my use of this word, or that construction, could lead people to misunderstand what I'm trying to say? If the answer is yes, then the question of whether it's "good" or "bad" usage doesn't arise: find another, clearer way of saying what you mean.

The second question is **Do reputable writers accept this usage?** Here your best guide is not (or not necessarily) the manuals on usage listed in the Bibliography, though some are more useful than others. At most, they will tell you what reputable writers do *in the author's (or usage panel's) opinion.* Sometimes these opinions are right; sometimes they're wrong—usually because those giving the opinions have mentally rephrased the question. Rather than ask "What do reputable writers do?" they think "What do I—who am, of course, a reputable writer—do?" And sometimes the opinions are not just wrong but wrongheaded: the writers know perfectly well that many or most reputable writers don't do as *they* do, but nonetheless insist *their* usage is the only correct one (see **AGREEMENT**).

When it comes to what people do—as opposed to what they "ought" to do—we are (or should be) dealing in facts, not opinions. So go after the facts. The very best source for these facts is the *Oxford English Dictionary*—the unabridged version, of course, including its four supplements, which you will find in most good-sized libraries. The quotations attached to its hundreds of thousands of entries will give you a good sample of who has used a particular word in a given sense, or a particular grammatical construction, and when. If you find, for example, that **CRITIQUE** has been used as a verb since the eighteenth century, and is still so used, then the question of whether someone thinks it "ought" to be a verb is, as the lawyers say, **MOOT:** not worth arguing about.

A much more compact sourcebook for *recent* usage is Margaret M. Bryant's *Current American Usage.* Unfortunately, it's out of print, and a little out of date—but still worth consulting if it's in your local library.

It may well occur to you at this point that digging out the facts of usage for yourself will mean work—a lot more work than simply taking somebody's word for them. It will. But face it— making up your own mind about anything is always more trouble than letting someone else make it up for you.

The third question is a tougher one: **Will this usage label me in a way I dislike?** For example, will some critic or usage expert call me **ILLITERATE,** "ignorant," "uneducated" or any of the other nasty epithets such people apply to those who don't use English as they do? I have dealt with many of these "labeling" usages in the text (e.g., **LAY/LIE**); for those not included, probably the simplest solution is to consult one of the dictionaries or usage manuals mentioned in the Bibliography. As I've indicated, they are far from infallible on the facts, but will usually give you a good sense of what "respectable" people *feel* about the problem in question. And when it comes to labeling, it's feelings that matter, not facts.

Of course you may simply not give a damn what the respectables think, which is fine with me. But in language as in anything else, you can't thumb your nose at the Authorities without also sticking your neck out. It's your neck!

When it comes to usages that make you look like a stuffed

shirt, you won't get much help from most standard usage manuals—which, perhaps, tells us something about the kind of people who write or contribute to these manuals. I have dealt with some of these in the text; otherwise, when in doubt remember what Caxton said five centuries ago: "the common terms that are daily used are lighter understood . . ." Certainly there are times when uncommon words can say things that common ones can't—but a few of them go a long way.

Indeed the overuse of long or obscure words can in itself label you, as someone trying to impress or overawe the reader rather than inform him or her—as a smart-ass, in fact. Alternatively, it will suggest that you aren't really confident about your own knowledge of English, and are using overelaborate terms to cover up your own insecurity. In either case, a little self-analysis is in order. Ask yourself: am I trying to say something clearly, or just to show off—or perhaps reassure myself?

All of us, of course, try to suit our diction to our company: we're not likely to address a college dean in the same terms as an old and dear friend. Most usage manuals, in fact, distinguish between "formal" and "informal" usage—though I'm not sure that this particular distinction is of much use to most people. Thus William and Mary Morris, in their useful if sometimes wrongheaded *Harper Dictionary of Contemporary Usage,* use "formal" to identify usages appropriate to "diplomatic messages, legal briefs and sermons."

Since I doubt that many of you will be writing such documents, I have pretty much ignored this distinction. For that matter, I think the style of legal briefs and diplomatic notes would be much improved by eliminating most of their overelaborate diction, which often serves—designedly—to obscure rather than clarify what the writer is trying to say. As for sermons, I stand on the First Amendment: the language people choose for their prayers or religious observances is entirely their own business, and I don't propose to offer advice on the subject. (Worth noting, however, is that the King James Bible, one of the greatest achievements of English prose, was deliberately written in the simplest kind of English. I think the eminent churchmen who wrote it knew what they were about.)

As I've already indicated, my main aim has been to help you write clearly. But I've also devoted some attention to helping you *read* clearly, by pointing out certain expressions that are widely misused and often *abused*—used deliberately to misinform rather than inform. Terms like **PATRIOTISM** are Humpty-Dumpty words that mean pretty much what the writer wants them to mean; others, like **CLAIM,** have overtones you won't find in dictionaries—connotations that can subtly mislead you if you're not aware of them.

Some readers may feel that these discussions are "political," and wonder what politics is doing in a book on usage. They *are* political—and I make no apologies for including them. Language, like most other things, has its political dimension; that is, people's opinions on its use and misuse reflect their attitudes toward their fellows and to society in general. A good, if obvious, example is the class attitudes, discussed earlier, that shape people's conceptions of what is and isn't "good English."

Moreover, as George Orwell long ago pointed out, political discourse in its broadest sense (which includes not only politicians' speeches but also statements by corporations and other large organizations, and writings on political and social problems) is a major source of bad usage. Some of this is deliberate, but much is unconscious—and therefore all the more pervasive.

Orwell noted, for example, that the clichés so common in political discourse reflect clichéd thinking, just as its mixed metaphors reflect mixed-up ideas. He also makes the equally important point that unclear writing not only grows out of unclear thinking but actively encourages it: if you can't say clearly what you mean, you won't know whether it makes sense. Conversely, he says, "If you simplify your English . . . [then] when you make a stupid remark its stupidity will be obvious, even to yourself."

Orwell's essay "Politics and the English Language" is required reading for anyone interested in the sociology of bad English (its collection of "horrible examples" is by itself worth the price of admission). You probably won't agree with everything he says—I certainly don't—but his acid remarks should stimulate your own thinking on where "bad English" comes from and what it does.

In selecting "political" examples of bad usage, I've tried not to play favorites; nonsense is nonsense, whether it comes from the "right" or the "left." However, I have deliberately said almost nothing about the sort of nonsense one finds in *Pravda* or its minuscule English-language counterparts; I don't care to waste my time, and yours, in beating dead horses.

Throughout this book I have dealt critically, sometimes harshly, with some of the experts who have written, or expressed public opinions, on usage questions. I've done so not simply because I like a good argument but, more important, as a way of encouraging you, the reader, to *make up your own mind.* Until you recognize that experts (including me), in language or anything else, are human (meaning that they are on occasion prejudiced, confused or just plain wrong), you will be reluctant to challenge their opinions—and this book will have been less than totally successful.

However, I would not want anyone to get the notion that the amount of criticism I've devoted to particular experts or books reflects my opinion of their overall worth. For example, I have a lot to say about both the late Theodore Bernstein's *The Careful Writer* and the *Harper Dictionary of Contemporary Usage,* but a major reason is that *they* have a lot to say about a great many topics. Some of what they say is wrong, as I see it—but a great deal is both right and useful. Conversely, I have completely ignored certain other books on usage, not because I agree with them but because I don't think they're worth bothering with. (For further information, see the Bibliography.)

John Simon is a special case. As a literary critic, he can be both sensitive and perceptive, but his writings on usage are often nonsense—and nastily worded nonsense at that. "Experts" who are not only wrong but abusive to boot are asking for rough treatment, and whenever I get the chance I try to give them what they're asking for.

Any book on usage is bound to reflect the writer's personal opinions and tastes, and this one certainly does. I have, however, tried throughout to label my opinions as such—not (as some experts do) the latest word from Mt. Sinai.

This book will not teach you to be a writer. In particular, it won't and can't tell you the most important thing any writer needs to know: exactly what do I want to say? Unless you yourself are clear on what you mean, no book is likely to be of much use in helping you to say it clearly. (Equally, if you persistently have problems in putting together a clear sentence on a particular subject, it's worthwhile asking yourself: just what in hell *am* I trying to say?)

But assuming that you know what you mean, this book should help you say it clearly, whether you're writing a letter or a treatise. It will also help you say it in ways that will incidentally convey to the reader the kind of person you are—or want him or her to think you are.

P. 11:   The Knoblauch/Brannon quotation is from their *Rhetorical Traditions and the Teaching of Writing* (Boynton-Cook, 1984).

P. 12:   The Hall quotation is from his *Linguistics and Your Language* (Doubleday, 1960).

P. 13:   Simon's views on the evolution of English are scattered through his *Paradigms Lost* (Penguin, 1981).

P. 16:   On the changing meanings of "nice," "deer" and "soluble," see the *Oxford Etymological Dictionary.*

Pp. 17f: For more on English dialects and historical changes in the language, see my *Our Marvelous Native Tongue* (listed in the Bibliography) and Albert C. Baugh, *A History of the English Language,* (Appleton-Century—Crofts, 1957).

P. 17: "It is impossible for an Englishman . . ." is quoted in H. L. Mencken, *The American Language.*

P. 19: "the property of a once privileged . . ." is the invention of Stanley Berne and Arlene Zekowski, formerly of Eastern New Mexico University. They are quoted in Simon, *Paradigms Lost.*

Pp. 21f: The text of Caxton's preface (which is well worth reading in full) will be found in W. F. Bolton, ed., *The English Language,* vol. 1 (Cambridge University Press, 1966).

P. 24: "see no absolute necessity . . ." is quoted in Baugh; the full text of the document from which it was taken is in Bolton.
"to give definite rules . . ." is quoted in Baugh.

P. 26: Adams' proposal is quoted in Baugh.
Simon's proposal for an academy is in his *Paradigms Lost.*

Pp. 24f: The quotations from Cheke, Wilson, Mulcaster and Pettie will be found in Baugh. The complete text of Mulcaster's essay is in Bolton.

Pp. 29f: The rise of American English and English reactions to it are discussed at greater length in *Our Marvelous Native Tongue,* chap. 9.
The British comments on American English, as well as the Webster-Hall dialogue, are all quoted in Mencken, *The American Language.*

P. 31: Lounsbury's remarks are from his *The Standard of Usage in English;* they are quoted in Jim Quinn, *American Tongue and Cheek* (Pantheon Books, 1980).

P. 35: The example of "fearful" is from Isaac Asimov, *The Beginning and the End* (Pocket Books, 1978).
The Jonson quotation is from his essay in Bolton.

P. 36: "But his sex life . . ." is quoted from Claire Sterling, *The Terror Network* (Reader's Digest Press, 1981).

P. 37: The hotel lobby quotation is from *A Death in China,* by William D. Montalbano and Carl Hiassen.

THE GUIDE

———

The entries in this Guide are arranged alphabetically, but many of the words I've discussed aren't in their proper alphabetical place; that is, they're included in some other entry. Some usage manuals handle this problem by including dozens of cross-references; I have chosen to use a supplementary Index, which you'll find at the end. If, then, you're looking for information on some expression or topic and don't find a heading on it in the Guide, check the Index. If you don't find it there either, it's one of the many usage problems I didn't have space to deal with.

The index also gives page references to books and individuals mentioned in the text. However, in the interests of space I have seldom cited the *Oxford English Dictionary* by name, and have not indexed even these references. You can take it that *any* statement on the history of a particular word or usage is based on the *OED,* unless otherwise indicated.

Words within entries in **BOLDFACE CAPITALS** refer you to other entries.

References

The following abbreviations are used to identify books cited hereafter. Complete information on these works will be found in the Bibliography.

AHD	*American Heritage Dictionary*
Bernstein	Theodore M. Bernstein, *The Careful Writer*
Bryant	Margaret M. Bryant, *Current American Usage*
Follett	Wilson Follett, *Modern American Usage*
Fowler	H. W. Fowler, *Modern English Usage*
HDCU	William and Mary Morris, *Harper Dictionary of Contemporary Usage*
OED Supp.	*A Supplement to the Oxford English Dictionary*
OMNT	Robert Claiborne, *Our Marvelous Native Tongue*
RHD	*Random House Dictionary*
Simon	John Simon, *Paradigms Lost*

A

ABSTRACTIONS. All of us are sometimes forced to use abstract nouns, but some of us overuse them. Consider, for instance, "He showed great shrewdness in the negotiations" vs. "He negotiated very shrewdly." The first sentence is weaker because it emphasizes the abstract concept "shrewdness" rather than the important, concrete point: how he negotiated. In general, it's best not to use an abstract expression if you can substitute a concrete one; talking about the real world of things and people is both clearer and more forceful than talking about the ethereal world of concepts.

Some things can be either abstractions or realities, depending on circumstances. If we say "The U.S. government consists of three branches . . ." we are evidently talking about a real structure composed of real people. But when we say "The administration believes . . ." (or "The Pentagon believes" or "The business community believes"), we are sliding into abstraction. Neither these nor any other institutions or groups "believe"; only people do.

Journalists use (and often overuse) expressions like these as shorthand: "The administration believes" equals "The top figures in the executive branch believe"—or say they do; likewise, "The business community believes" means that a large majority of businessmen (or anyway, those willing to be quoted) believe—or say they do. Shorthand of this sort should be used with discretion: it saves space, but can also mislead the reader, deliberately or otherwise. It obscures the fact that what is true of most people in a group is seldom true of all of them—and the further fact that what people (especially public figures) say they believe often differs widely from what they really believe. Using abstractions of this sort can too easily lead you into the slippery area of **GOLDBRICK GENERALITIES.**

In short, abstractions can be useful servants, but bad masters: handle with care!

ACRONYMS. These are, of course, abbreviations formed from the first letters of a string of words. Some have passed into the language—for example, "RAdio Detection And Ranging" and "Self-Contained Underwater Breathing Apparatus." Some people are allergic to them. Thus Follett (or his collaborator, Jacques Barzun) disliked "scuba" and proposed to replace it with "gills." The suggestion was a dud, and deservedly so: a fish's gills are nothing like scuba apparatus in structure and resemble it only remotely in function. Objecting to new words on the ground that they're not needed seldom makes sense; objecting to *needed* words, coined to describe new things, never does.

Acronyms are widely used in professional **JARGON,** such as DOD (Department of Defense) among Washington bureaucrats and journalists, OB-GYN (obstetrics and gynecology) among doctors and GIGO (Garbage In, Garbage Out) among computer people. This last has spread fairly widely among the general public, since it concisely sums up a fundamental truth: false information leads to nonsensical conclusions. (It has also been described as the computerized version of "Ask a silly question and you get a silly answer.") Also fairly well known are the office worker's FYI (For Your Information) and TGIF (Thank God It's Friday!).

Like other "inside" terms, acronyms develop because

(among other reasons) they speed up communication among insiders. By the same token, however, they can seriously hamper communication with outsiders. Before using an acronym, then, ask yourself: will people recognize it *immediately?* If the answer is no, give the name in full. If you expect to use the name several times and want to avoid cumbersome repetitions, follow the full name with the acronym in parentheses —for example, "the Department of Defense (DOD)"—after which you can generally keep using the initials with a clear conscience.

Beware, however, of overloading your writing with such abbreviations; referring to DOD, AWACS, MIRV and SEATO in the space of two or three paragraphs is likely to numb the reader, even though all four have been defined previously. Beware, too, of using an acronym that was last seen a dozen paragraphs back; many readers will by that time have forgotten what it meant.

Another reason to "watch your acronyms" is that people have become acronym conscious, finding these abbreviations in unexpected and unintended places. That was why the Pentagon quickly renamed its plan for Deep Underground Missile Basing.

ADJECTIVES, UNCOMPARABLE. Words like "complete," **PERFECT, UNIQUE,** "equal," "full" and "dead" are a favorite stamping ground of purists, who insist that, unlike other adjectives, they can't, or anyway shouldn't, be compared. The experts reason that (for example) a person is either dead or not; (s)he can't be "more dead" or "very dead." Almost any usage manual has its list, long or short, of uncomparables. Bryant, however, points out that apart from some rule-conscious editors and writers, most people normally compare all these words at least some of the time.

You can make a good case for "dead" as uncomparable when it means "no longer living." ("Very dead"—meaning,

I guess, "obviously or conspicuously dead"—was mildly
amusing when it was first used in hard-boiled crime fiction
some sixty years ago; today it's a cliché, and should be avoided for that reason alone.) But when you're using "dead"
in one of its figurative senses (there are several dozen), you
need to think about the sense, not the word: it's perfectly
reasonable to say "the deadest [= dullest] party I ever went
to."

Words such as "full" and "complete" are normally and, I
think, properly compared even in their literal sense: to say
"My gas tank is *more nearly* full than yours," instead of "My
tank is fuller than yours," is pedantry.

"Equal" is often considered the ultimate in uncomparabil-
ity, yet most of us would quite naturally say "We need to
provide children with more equal opportunities." And then
there's George Orwell's deliberate and ironic comparison
"Some animals are more equal than others"—now, alas,
something of a cliché.

ADVERBS AND HOW TO SPOT 'EM. The construction of
adverbs in English is a vivid illustration of the principle that
languages aren't logical. "Normal" adverbs follow the pattern
ADJECTIVE + "-ly" (foolish/foolishly; sad/sadly), but some
adjectives can double as adverbs without the "-ly" (e.g., fast,
high, low), while some "-ly" words aren't adverbs at all but
adjectives (ugly, lowly, lovely, friendly, etc.). A few nouns are
equally duplicitous, since they can serve as adverbs in the
plural form ("He works nights"). These last are not "real"
plurals, but what are ponderously called "adverbial genitives"
—a survival from Old English syntax, in which the genitive
(possessive) form of a noun could sometimes be used to modify a verb. (See **INTERCHANGEABLE PARTS.**)

To complicate life even further, many adverbs come in two
flavors, ADJECTIVE + "-ly" and ADJECTIVE alone—for
instance, **SLOW(LY),** direct(ly), cheap(ly), wide(ly)—and

using some of the short (without "-ly") forms can label you as uneducated, for no very sensible reason. Would anybody really say "He swung wide*ly* around the turn"?

Yet another complication is that a number of verbs (notably, "be," "look," "feel" and the like) are normally followed by adjectives, not adverbs. At first glance, the sentences "He looks good" and "He drives good" seem to be constructed identically, yet the first is Standard English while the second is blue-collar English. The reason should be clear if you focus on meaning rather than formal structure. In the first sentence, "good" refers to the man, not the looking, meaning that an adjective is in order; in the second, it refers to the driving, not the man, meaning that using "good" (rather than the adverb "well") isn't educated usage. The same principle applies to "bad": a man with a sprained ankle limps badly—but feels bad.

In case you thought you were finally getting the hang of these complexities, note that while "good" is *only* an adjective (in Standard English), "better" and "best" are adjectives *and* adverbs ("He looks better because he's been sleeping better"). The same goes for "bad" (adj. only) and "worse" and "worst" (adjs. and advs.).

How can you best navigate this treacherous terrain? (1) Make sure what your modifier is modifying: if it's a verb or adjective, use an adverb; if it's the subject of the verb ("I feel sad"), use an adjective. For the same reasons, we say "He bought it cheap" but "He lived cheaply": "cheap" refers to what he bought; "cheaply," to how he lived. Similarly, say "I like my bread sliced thin" (not "thinly"): you're talking about the bread, not the slicing. (2) If the meaning calls for an adverb, check the dictionary to see whether it's one of those with two forms (with and without "-ly"). If it is, take your pick, bearing in mind that some people insist that only the "standard" ("-ly") form is kosher. Others (including me) feel that the standard version is overformal, if not pretentious, more often than not.

Whichever you choose, you're likely to annoy somebody; who that somebody will be is your decision. Personally, I use the short, informal forms as often as possible, since I prefer to come across as an informal type. In a few cases, such as "I'm flying direct to Los Angeles," the short forms are used by almost everybody.

The "-ly" in "firstly," "secondly" and so on is totally unnecessary, as it is in "thusly": say "first" and "thus," unless you're playing for a chuckle. (If you are, make sure they'll laugh with you, not at you!) In "overly," the suffix isn't even funny, just superfluous; don't say "overly cautious" but "overcautious."

ADVERTISINGESE. It is an article of faith among many usage experts that the advertising industry is corrupting, debasing and otherwise mucking up the English language. Thus Barry Bingham, Sr., of the *HDCU* usage panel denounced the verb **GIFT** as "vulgar advertising jargon. NO, NO, NO!" and the late Theodore Bernstein belabored another verb, **CRAFT,** in similar tones.

Earlier, the slogan "Winstons taste good, like a cigarette should" (rather than "as a cigarette should") evoked howls of disapproval, as, still earlier, did "Travels the smoke further" —this on the ground, first, that "travel" is not a transitive verb and, second, that "further" should have been **"FARTHER."**

To make a sensible judgment on how advertisingese has affected English—or whether it has affected it at all—we need to remind ourselves of some basic principles. First, many of the objections to advertising lingo clearly reflect the feeling that advertising people, or many of them, have bad characters —and therefore use bad English. Since I've already discussed this fallacy at length in the Introduction, I'll say no more about it here. And since the logic is faulty, we needn't concern ourselves with what kinds of characters, good or bad, advertising people actually have.

Second, the original source of a word tells us nothing whatever about the value of the word itself, or the propriety of using it. Words such as "fence" (receiver of stolen goods) and "phony" were first used by criminals, yet nobody today hesitates to use them any time, anywhere (see also **CONTACT**).

Thus far we're talking about virtual truisms. My third point is more controversial: I believe that the influence of advertising, on English or anything else, has been grossly overrated —especially by the advertising industry. On occasion, advertising *abuses* language to sell goods that are shoddy or overpriced or simply unneeded—but that sort of thing has been going on since the first Mesopotamian merchant palmed off junk jewelry on a country cousin come to the big city of Ur.

More specifically, I don't believe that the use of "ungrammatical" English in advertising ("like a cigarette should") encourages people to use that sort of English. Rather, it's the other way round: advertising copywriters use "ungrammatical" English because they believe—correctly—that most people talk that way. Addressing itself to the "common people," it adopts the language (or what it conceives to be the language) that such people use—and were using long before advertising was invented.

Conceivably, this sort of thing does set a bad example to some young people. But advertisers, after all, are engaged in selling goods, not in moral or educational uplift. One may, I think, quite reasonably question whether selling goods is, or should be, as important in our society as advertising agencies and their clients obviously think it is. But this question, interesting though it is, has nothing to do with usage.

There are a few words so intimately associated with advertising that they carry inescapable overtones of phoniness; "zesty" and "crispy" are a couple that occur to me. Such words—you can make your own list—should obviously be avoided, unless you don't mind coming across as a phony.

Another common advertising locution is what Bernstein

calls "the hanging comparative," in which words such as "better" are used as absolutes: "better-grade motor oil" (better than what?) and so on. Personally, I can't get very excited about this: "better-grade motor oil" clearly means oil better than the maker's (or somebody's) lower-grade oil. Then why not say so directly? Simple prudence! If Conglomerate Oil Co. says its expensive oil is not just "better" but better *than* its cheaper oil, people may conclude that the latter is junk and quit buying it, thereby depriving Conglomerate of a sizable part of its sales. If Conglomerate says its stuff is better than the stuff sold by Octopus Oil, its competitor, it's likely to hear from Octopus's lawyers—assuming, that is, that the two firms haven't merged in the meantime. Finally, if it says its oil is the *best,* some nosy government bureaucrat may suggest that it prove the statement in court.

These minor points aside, the usage experts' perennial complaints about "advertising jargon" strike me as missing the important point. Any damage to the language wrought by "travels the smoke further" is very small potatoes compared to the damage induced by the smoke itself. And the phony folksiness of some advertising lingo is even smaller potatoes compared with the phoniness of some politicians that the industry promotes with spot commercials. In short, if the worst thing you can say about advertising is that it's corrupting the language, you don't know much about advertising— or language.

ADVISE. In the sense of "inform," it is a favorite word with bureaucrats ("Kindly advise me immediately"), and should therefore be avoided unless you're writing to a bureaucrat. (In correspondence of that sort, a judicious use of **BUREAUCRATESE** can give your letter a stuffy, legalistic tone, suggesting that you're someone it pays to get along with.) If you're giving somebody *advice,* of course, anyone would agree that you're advising them—though in my experience this should generally be avoided, on grounds not of usage but of prudence.

AFFECT/EFFECT (nouns and verbs). Not synonyms, though some people think so. "Effect" (the verb) is a rather pompous way of saying "bring about" or "produce" ("effect a change"); if that's what you mean, say so. There is, however, nothing wrong with the noun "effect"—meaning, of course, the change *effect*ed in something by whatever has *affect*ed it. Avoid the noun "affect"; nobody but a psychologist is likely to understand what it means.

AFICIONADO. Borrowed from Spanish in the mid-nineteenth century as a semitechnical term referring to a devotee of bullfighting, it became—thanks in part to the influence of aficionado Ernest Hemingway—a trendy synonym for "enthusiast," "devotee" or "fan." Today, it's simply pretentious. If you use it with a straight face, you're labeling yourself as a compulsive Hemingway aficionado—or somebody who didn't get off the trend in time.

AGGRAVATE. For a case history of how usage panels work, and why they often work badly, you can do no better than consult this entry in *HDCU*. It begins as follows: **Aggravate originally simply [*sic*] meant to make worse. . . . It is also widely used in the sense of "to exasperate" or "to vex."** Then it asks the panelists **Do you accept this second sense?** The first statement is false: the *real* original meaning of "aggravate" (dating from 1530, and now obsolete) was "make heavy" (the "-grav-" is the same root we find in "gravitation," which is what makes things heavy). The *HDCU*'s "original" meaning (make worse) and its "newer" meaning (annoy) developed almost simultaneously—some four centuries ago! This kind of sloppiness with facts aggravates the hell out of me. (If you've been wondering what that *"sic"* meant, see **PIGGYBACK MODIFIERS.**)

By ignoring the facts, the editors have constructed what amounts to a loaded question, saying, in effect, "A is the original meaning, B is a relatively recent though widely used meaning; which do you prefer?" If you know anything about the kind of people who get asked to sit on usage panels, you shouldn't have much trouble guessing the result: a majority flatly condemned use of the "recent" meaning in writing, a near-majority condemned it in speech—and even most of those who accepted it did so with the air of biting into a wormy apple. Ask a loaded question and you get a predictable answer. (Simon is even harsher: he calls the second use "manifest . . . linguistic ignorance and nonsense." There's a lot of that going around these days.)

I wonder what would have happened had the question been phrased factually rather than fancifully: **For nearly four centuries, "aggravate" has been used in two senses: (1) make worse, and (2) annoy. Sense (2) is often considered "substandard," though it has been used by such writers as Richardson, Dickens and Thackeray. Would you yourself use it?** No prizes for guessing *my* answer!

Among the noteworthy comments of the panelists is the statement that the "new" meaning should be rejected because we "need" the old one, and "have enough words meaning vexation." Shades of Captain Basil Hall, who told Noah Webster that "there are words enough already" (see the Introduction)! As for needing the "older" meaning—who ever suggested we were about to lose it? The two meanings have been coexisting happily since around 1600; clearly neither one is going to crowd out the other.

And for good reason: the two senses are (or should be) clearly distinguished by the context. In the sense of "make worse," the verb applies only to situations; in the sense of "annoy," only to people or, occasionally, animals ("The doctor's treatment aggravated the patient's condition; his manner aggravated the patient").

An interesting question is how the "annoying" meaning of "aggravate," acceptable to reputable writers a century ago, acquired its present, dubious reputation. One reason, I'd guess, is that it is used in this sense by nearly all Southerners —and Southern English is considered rather uncouth by many educated people outside the region. Since my own family is rooted in Virginia, I don't share this view. How you choose to deal with this particular linguistic hassle will depend on the kind of person you are. If, like me, you don't mind aggravating the purists, use it in both senses—with due attention to context of course; don't say that the doctor's *treatment* aggravated the *patient,* unless it, rather than the doctor, caused the annoyance. Should you get some flak (as you probably will), cite the facts given above. If, on the other hand, you prefer not to upset the Authorities, say "annoy" or "irritate."

AGNOSTIC/ATHEIST. You won't get much help from the dictionary in using this confusing pair; some things aren't in dictionaries. Literally, "atheist" means "one who denies or disbelieves in the existence of God"; agnostic, one who feels (s)he doesn't know one way or the other. (Friedrich Engels once defined agnosticism, wittily but unkindly, as "shamefaced atheism.") Practically, however, "atheist" now has overtones of amorality: many religious people are certain that if you reject God (or even their particular God) you must obviously reject any kind of moral code ("Where there is no God, there is no virtue"—Ronald Reagan).

In addition, atheists are often seen as people who not only don't accept religion but want to abolish it—to the point, sometimes, of padlocking churches and harassing or even jailing believers. This feeling derives in part from the record of "Atheistic Russian Communism"—which I suspect has less to do with atheism than with Russian history: no Russian government, Soviet or otherwise, has ever allowed what we would call religious freedom.

As a card-carrying atheist of many years' standing, I say that we unbelievers have been handed a bum rap. I consider myself as moral as most people—more moral, indeed, than some believers I know of. In particular, I have great admiration for much of the Judeo-Christian moral system, and wish it were more widely and consistently observed among practicing Jews and Christians. And I have absolutely no interest in interfering with anyone's religious activities—unless, of course, those activities threaten to interfere with me.

Unfortunately, my say-so is not going to abolish the bad vibrations of "atheist." If someone asks me whether I'm one, therefore, I'm likely to ask "What do you mean by 'atheist'?" (If some official asks the question, I will naturally refuse to answer on the ground that it's none of his or her business.) The moral (you should excuse the expression) is that if you describe somebody as an atheist, make sure you make clear what kind of an atheist (s)he is. If you don't, you're inviting a libel suit—or, conceivably, a knuckle sandwich.

AGREEMENT, INDEFINITE PRONOUNS. "Anybody" "anyone," "everybody," "everyone," "somebody," "someone," "nobody," "no one" and "none" are almost guaranteed to raise hackles at any gathering of usage experts. The textbook rule is that all these pronouns are singular, hence must be followed by singular pronouns: "Everybody get his hat and coat." The actual fact is that most people, at least part of the time, think of them as plural: "Everybody get their hats and coats." As a further complication, the pronouns usually take a singular *verb:* "Everybody needs [not "need"] to get their hats and coats."

An important exception to the "singular verb" rule is

"none." Purists insist that the word means "not one," hence we should say "none of them has a hat." In fact, "none" means "not any," which clearly implies that we're talking about more than one thing ("none of them have hats"). To use a singular verb here is pedantry.

Purists claim that usages of this sort are illogical—as if languages were ever constructed logically. Simon, for instance, declares that "English thinks of 'everyone' and 'everybody' as being a single one or body," so that "it is illogical to say . . . 'Everyone returned to their seats.' " Of course English doesn't "think" anything of the sort; languages don't think, though people (sometimes) do (see **ABSTRACTIONS**). But this bit of nonsense is useful, since it enables Simon to talk about the imaginary thoughts of English rather than the real actions of the people who use it. Let *us* stay in the real world.

"Everybody," according to the *OED,* is "sometimes used incorrectly" with plural pronouns. But "sometimes" turns out to be an understatement. Of the dictionary's ten quotations illustrating the use of "everybody," dating from 1530 to 1871, the word is followed by a pronoun in seven—and *all seven* pronouns are plural. Among the "incorrect" writers quoted are Sir Philip Sidney, Byron and Ruskin.

Simon is evidently aware of these facts; indeed he adds Shaw and Scott Fitzgerald to the list of "pluralists." But, he says, "the lapses of great ones do not make a wrong right." This, of course, is a heads-I-win, tails-you-lose argument: if good writers do as Simon says, that proves he's right; if they don't, that proves they're wrong.

There is this to be said for rigid, logical rules, in grammar and other things: they save you from thinking—specifically, thinking about the sense of what you're saying rather than the rules. And in sense, if not in logic, "everybody," "anyone" and the rest of these troublesome pronouns are plural at least as often as not. "Everyone get their hats and coats" is equivalent to "All members of the group should get their hats and coats," and "None of them are hatless" equals "All of them have hats." The "one" in "every*one*" and "*none*" is a linguistic fossil, like the "grav-" in the adjective "grave" (from the Latin *gravis*, heavy): when a doctor says a patient's condition is grave, he doesn't mean that the sufferer is overweight.

The INDEFINITE PRONOUN + PLURAL PRONOUN construction conforms with most people's usage and is (of course) perfectly clear; for those reasons alone it deserves even wider use. It has a further advantage: it helps bridge the **GENDER** gap. Specifically, it saves you from saying, to a mixed crowd, "Everyone get his hat and coat," which is arguably sexist, or "Everyone get his or her hat and coat," which is unquestionably cumbersome. Here custom has filled a real need: a concise way of referring to groups including both sexes. And this usage, too, has abundant historical sanction: see the *OED* under "Every."

Be warned, however, that everyone who uses this eminently sensible construction is certain to have the purists on their backs. *I* can stand it; what was good enough for Byron, Ruskin, Shaw and Fitzgerald is good enough for me. But *you* may, reasonably, prefer to dodge the flak and conform to "logic." Nobody who takes this prudent course will have *me* on their backs.

AIN'T. When I was a kid, we used to say " 'Ain't' ain't a good word to use because it ain't in the dictionary. That's why I ain't going to use 'ain't' any more." Whether it actually *was* in the dictionaries in those days I don't remember, but it certainly is now—and is almost invariably marked "substandard," or "illiterate."

How and why "ain't" acquired its present low-life reputation is a puzzle. Anyone who's read Anthony Trollope knows that his mid-Victorian aristocrats said "It ain't" and "He don't" quite unselfconsciously—and would have frigidly snubbed anyone suggesting that their speech was anything but impeccable. Yet today, as for well over fifty years, nobody has a good word to say for "ain't." Or hardly anybody: the controversial *Webster's Third International Dictionary* claimed (to the outrage of many critics) that the word "is used orally in most parts of the United States by many cultivated speakers." ("Where," asked one wit, "did Webster cultivate those speakers?" My own guess would be mainly in the South, where "ain't" ain't as unspeakable as in many other regions.)

Most Americans—including many college graduates—use "ain't" in conversation. But it *ain't* a good word to use in writing, unless you're willing to buck 97 percent of the *HDCU* panel and 99 percent of the *AHD* panel—plus generations of schoolteachers. Like it or not, the word labels you as uneducated—and that, for most of us, ain't good.

ALL THAT. Say "It's not as bad as all that" and nobody will notice; say "It's not all that bad"—giving you seven words' worth of meaning for the price of five—and you'll collect a raised eyebrow or two. The experts' consensus is that it's O.K. in speech but not in writing; *I* don't consider the difference all that important.

ALTERNATE(LY)/ALTERNATIVE(LY). The distinctions between these two pairs are often confusing, but still important. The first thing to keep in mind is that the central idea of the adjective "alternate" (ancestor of all the rest) is "by turns." In summer, my wife and I usually go for the mail on alternate days; I go one day, she goes the next, and so on. That is, we get the mail alternately and thus alternate in going to the post office.

The central idea of "alternative" is choice: thus when it's my turn to get the mail I have the alternative of not bothering. That is, I can choose either to get it or not, and those are the only alternatives. (Usually, though not invariably, the choice between alternatives is inescapable, as it is here.)

In practice, people often use "alternate" and "alternative" interchangeably—and therefore, on occasion, confusingly. If you refer to "an alternate procedure" the reader may be uncertain, at least momentarily, whether you're talking about choosing one alternative procedure or the other, or using both of them alternately.

A few ultra-purists still insist that "alternative" refers to *only* two choices. This distinction neither contributes to clarity nor reflects actual usage: writers have been referring to three or more alternatives for well over a century.

"Alternate" can also double as a noun, with a special meaning, "substitute"; most political conventions are attended by both delegates and alternates. This usage, I suspect, developed because a substitute sounds (and often is) inferior to the real thing. Much better to be an alternate.

AMERICAN. Most residents of the United States use this word as if it applied only to them. In fact, all residents of the Americas, from the Canadian Arctic to Tierra del Fuego, are just as "American" as we are—and are likely to resent our appropriation of the term. Unfortunately there is no easy solution to this problem of linguistic etiquette: nobody speaks of "United Statesians." Natives of Hispanic America usually say *Norteamericanos, Yanquis* or, less politely, *gringos.* Probably the best solution is, when you're in that part of the world, do as the locals do.

Some people claim—how accurately I don't know—that some south-of-the-border Americans even object to being called "Latin Americans." The term, however, is needed: it refers collectively to peoples of Central and South American whose official language is of Latin descent (Spanish, Portuguese, French); I find it hard to imagine how this wholly factual expression could offend anybody. (Note that some Latin American immigrants in this country refer to *themselves* as "Latinos.") I shall therefore continue to use it unless some Latin American can suggest an equally precise and concise substitute.

During the 1960s and 1970s, some alleged radicals began referring to "Amerikan" and "Amerika"; a few still do. The Germanic spelling suggested, without actually saying so, that "Amerika" was like Nazi Germany. Since the United States at its worst has never been anything like as horrible as Nazi Germany at its best, the spelling is ridiculous. I'd say slanderous—but it's too silly to take that seriously.

AMONG/BETWEEN. The second of these is a favorite stamping ground of linguistic fossil hunters, who insist that "between" somehow includes the notion of "two"—meaning that it can't be applied to more than two things. (Everyone agrees that "among" can't be used with less than three things.) Thus Simon, denouncing "our sadly permissive dictionaries," asks "Who cannot hear the 'twain' in 'tween'?" His question was intended to be rhetorical, yet the correct answer is surely "Almost nobody can, unless it's specifically called to their attention." Anyway, who—to pose another rhetorical question—uses "twain" nowadays?

In fact, as the *OED* points out, "between," in all its senses, "has been extended, from its earliest appearance, to more than two." (The fossil, like the bones of "Piltdown man," isn't even a legitimate fossil.) Moreover, "It is still the only word available to express the relation of a thing to many surrounding things severally and individually . . . [rather than] collectively and vaguely." As examples where "among" is clearly wrong, the dictionary cites "the space lying among the three points," and "a treaty among three powers." Bernstein, unlike some other experts, evidently took the trouble to check out the word in the *OED*, and his discussion of it is worth reading.

For a bit of high literary comedy, take a look at *HDCU* under AMONG/BETWEEN —specifically, the hassle over the sentence "In the new subdivision, there was a driveway between every house." Most of the panelists agreed that the sentence was wrong, and that "among every house" would be worse, and they were right on both counts, but none of them offered a solution.

The real problem with the sentence is not its use of "between" but simple unclarity. If the anonymous writer meant the common arrangement of house, driveway, driveway, house, (s)he should have said ". . . driveways between each two houses"; if the layout was house, driveway, house, driveway, then it should have been "driveways between the houses" or, even simpler, "the houses were separated by driveways."

In short, if you find yourself forced to choose between (or among) several alternative usages and none of them sound (or sounds) quite right, look for another alternative that does.

AND & BUT, beginning a sentence with. When I was a kid in school, the rule was never to begin a sentence with either word, for no very good reason: other conjunctions (e.g., "moreover" and "however") were used at the beginning of a sentence as often as not. I strongly suspect that this "rule" never had much reality outside the schoolroom, but in any case everyone agrees that it's now completely inoperative. But they also agree that the device shouldn't be overused: sentences beginning with "and" or "but" may sound choppy. And that should be avoided.

AND/OR. Follett calls it "ungraceful," Bernstein calls it "a visual and mental monstrosity." *I* call the second comment confusing (a "mental monstrosity" surely implies something like a nightmare)—and uncharacteristically strident; Bernstein, even when he's wrong, is almost always charming. The expression has a very precise meaning (probably the reason lawyers are so addicted to it): A alone, B alone, or both of them. "A fine not exceeding $100 and/or five days in jail" means that the judge may fine you if he's feeling mellow, toss you in the slam if he's not, or, if he's feeling really nasty, take both your money and your liberty.

But the very fact that lawyers love the term is a persuasive reason for the rest of us to avoid it. Saying "A, B or both" is just as concise as "A and/or B."

ANGST. If you're trying to say "anxiety," using "angst" is pretentious; if you're trying to say something else, it's unclear. On either ground, skip it.

ANXIOUS/EAGER. They don't mean quite the same thing, but the difference is hard to state precisely. The simplest way of putting it is that the two words are "negative" and "positive" respectively: feeling anxious is unpleasant, feeling eager is pleasant. They also generally take different constructions: you may be either eager *to go* on a trip or anxious *about going.* For maximum clarity, use "eager" about something you want to happen, "anxious" about something you'd rather avoid.

ANY MORE. Combined with a negative verb ("Don't get around much any more"), it's standard, meaning "not now, though formerly." Without the negative, meaning simply "now" or "nowadays" ("We are so sophisticated any more"), it seems to be a regionalism. If it sounds weird to you, you've got company: *I'd* never heard of it until I unearthed it in *HDCU*—though a few months later I heard it used in conversation. Even more surprisingly, I find that it's by no means new: the *Dictionary of American Regional English* traces it back to 1859. If by any chance you've been using "any more" in the second, confusing sense—that is, without a negative—don't use it any more.

AREN'T I? is common in Great Britain but not here, at least not among the literati: it was accepted by only a bare majority of the *HDCU* usage panel, and then often reluctantly. Comments included "awkward," "strained," "a bit elegant" (!), and even "loathsome"; the late Red Smith called it "nice Nelly usage" and declared "I'd rather commit adultery"—a statement that may have been true but was hardly relevant.

A page and a half of conflicting opinions left the experts painted into a corner: "**AIN'T I**" was obviously impossible, "amn't I" is very rare (I've seen it in print only once in fifty years) and "am I not," though recommended by several panelists, sounded stuffy to others, as it does to me. "Aren't I" is unquestionably illogical—nobody says "I aren't"—but is useful enough to use if you feel like it.

AS LARGE AS, etc./LARGER THAN, etc. Used alone, these phrases obviously mean quite different things. Used with numbers, however, they become synonyms to some people: "three times larger than" substitutes for "three times as large as." Here the confusion is minor, but it gets worse with percentages. You can say that A is 150 percent the size of B, or (better) that A is 50 percent larger than B, but you can't—or shouldn't—say that A is 150 percent larger than B unless you mean that it is two and a half times the size of B. And note that it's "X times as much *as,*" not "X times as much *than*" (which I've seen in print).

When it comes to "small" and "smaller," using the wrong variety of number can produce total confusion: "three times as small as" *probably* means "one-third the size of," but what on earth does "three times smaller than" mean—let alone "150 percent smaller than," which I've also seen in print? To avoid muddles of this sort, remember that "as large as" refers to *relative* size, "larger than" to the *difference* in sizes; if A is twice as large as B, it's still only 100 percent larger than B, not 200 percent.

With "smaller than," use percentages if you really must ("50 percent smaller than"), but don't use "as small as" with any kind of number; say "half as large as" instead. Bear in mind, too, that "more than" and "less than" will often do the same job as "larger than" and "smaller than"—and do it better.

ASIATIC (noun and adjective). Some people of Asian ancestry object to this word on the ground that it is derogatory; their objection strikes me as somewhat paranoid. But on the principle that people or peoples have the right to name themselves (see **BLACK** and **GAY**), you might as well save two letters and say "Asian." On the other hand, the objection some Asians have to being called "Orientals" seems to me perfectly reasonable, because the word lumps together just about everybody east of Suez. Since the peoples in question are at least as diverse as we "Occidentals," I find it hard to imagine any statement about them that would be both true and meaningful. See also **MONGOLISM.**

ASSURE/ENSURE/INSURE. I insure my life to ensure my wife's financial security—and I assure you that's the only reason. In standard American (though not British) usage, only "insure" refers to insurance—and never mind the name of the Something-or-Other Life Assurance Society, which is a nineteenth-century relic. "Ensure" refers to making sure of something; "assure," to making *somebody* sure of something. Mixing up the three terms isn't likely to confuse anyone seriously, but sticking to the standard will guard against even momentary confusion—and mark you as a precisionist.

AUTHORITARIAN/TOTALITARIAN. Two buzzwords in considerable vogue among political spokespersons during the early 1980s. If you find the distinction confusing—join the club. Both refer to intensely repressive governments, under which most people have few legal rights even in theory and none at all in practice. But in current usage, an "authoritarian" regime is often assumed to be, well, not *nice,* but still not as bad as a "totalitarian" one.

What this generally boils down to is that the authoritarian government is on "our" side, the totalitarian one on "their" side. As not a few U.S. officials said of the Dominican dictator Rafael Trujillo, "Sure, he's a son-of-a-bitch—but he's *our* son-of-a-bitch."

Some people argue that under authoritarian governments *some* people have some rights, while under totalitarian ones, nobody—except the governing elite, of course—has any. This is no doubt a significant distinction if you're one of the minority (usually affluent to rich) with some rights, but not if you're one of the majority (often the overwhelming majority) with none.

Indeed it can be argued that in some "totalitarian" countries (Cuba, for instance) the majority *lives* a good deal better, in terms of food, education and health, than in some "authoritarian" ones (Chile, for instance). Obviously this doesn't make the Cuban government "good"—but whether it's "better" or "worse" than the Chilean government clearly depends, like many such judgments, on who you are and where you're sitting. See also **FASCIST.**

AVERAGE (adjective and noun). A word that is often confusing —sometimes deliberately so. Loosely, it's generally understood to mean "typical." More precisely, it means what statisticians call the arithmetical mean—the sum of a series of quantities divided by the number of quantities. And the mean isn't necessarily typical.

Suppose, for example, you read of a country in which the average per capita income is $5,450 a year. On the face of it, this sounds fairly prosperous. As it happens, however, the top 10 percent of the population average $50,000 a year, while the remaining 90 percent average only $500—meaning that the "average" (typical) citizen is only a jump or two from starvation. Equally, the fact that the average (mean) annual temperature in New York City is fifty-odd degrees doesn't prepare you very well to deal with either a January blizzard (temperature 20° or less) or an August heat wave (temperature 90° or more).

Unless you're deliberately trying to befuddle the reader, then, don't use "average" unless it gives a reasonably accurate picture of the group you're describing. An often useful substitute is "median," the figure that divides your group into even halves. For our first example, the median income would probably work out to something like $1,000 a year, which would give a rather more accurate picture of how the "average" citizen of that country lives.

Another misleading phrase is "the law of averages." Everyone knows that a flipped coin will come up heads half the time, on the average. But many people believe that if the coin has come up heads a dozen times in a row, then by "the law of averages" it's likely to come up tails the next time. There is no such law (unless you're flipping a two-headed coin), and betting on it can lose you your shirt.

B

BACK FORMATION. If you've ever thought about the origin of the word "scavenger," you probably assumed that it derived from the verb "scavenge," as "teacher" derives from "teach." In fact, it was the other way round: "scavenger" came into English in the sixteenth century; "scavenge," a century later. Doubtless it was coined by someone who assumed (as you did) that if there was a person called a scavenger, there must be a verb to describe what he did. Well, from then on, there was. This process, called back formation, is one of the many ways that languages form new words. As such, it reflects one of the most remarkable features of language.

Linguisticians have long drawn attention to the fact that all of us can both construct and understand sentences *we have never heard before.* When Gelett Burgess remarked "I never saw a purple cow," he was surely the first person in the world ever to make that statement—yet nobody reading it was in the slightest doubt about what it meant. The sentence was immediately understandable because it was constructed from familiar words, arranged according to the familiar rules of English syntax.

The same principle applies to individual words: we can and do understand words we've never seen or heard before, provided they are formed from familiar linguistic elements (words, prefixes, suffixes), according to familiar rules. Take "antidisestablishmentarianism," for instance. I doubt if more than one reader in a hundred can define this famous jaw-breaker, or more than one in ten thousand has ever used it. Yet if you know what "establishment" means you can, bit by bit, link up all the parts to produce a meaningful whole.

As used here, "establishment" means government support of a particular religion (specifically, the Church of England); "disestablishment," then, must mean the removal of such support. A "disestablishmentarian" is evidently one who favors such removal, and "disestablishmentarianism," the principles or doctrine favored by such a person. Add the "anti-" and you're home free.

Just as we can understand words we've never seen before, so we not infrequently construct words we've never seen (or heard) before—again, using familiar elements combined according to familiar rules. If (as usually happens) the word is already in the dictionaries, we have, in effect, reinvented it. If it isn't—we've produced a new back formation.

Sometimes "new" formations turn out to be very old. When I was in college, some of us had fun transforming existing words into what we thought were new ones, such as "couth," "kempt" and "gruntled" (from "uncouth," "unkempt" and "disgruntled," of course). Much later, I discovered that all our "new" words were in fact obsolete ones that we had, quite unwittingly, reinvented.

Back formation, then, starts with a word like "scavenger" that apparently, but not really, derives from another word, and then turns appearence into reality by introducing the "original" word into the language. If a doctor makes a diagnosis, he evidently has *diagnosed* the patient; a lazy person *lazes,* a drowsy one *drowses.* And if you've ever made jelly, you know that it either *jells* or doesn't.

I cite these particular words because though they were originally begotten by back formation (a process that some purists take a dim view of) they are absolutely acceptable

English. Others, like **ENTHUSE**, "donate" and "commentate," are still considered questionable in some quarters, while **BURGLE, EMOTE, SCULP(T)** and "but(t)le" (what a butler does) are often described as acceptable only in a humorous context. As always, usage is king—or queen.

Some of these words will be discussed individually later on. As a general rule, the first question to ask about any back formation is "Is it necessary?" Words like "commentate" and "conferencing" should be avoided because fully acceptable, and shorter, alternatives already exist ("comment" and "conferring" or "meeting"). The same goes for "orientate," used by many British writers, though they and we already have the shorter "orient." Second, many back formations (like "couth" and "gruntled") have humorous overtones, whether or not intended. And as always when you're making with the jokes, make sure the laugh won't be on you.

BALANCE (noun). In the sense of "rest" or "remainder" ("I'm returning the balance of the tickets"), the word was originally commercial slang, for which reason, probably, Follett (among others) looks down his nose at it. (The fact that a word was originally **SLANG**—or commercial—is, of course, no argument either for or against it; see **ADVERTISINGESE**.) In favor of "balance" is that it is both shorter and less pretentious than "remainder"; against it is that "rest" is still shorter, and can substitute for it at least nine times out of ten. Balancing the alternatives, I'd say save yourself a syllable—and give the critics a rest.

BARMY. A somewhat slangy British term that has recently crossed the Atlantic, on the way acquiring the spelling B-A-L-M-Y. What happened, I think, is that the Americans who picked it up assumed that "barmy" was a Cockney mispronunciation (Cockneys often inject an extraneous R after certain vowels, as in the old song about a girl who repeatedly "lorst

[lost] 'er nyme"). In fact, "barmy" is a respectable word of considerable antiquity, meaning originally "frothy, yeasty" (from the "barm"—froth—that forms in beer-making), whence the "barmy" individual with frothy or fermented brains—a bubblehead, you might say. This fine old metaphor is worth preserving, by spelling the word with an R, not an L.

BASAL/BASIC. According to *HDCU,* the first of these has become a supposedly "elevated" substitute for the second ("the basal parts of a sentence"). Whenever you're tempted to replace a familiar word with a high-toned equivalent, or supposed equivalent, think of the old, allegedly Chinese saying "Higher monkey is climbing tree, more is showing his behind."

BE ABLE TO/CAN. "Can" is one of the rare and curious creatures known as "defective verbs." Specifically, it possesses *only* a present and perfect tense ("can" and "could"), with no future, no past or present participle and no infinitive. ("To can," or "she was canning" or "I will can" concern food, not capability.) The only way of expressing future capability, and similar concepts requiring these missing parts, is to say "I will be able to," "I used to be able to" and the like. The result is that one easily falls into the habit of saying "I am able to" or "they were able to." Save words with "I can" or "they could." See also **CAN/MAY.**

BEAT (verb). Used as a past participle instead of "beaten" ("The team was badly beat"), the word has been described as "illiterate" *(HDCU).* I'd say rather that it's confusing, since it fails to make clear whether the team was defeated or exhausted—or (most likely) both.

BETTER THAN. This expression is often used informally to mean "more than" ("It took us better than four hours to get there")—but also "less than" ("We made the trip in better than four hours"). Obviously, a phrase that can mean opposite things should be handled with care. Further confusion can develop out of the other meaning of "better"—superior, or more desirable—which is implied by the second sentence but certainly not by the first, since a shorter trip would have been better.

Another example is "He sold it for better than $50,000" vs. "It cost him better than $50,000." In the first case, the price was clearly better from "his" (the seller's) standpoint; in the second, where we're talking about the buyer, a lower price would have been better.

In most cases, the context will make clear whether you mean "more than" or "less than." But to avoid any chance of confusion, make sure that more (or less) is really better; that is, don't say "better than" unless it really *was* better.

BILINGUALISM. A potentially confusing word because of its multitude of meanings—and a potentially dangerous one because some of these meanings evoke political acrimony. Its standard sense in both England and the United States is simply the ability to speak two languages, but it can also refer to the policy of having two "official" languages within a single country (e.g., English and French in Canada, French and Flemish in Belgium).

Most recently, it has in this country taken on various educational meanings: (1) the policy of giving special educational help to children whose native tongue is not English; (2) one form of this policy, consisting of teaching such children in their native tongue temporarily—that is, until they have mastered English; (3) an extension of (2), proposed by some leaders of Hispanic groups, involving the compulsory teaching of Spanish grammar and literature, and "Hispanic culture," to such children, *in Spanish*. Whether you're writing or (especially) reading the word, you obviously need to be sure which meaning is intended.

Some people are convinced that educational bilingualism will somehow lead to "official" bilingualism, and accordingly have proposed a constitutional amendment making English the only official language of the United States. This strikes me as pure paranoia: the chances that Spanish (or any other tongue) will offer serious competition to English in American life are virtually nil for the foreseeable future. What these people really have in mind is suggested by another of their proposals: ballots and other electoral materials should not be supplied in any language but English. It doesn't take a genius to see that the real idea here is to prevent non-English-speaking people from voting.

As for the various educational meanings of bilingualism, (1) seems to me elementary common sense, but (2) seems ill conceived, since it is likely (for reasons I've discussed in *OMNT*) to hamper children in learning English—meaning that they will be seriously handicapped as adults. Bilingualism (3), finally, seems reasonable enough—provided the compulsory feature is dropped.

BIMONTHLY, SEMIMONTHLY et al. One of these words means "twice a month"; the other, "every two months"—and I'll bet you three to one you're not completely sure which is which. If you're not, you've got plenty of company: over a dozen members of the *HDCU* usage panel admitted to similar uncertainty, and nearly a dozen more, though insisting that *they* knew the difference, classed them as confusing and therefore to be avoided. The confusion has existed for well over a century; "bimonthly" has been used with both meanings since the 1840s.

The problem here is with the two prefixes, "bi-" and "semi-." The first, as practically everyone knows, has something to do with "two," as in "bicycle"—but as applied to "monthly" and similar adverbs, does it mean "two" or "twice"? (If you have a firm opinion on this question, maybe you can give me a sensible reason why "biannual" means "twice a year" while "bi*ennial*" means "every two years.") Matters are even more muddled with "semi-," which can mean either "half" (as in "semicircle") or "partly" (as in "semiconscious"). Well, if a semiconscious person is less than conscious, it follows "logically" that a semimonthly magazine is published less often than a monthly one.

The only way out of this labyrinth is simply to quit using these words and all their kin ("biannual," "biennial," "semi-weekly," etc.). Indeed, Fowler suggested just this nearly forty years ago ("there is no reason why the *bi*-hybrids should not be allowed to perish"). However, his proposed substitutes, "two-monthly" and "half-monthly," don't make matters much clearer, which probably explains why they never caught on. Here, as in many other cases, the simplest solution is the best: if you get two paychecks a month, then you're paid *twice a month;* if a magazine is published in January, March, May, July, September and November, it's published *every two months* or *every other month.* As for "bimonthly," "semimonthly" and the rest of their adverbial tribe, the best we can do for them is provide a decent burial.

A minor exception to this "better off dead" judgment is "bicentennial," which unambiguously refers to two hundred years, never twice in a hundred years. (For the same reason, it's not used often!) If you're talking about the widespread U.S. celebrations during the year 1976, you'll be quite safe in calling them the Bicentennial.

BITTER(LY). " 'It's bitter cold,' he said bitterly" illustrates the fact that both words can serve as adverbs in certain contexts ("bitter" is also an adjective, of course)—see **ADVERBS**

AND HOW TO SPOT 'EM. "Bitter cold," however, is perhaps a bit tired, and certainly uses an extra word: if somebody asks you what the weather's like outside, all you need say is "It's bitter!"

Also somewhat tired is the "bitter end"—which has nothing to do with bitterness: it originally referred to the end of a rope attached to the bitts—stout posts set into the deck of a ship or boat to which anchor or mooring lines are fixed. If you've reached the bitter end, you are at the end of your rope—literally or figuratively.

BLACK/NEGRO. When I was a kid, I was carefully taught by my (Southern) parents never to say "nigger"; the only polite term for colored people was "Negroes." The lesson served me in good stead for forty-odd years in my dealings with people of color: all of them called themselves "Negroes," whereas racist whites (whom I also encountered) called them "niggers." Neither Negroes nor anyone else spoke of "blacks."

During the 1960s, some Negro militant announced that "Negro" was a "white man's word," and that the proper term was "black." How he reached this conclusion is a mystery, since both terms are English (and therefore, presumably, "white man's") words. "Black," dating from the seventeenth century, means "black"; "Negro," from the sixteenth, is a borrowed Spanish or Portuguese word meaning—you guessed it—"black."

But granting that the reasoning makes no sense, I think the rest of us should go along with it anyway, out of common courtesy if nothing else. Most black people in this country have few choices as it is; the least we can do is let them choose their own name for themselves.

There is, however, one minor hitch in the shift from "Negro" to "black": few of the people in question are literally black. And while the phrase "a light-brown Negro" made perfect sense, "a light-brown black" sounds a bit weird. Suggestions on how to get out of this bind, from readers of any color, will be welcome.

As a parenthetical note: I've heard some (white) people claim that "light-brown black" is itself "racist," a theory that completely baffles me. To me, "light-brown black" is no different from "dark-complexioned white": it's a purely descriptive term. If anything, I'd call it anti-racist, since it reflects the fact that blacks do *not* (as some whites believe) all look alike. One of the ways they don't look alike is in their color.

Some blacks also object to the figurative use of "black" in the sense of "threatening," "evil" and the like ("a black day," "blackmail"), calling it "racist." Here again I drag my feet. These usages go back to a time when few of the English had even seen black people, or had any very strong feeling about them one way or the other. They derive not from anyone's black skin but from the blackness of threatening storm clouds, and (especially) of night, when both evil spirits and evil people were abroad. (The Zulus, I'm told, also use their word for "black" to mean "evil".)

I simply don't believe that anyone reading the word "black-mail" supposes that it has anything to do with black *people*. However, I did enjoy the remark of a black political leader who, having suffered some arm-twisting from white politicians, called it—"whitemail."

BOTH. This one can get you into trouble in several ways. First, many people either use "both" unnecessarily or, having used it, add other elements to the sentence that simply repeat the same idea. Since "both" means "the two," you don't need it in "Both the children look alike"; if they look alike there obviously must be at least two of them (if there's any doubt about the number, say "The two . . ."). Nor do you say "The President's remarks demonstrated both ignorance *as well as* irresponsibility"; either replace "as well as" by "and" ("demonstrated both ignorance and irresponsibility") or drop "both" ("demonstrated ignorance as well as irresponsibility"). You might also consider dropping the President.

"Both" can also trip you up in the sequence "both . . . and." These are what the grammarians call "correlative conjunctions"—that is, the sequence of words directly following "and" must have the same syntactic structure as that following "both." This may sound like one of those meaningless schoolroom technicalities, but it isn't.

If you say "He gave a dollar both to John and Mary" (instead of "both *to John* and *to Mary,*" or, still better, "to both John and Mary"), your meaning will be clear, but some people will consider you a sloppy writer. A more serious mistake is a sentence like "Both from the standpoint of commonsense and morality, the statement was ill-advised," because it hangs the reader up. Mentally, (s)he expects that "Both from the standpoint of commonsense and morality" will be followed by "and from the somethingelse of somethingelse," and is likely to be confused when the expected clause fails to show up. Saying "From the standpoint of both commonsense and morality . . ." will tell the reader immediately what you mean, with no hangups.

BRING/TAKE. Some people say "I'll bring those bottles back to the store"; others, "I'll take them back to the store," and in neither case will anybody be in any doubt about what's going to happen to the bottles. *HDCU* insists that "bring" implies motion toward the speaker; "take," away from the speaker—which is as may be (in the sentence under discussion, the bottles are evidently going neither toward or away from the speaker but right along with her). It also describes the use of "bring" for "take" as "a debasement of our language"—which I see, with no maybes, as overkill at best, nonsense at worst. Debasement, according to the dictionary, means a lowering in quality or value; I fail to see how this alleged misuse of "bring" lowers the quality or value of English—though it may well lower *your* value in the eyes of purists.

A footnote: the editors of *HDCU* refer to the distinction between the two words as "honored in the breach almost as often as in the observance"—which is itself a solecism, though one now ingrained in the language. See **MORE HONORED IN THE BREACH.**

BRIT/BRITISH(ER)/BRITON. Natives of Great Britain normally call themselves either British or English—unless, of course, they happen to be Scots or Welsh. Strictly speaking, "the English" refers collectively to the natives of England only; if you want to be more inclusive, then it's "the British." One inhabitant of England is an Englishman, -woman or (if you insist) -person, but "Britisher" lets you say much the same thing while leaping the **GENDER** gap. "Brit" does the same job, but very informally. Originally an American term, it now has some currency among the British themselves.

"Briton," however, is somewhat ambiguous. Its original meaning was a non-English native of Great Britain, speaking a Celtic language ancestral to modern Welsh and Breton; much more recently, it acquired the additional meaning of *any* inhabitant of Great Britain ("Britons never, never, never shall be slaves!"). I prefer to stick with the original meaning—the more so in that the more recent sense, ironically, now has a somewhat archaic flavor. If I mean a modern native of Great Britain, I say "Britisher" (or Scot, or Welshman)—but not "Brit," which to me has a somewhat patronizing flavor.

BUG (verb and noun). In the sense of "annoy" or "upset" ("What's bugging you, man?"), it's a slang term taken over from Black English (ultimately, from a West African word *bagu,* annoy); whether you use it depends on how you feel about **SLANG.** In the sense of "insect" it is, of course, Standard English—though in England it often means specifically a bedbug.

In recent decades, the word has been applied to the small, pestiferous listening devices planted—often illegally—by "law enforcement" or "national security" agencies in homes and offices, and then, by extension, to devices used to tap telephone lines. Some purists object to these recent meanings, preferring "wiretap" or "tap." But while all wiretapping is bugging, bugging is not necessarily wiretapping: some bugs work by wireless. In short, say "wiretapping" only if that's what you mean; for other forms of electronic eavesdropping, or for all forms collectively, say "bugging"—unless the term really bugs you.

BUNK. Described almost universally as **SLANG**—a statement I consider bunk. Does anybody really say "bunkum" or "buncombe" nowadays, except with tongue in cheek?

BUREAUCRATESE. Most books on usage include a number of horrible examples—and they *are* horrible—of bureaucratic jargon. The bureaucrat is certainly a sitting duck for anyone seeking to demonstrate their linguistic marksmanship; indeed, criticizing bureaucratese amounts to shooting fish in the proverbial barrel.

What the experts don't seem to be curious about is why bureaucrats talk the way they do. Bureaucratese has been criticised, denounced and mocked for well over a century (Dickens referred to a fictitious Circumlocution Office as "the most important Department under Government"), and for all I know much longer. Yet bureaucrats continue to go their circumlocutious ways, untroubled by the fact that other people find their language irritating at best, appalling at worst.

It's easy to assume, as many authorities seem to, that bureaucrats write the way they do because they are stupid, ignorant or both. Doubtless some are—but many demonstrably are not, meaning that they write bureaucratese because they want to. One reason they want to is that their curious dialect, like other kinds of **JARGON,** serves to separate insiders from outsiders.

An even more important reason was summed up centuries ago in a remark of the Elizabethan critic Thomas Wilson; he described circumlocution as designed "either to sette forth a thyng more gorgeouslie or to hyde it." Bureaucratic language, then, seeks either to set forth commonplace ideas "gorgeouslie" (thereby inflating the writer's importance) or —even more important—to "hyde" what the writer is really getting at (thereby covering his or her rear from possible attack, whether by higher bureaucrats or by outsiders).

Since I've already discussed the reasons for this self-protective drive at some length in *OMNT,* I'll say little about them here, but an example of bureaucratese may suggest their nature. Consider the following reply to a request for a government grant:

> As I review the growing constraints of the new year, I have to conclude with the greatest of regrets that we simply are not in a position to direct any funds from the established priorities for this purpose.

In plain English, this means "Sorry, but they've given us less money than last year ['the growing constraints of the new year'] and what there is has already been spoken for by people who were ahead of you in line ['the established priorities']."

But why not say so directly? Well, if you say flatly that "they've given us less money than last year," then "they"— presumably the legislature—may feel you're criticizing them, especially if the recipient of the letter (who doubtless still wants the money) writes to his or her representative wanting to know how come. "Growing constraints," on the other hand, criticizes nobody. Likewise, to say "people who were ahead of you in line" might lead to questions about just who these people are and how they got into the line—meaning, at best, further correspondence and, at worst, the revelation that they elbowed their way in through political **CLOUT,** not merit. "Established priorities" provides no such clear target, and thus exemplifies the bureaucratic maxim "Cover Your Ass."

As a sort of "usage antimanual," here are some of the principles of bureaucratic style:

1. Never use a short word where a long one will do.
2. Never use one word if you can use three.
3. Use abstract terms, not concrete ones, and general, not specific, ones.
4. Avoid flat statements: hedge!

With careful attention to these principles, you can write as badly as any bureaucrat. Of course people will criticize your style, but they probably won't criticize the substance of what you're saying—because they won't be sure what it is.

BURGEON. According to *HDCU,* a word widely misused in recent years, "in the opinion of purists," to mean "grow" or even "mushroom" (= grow rapidly); supposedly, it means only "to bud." Here, as in many other cases, the purists are being purer than the facts: "burgeon" has meant "grow" since the fourteenth century. *I* object to it, first, because it is imprecise: does "rapidly burgeoning" mean "rapidly growing" or, redundantly, "rapidly mushrooming"? In addition, it's pretentious; why use a two-dollar word when a two-bit one will do just as well? Texans may conceivably refer to "the rapidly burgeoning city of Dallas"; for the rest of us, "fast-growing" does well enough.

BURGLE/BURGLARIZE. The first is a **BACK FORMATION** of the Victorian era, originally used with humorous intent to describe breaking into a house with felonious intent ("When the enterprising burglar's not a burgling"). *Some* word is certainly needed to describe what a burglar does (which is not the same thing a robber does—see your dictionary). But "burgle" gives a faintly comic air to a not very comic subject, while "burglarize" could get you into trouble with the **-IZE**-phobiacs. You pays your money—if the burglars have left you any —and you takes your choice.

BUSINESS. Bernstein considers that this word should not be applied to a profession, and asks "Would you say that your family doctor was in the medical *business?*" As a matter of fact, I might well say so—of him and of many other doctors. Some doctors, lawyers and other professionals dislike "business" as applied to their work—mainly, I suspect, because it suggests that they are not simply concerned with serving their patients or clients but, like other businessmen, are also interested in making money. If you've recently paid a doctor's or lawyer's bill, you'll no doubt be able to make up your own mind on this. *I* call myself a writer by profession—but also, since I make my living by it, feel not the slightest embarrassment in saying that I'm in the writing business.

C

CAN/MAY. Remember in school when you asked "Can I leave the room?" and teacher replied sweetly "Don't say 'can,' say *'May* I leave the room?' " Since "can" is from the same root as "know," its central idea was originally know-how—that is, ability ("I can call spirits from the vasty deep!"). "May" began with a very similar meaning, but soon moved toward the sense of possibility ("It may rain tomorrow"), whence its additional sense of permission. Thus "May I leave the room?" = "Is it possible (that you will permit me) to leave the room?"

For more than a hundred years, however, "can" has been used for "may" in this last sense, and I can't see why we can't continue using it that way, even though some people feel that the tone (if not the meaning) isn't quite the same. Remember, however, that the two verbs are interchangeable *only* if you're asking permission; use "can" if you're talking about ability ("I can fix the car; I don't need a mechanic"), "may" if you're talking about possibility or uncertainty ("I may fix the car— or I may send it to the garage"). Note, too, that "can" may occasionally be ambiguous: "You can fix the car" may mean either that you have the know-how to do it or, as an order, that you should get on with the job. See also **MAY/MIGHT.**

CANCEL OUT. *HDCU* calls the "out" redundant; I say yes and no. "Cancel" alone is fine if the idea is simply to erase or delete something ("Please cancel my order"), but if you're talking about one thing balancing or offsetting another ("His experience cancels out his lack of formal training") the "out" adds a nuance of completeness, indicating that the cancellation has produced, as they say, a wash.

CAN'T HELP BUT. Bernstein doesn't mind this, *HDCU* does, and the *AHD* and *RHD* usage panels can't make up their minds. I can't help but go along with Bernstein.

CAREEN/CAREER (verbs). The first of this troublesome pair originally meant to heave a boat over on its side in order to work on its bottom; the second (completely unrelated), to run at full speed ("careering along the road"). Nowadays, people are much more familiar with the personal *careers* that they and others pursue, and are thus likely to be confused by the apparently unrelated verb (there *is* a relationship, but you have to dig deep to find it). They have therefore substituted the phonetically similar "careen," whose original meaning is also little known; since there seems to be no very good alternative, the usage is now widely accepted.

If, like me, you know something about boats, you'll probably prefer to stick with the original, maritime sense of "careen"—and incidentally one-up your landlubber friends. If you're a landlubber, "careening" down the road is O.K.— provided you're sober, fasten your seat belt and keep an eye out for the cops. And—if you should have an accident, *don't* say that the car "careered " onto its side—which I've seen in print.

CASUALTIES/DEATHS. Bad usage is sometimes deliberate. During the Vietnam War, official U.S. spokesmen sometimes used "casualties" in the sense of combat deaths only—the point being that this figure was much lower, and therefore less alarming to the public, than the total number of casualties, which included wounded, missing and captured. One hopes there will be no future occasions for such bad (in every sense) usage.

CENTER AROUND/CENTER ON. The first is widely used, and almost as widely disapproved, on the ground that "center means to be collected or gathered to a point" (Bernstein). However, it has long had the additional meaning of "to gather or collect as round a centre" (*OED*—note the British spelling), which would make "center around" (= collect around) reasonable enough.

As an example of the incorrect usage of "center around," Bernstein gives the sentence "The strikers are at odds over their actual grievances, but these appear to center around the vacation provisions of the contract." The sentence is certainly a bad one—but replacing "around" with "on" doesn't help a bit. It describes the strikers as simultaneously disagreeing ("at odds") and, implicitly, agreeing ("their . . . grievances center around the vacation provisions"), while "actual" adds a further note of confusion ("actual grievances" versus what other kind of grievances?).

What the writer probably meant to say, but didn't, was something like "The strikers showed little agreement on their grievances, but most of them expressed special dissatisfaction with the contract's vacation provisions." The moral is that if you center your thinking around niceties of usage you can lose sight of what you're trying to say.

CHAISE LOUNGE. A good example of "popular etymology"— turning an unfamiliar foreign word into a respectable native-sounding one. The same process converted the outlandish "musquash" (borrowed from Algonquian) into "muskrat"— quite reasonably, since the creature looks like a large rat and has a musky odor. The chaise longue was borrowed from France, where its name means simply "long chair"; since it's also a chair you lounge in, the "longue" is, not unreasonably, becoming "lounge." If, like me, you know some French, you'll stick with the original name; just make sure you pronounce it "long," not "lonj." If you don't know French, and don't care if people know you don't, you'll say "lounge."

CHAUVINIST. Nicolas Chauvin, a French soldier in the Napoleonic wars, won the mockery of his comrades through his mindless and vociferous loyalty to his leader. His name has given both French and English a term for the sort of patriot who gives **PATRIOTISM** a bad name. Your true chauvinist goes far beyond the dubious principle of "My country, right or wrong"; he (and he almost always *is* a he) would never concede that his country—or its leaders—*could* be wrong.

During the 1930s, radicals began referring to "white chauvinists" and "male chauvinists"—meaning people with a similar blind commitment, or supposed commitment, to white or male supremacy, or even with mild tendencies in that direction. The second phrase moved into general usage with the rise of feminism, some of whose adherents pronounced it "malechauvinistpig." Later, it was shortened to plain "chauvinist"—or M.C.P.

This use of "chauvinist" naturally evoked the ire of John Simon, who called it yet another example of a **SPECIAL INTEREST GROUP** (i.e., feminists) "perverting the language to its own presumed benefit." The *HDCU* usage panel (92 percent male) also disapproved of it almost unanimously, and had a good deal of literary fun doing so.

Their badinage ignored two important facts. First, "chauvinist" is becoming a rare word in its original, nationalistic sense; people are more likely to say "jingo" or "superpatriot." Second, if the word is used to mean "male chauvinist," the context will make its sense clear at least four times out of five. The fifth time, say "male chauvinist"—or simply call the pig a sexist. See also **GENDER.**

CLAIM/REPORT/STATE (verbs). All of these are synonyms for "say," but they don't mean precisely the same thing. "Claim" in particular is one you need to be careful of, whether you're writing it or reading it. Bernstein, following H. L. Mencken, describes it as "newspaper jargon"—but Mencken's been dead a long time.

Today, "claim" is a perfectly acceptable word, provided you're aware of its distinctive overtones. When a writer tells you that so-and-so "claimed" such-and-such, (s)he's hinting that so-and-so may not have been telling the truth, the whole truth and nothing but the truth. "State" is more noncommittal; it says, in effect, "That's what the man said; make what you like of it." "Report," finally, has mildly positive overtones. In particular, it is often used of more or less formal statements by officials—who, as we all know, always tell the truth.

During the Vietnam War, the press almost invariably told us that the North Vietnamese "claimed" to have shot down various numbers of American planes, whereas the U.S. military "reported" that they had killed a certain number of the enemy. As we now know, of course, the U.S. "reports" were every bit as inaccurate—or fictitious—as the Vietnamese "claims."

A careful, conscientious writer will never tell you that something happened unless (s)he personally saw it happen, or was told of it by somebody (s)he considers both knowledgeable and truthful; otherwise (s)he'll say that so-and-so reported or stated that it happened. If (s)he has any doubts about the statement, (s)he'll say "claimed." Unfortunately, not all writers are both careful and conscientious; a few are neither.

A final nuance is that "report" properly applies only to statements of fact or alleged fact. A political spokesman can state or claim that his candidate will win by a landslide, but he can't report it, because the statement is a matter of opinion until the votes are in. See also **TOM SWIFTIES.**

CLICHÉS. It's almost impossible to say anything about clichés that is both brief and sensible. Everybody has the feeling they're something to avoid, but most people also know that they can't be avoided completely. And when it comes to identifying what is and what isn't a cliché, the mind (you should excuse the expression) boggles. Is **DO YOUR OWN THING** a cliché, a bit of dated 1960s slang, or both, or neither? (*HDCU* offers almost as many opinions as there are panelists.)

Dictionaries of clichés (e.g., Eric Partridge's) are sometimes helpful, but date rapidly: hackneyed expressions, like crabgrass, spread too fast to be weeded out by even the most assiduous lexicographer. As a further complication, even a certified, dyed-in-the-wool *(sic!)* cliché can often be sanitized by using it tongue in cheek—as I've just used "dyed in the wool" and, earlier, "the mind boggles." The late Frank Sullivan, in his periodic articles on Mr. Arbuthnot, The Cliché Expert, showed that clichés can be fun—provided you know what they are, and your audience knows you know.

Broadly speaking, a cliché can be defined as a once-colorful phrase whose color has faded with time and use—as often happens with colorful things. The result is that words which once enlivened communication serve instead to deaden it; instead of stimulating thought, they inhibit it. When we speak of someone as "thinking in clichés," we mean that (s)he simply regurgitates the hackneyed thoughts and phrases of others without thinking about their sense.

Yet these generalities, though true, aren't of much help when it comes to spotting clichés on the wing, as it were. The phrase "sour grapes" has been used for centuries, yet I certainly wouldn't call it a cliché; it's just part of the language. "Dyed-in-the-wool," on the other hand, seems to me a tired way of saying "thoroughgoing," "out-and-out" or "inflexible" ("a dyed-in-the-wool conservative")—and its less-than-precise meaning is perhaps the best reason for avoiding it.

Ultimately, I think, cliché spotting depends on personal

taste and experience. If a particular expression sounds tired to *you,* it may well sound tired to the reader. Unfortunately the reverse isn't true: an expression that *you* find well worn but still useful may strike someone else as worn out. Recently, for example, I saw "hidden agenda," "conspiracy theory" and "trickle-down theory" described as clichés—yet to me the last two, at least, seem needed: there's no other concise way of expressing their sense. For that matter, is "hidden agenda" any more of a cliché than its older equivalent, "[one's] own axe to grind"? Dictionaries of clichés can give you a general sense of the *kind* of expressions to avoid, but when it comes to particular cases, you're on your own.

CLIMAX. Derived from a Greek word meaning "ladder," it originally (sixteenth century) meant an ascending series, roughly equivalent to a **CRESCENDO.** Nowadays, however, it means the peak reached at the end of the ascent. Both Bernstein and the *OED,* for some reason, consider this sense a misuse of the word, though it has been current for two centuries. The original meaning has been dead for a century (except, possibly, among classicists), and any attempt to resurrect it can produce only confusion. After all, just about everybody *knows,* from personal experience, what a climax is.

CLOUT (noun). A good example of the clouded crystal ball in language. As late as 1975, *HDCU* called it a vogue word, though it probably wasn't then and certainly isn't now. Its value, as a succinct term for the off-the-record influence that plays so regrettably large a role in both politics and business, is shown by its persistence in American English as well as by its rapid adoption in Britain.

COHORT. If you know anything about Roman history, you probably know that the word originally meant a unit of infantry about the size of a modern company. Later, the meaning was extended to various other kinds of groups, and still later acquired the sense of *one* associate or assistant ("The dead gang leader and his cohort were found in the trunk of a car"). This last usage may originally have been either sloppy or a would-be witticism; if the latter, it wasn't very funny then and certainly isn't now. "Cohort" in the sense of a group has a specific, technical meaning in the sciences; elsewhere, it strikes me as overblown. Handle with care—if at all!

COLLIDE. Bernstein believes that you can't have a collision unless *both* the colliding objects are moving—that is, you can't properly say "The car collided with a tree." *HDCU,* on the other hand, considers that usage "perfectly acceptable." Bernstein is wrong on the facts—moving objects have been colliding with stationary ones in English since the eighteenth century—but right stylistically: "The car hit a tree" says the same thing a lot quicker.

What you can't say is that the car and the tree "were in collision," since that definitely implies that both were moving. And you *shouldn't* say it even of two moving cars, since the extra words make the phrase move slowly—and the cars didn't: just say they "collided."

An interesting sidelight on this word is that in the 1860s, when it began to be used of colliding trains or ships, English critics attacked the "new" usage as an "Americanism"—meaning, of course, something to be shunned by all decent people. The criticism was even sillier than most such, since the only thing new about the usage was the trains. A century earlier, Johnson's dictionary had defined "collide" as "strike against each other"—and what else were the trains doing?

COMMAS AND RESTRICTIVE CLAUSES. Improper or unconventional punctuation will seldom do more than momentarily confuse the reader; in this case, however, it can change your meaning.

A restrictive clause, as its name indicates, restricts or limits the word it refers to; Fowler coined the useful term "defining" clause. You use such clauses, then, if there is *more than one* of whatever you're talking about, to define which of them you mean. Thus "the woman that I married" usually defines one woman out of several billion on earth, and the clause beginning with "that" isn't set off with commas. (If it defines more than one woman, be sure you've made clear which marriage you're talking about.) "The woman, who I married," means a specific woman, already identified, who—incidentally—you married; that is, the commas are required.

The touchstone for a nonrestrictive clause, as Bernstein notes, is whether it can be omitted without turning the sentence into gibberish—which is the case with "as Bernstein notes": the sentence makes perfect sense without it. Similarly, if you write "Bernstein, the word expert, says . . ." you can drop the words between the commas and still make sense. But if you write "Bernstein the word expert says A, but Bernstein the conductor says B," the two modifying clauses are restrictive; if you dropped them, you'd end up saying "Bernstein says A, but Bernstein says B." See also **THAT/WHICH**.

A widely noted example of how the "nonrestrictive comma" can radically change meaning occurred at the 1984 Republican convention. The draft of the party platform opposed "any attempt to increase taxes which would harm the recovery." Since there was no comma after "taxes," the "which" clause was restrictive: that is, the draft didn't oppose all tax increases, just those "which would harm the recovery"; other increases were presumably O.K. Since there was little agreement on what sort of tax increases would actually hinder recovery (if any would), the plank committed the party to practically nothing.

But the more fanatical delegates wouldn't buy this restriction; they insisted on the comma, which put them on record against "any attempt to increase taxes, which would harm the recovery." That is, *any* such attempt would harm the recovery, and should therefore be resisted.

The revised sentence was clearer, but was also nonsense: the harm to recovery (if any) would flow not from an "attempt" to increase taxes but from the increase itself. Nor, indeed, did most party leaders take the added comma very seriously; thus Senator Robert Dole dismissed it as a "typographical error," thereby demonstrating his knowledge of both political reality and political **EUPHEMISM.**

COMMUNIST. A word that covers a multitude of sins, both real and imaginary—witness this story. In 1965 I was having lunch in a San Diego hotel and found myself eavesdropping on a conversation among four middle-class ladies. They were discussing President Lyndon Johnson, then engaged in bombing the hell out of (communist) North Vietnam. Yet to these ladies, LBJ was a communist. None of them actually *called* him one; they simply took it for granted—and were busily discussing his role in the **INTERNATIONAL COMMUNIST CONSPIRACY.**

In its most precise sense, "communist" means a member of some communist party or sect, but even this is fairly loose: communist parties (and governments) can and do differ abusively over many things, including who is and is not a "communist." (Some political splinter groups insist that *they* are communists, but Soviet and Chinese communists aren't.)

More loosely, "communist" means an adherent of some communist doctrine. Given the many varieties of those doctrines, the word won't tell you very much about what the person in question really thinks. Still more loosely—as used by those San Diego ladies, for instance—it means just about anybody you disapprove of. Lyndon Johnson was such a "communist," so was Nelson Rockefeller and so—I'm not making this up—was President Eisenhower.

Whenever you read the word "communist," then, try to

figure out (if you can) just what the writer means by it. And if you're tempted to write it, make sure you know what *you* mean by it—and that your readers will too. Bear in mind also that if you call someone a communist in print, you may be invited to prove it in court.

COMPARATIVES/SUPERLATIVES. The old rule is that if you're referring to only two things, you can't use superlatives like "best" or "youngest" or "fastest"; it's the *better* candidate, or *younger* child, or *faster* runner. The rule, however, is clearly on the way out—and not surprisingly, since the sense will be clear whichever form you use. The distinguished grammarian C. C. Fries says categorically that "The use of the superlative for two . . . is Standard English usage"; most of the usage experts have reservations. Indeed *HDCU* goes so far as to propose "May the *better* man win"; I doubt that any English-speaking referee or sports fan—or even the *HDCU* editors themselves—ever said this.

COMPOSE/COMPRISE/CONSIST. Everyone agrees that "is composed of" and "consists of" mean the same thing. Many people use "comprised of" as a synonym for "composed of," though many others object, saying (correctly) that in standard usage "comprises" means "is composed of"—or "consists of." The best way out of the confusion is to drop "comprise" entirely; whichever sense you use it in, it'll sound wrong to somebody. Equally dispensable is "is composed of," since it takes three words to say what "consists of" says in two.

But whatever you decide to do, don't substitute "includes" for any of these expressions, since it implies something rather different. The United States *includes* the states of New York, Pennsylvania and California, but it *consists of* (or comprises) these and forty-seven other states, plus the District of Columbia. Some dictionaries (e.g., *AHD*) will tell you different —but why take a chance? "Consists of" makes clear that you're talking about *everything* included in whatever you're talking about; "includes" doesn't.

CONNIVE. When I read in Bernstein that this word means only "wink" (at someone's misconduct), not "plot" or "conspire," I was startled, since I'd been using it in the second sense for years. It turned out that Bernstein was right—but only prior to 1800, which is when the second sense came into use. The additional meaning undoubtedly developed because if you're conniving (winking) at somebody's misdeeds, you are also, speaking loosely, conniving (conspiring) with them.

Fortunately, the ambiguity seems to be on the way out because the verb is not much used nowadays, in either sense. To speak of someone "conniving" at a crime sounds pretty musty, while to say that two people are "conniving" together is unclear; better to say "conspiring." About the only form in which you're likely to encounter the word is in the verbal adjective "conniving," meaning devious or sneaky, or the derived noun, "conniver," meaning that sort of person.

CONSENSUS. The often-used phrase "consensus of opinion" is a redundancy: you can't have a consensus of anything *but* opinion. (The phrase resembles "a Jewish rabbi," which I've seen in the *New York Times;* I wonder how many non-Jewish rabbis the *Times* editors know?) Most authorities are equally harsh with "general consensus," but here I'm not so sure. To me, at least, the phrase, depending on context, implies either a general agreement, but with some dissenters, or complete agreement on general principles, with some disagreement on details. In either case, however, "broad consensus" might be clearer. However you use consensus, make sure you spell it with two N's—coNseNsus, not coseNsus.

CONSERVATIVE. The word derives, of course, from "conserve," and in its original sense described people or groups wishing to preserve existing customs, institutions and the like. In recent years, it has increasingly been applied to—or adopted by—people who want to do away with existing institutions in favor of the supposedly better ones of the Good Old Days. We can ignore the question of whether the Good Old Days were all that good, and who they were good for, and merely note that people who want to change things back to an earlier state are not really conservatives but reactionaries (the sense of which, by the way, has nothing to do with "react"). "Conservative," however, is an O.K. thing to be; "reactionary" is not. If, then, you hear people described as conservatives, or are moved to so describe them, make sure you're clear on what (if anything) they actually want to conserve.

CONTACT (verb). I'd guess that more ink has been spilled over this word than over almost any other supposed barbarism in English: it has been furiously controversial for half a century. Alexander Woolcott detested it; Rex Stout (or at least his alter ego, Nero Wolfe) abominated it, and as late as 1975 two-thirds of the *HDCU* usage panel refused to accept it in writing, while one-third barred it even from casual speech. Indeed, many of those who accepted it did so only under protest; one announced that he used it, but didn't like it (I wonder who was twisting his arm).

A venerable objection to the word is that " 'contact' is a noun, not a verb." Well, it *is* a noun, of course, but, like thousands of other English nouns, it is also a verb (see **INTERCHANGEABLE PARTS**). The usage is no newfangled barbarism either: it dates from 1839 ("the spark and the powder contacted"—*OED*). Its modern, transitive sense ("Mr. Dickey contacted every family") dates from the 1920s.

Why, after more than half a century, does this usage still evoke passions, while many newer ones have slipped into the language with no commotion? The reason is pretty certainly its association with businessmen, for whom many literary people had and have a rooted contempt—which is, of course, returned with double-digit interest by many businessmen.

The word's commercial connections, real or imagined, are clearly much on the minds of the experts. Several *HDCU* panelists called it "business jargon," and Bernstein suggested that only businessmen need the word. (In England the usage had another strike against it: it originated in America.)

"Contact" is certainly used widely in the business world, and quite possibly originated there. Salesmen and similar low types who frequently had to *get into contact with* customers and suppliers found that saying *contact* saved time—which to the businessman is proverbially money. But—so what? The word has stuck, and spread—even in England—because there is no really good substitute. "Get in touch with" uses four words instead of one, and terms like "phone" or "write" are too specific: contacting someone may involve a phone call, a letter or a personal visit.

Myself, I "contact" people any time I need to because it's a clear and concise way of saying what I mean. If that marks me as a low, money-grubbing type—well, better that than the pretentious, verbose type who says "get into contact with."

CONTENT/CONTENTS (nouns). Theoretically, one word is merely the plural of the other; practically, they are—and should be—used in different senses. "The contents of the box" means the physical objects (or even one object) literally contained in it; "the content of the speech," on the other hand, means the ideas or emotional themes figuratively contained in it (as contrasted with the words or style in which those ideas were expressed). The content of a painting or piece of music means much the same thing—though many modern painters and composers would deny that their productions have, or should have, any content whatever.

HDCU's suggestion that "content" is formal, "contents,"

informal, is simply wrong. Would even the most pedantic judge declare that "the content of the box was damaged"?

CONTINUAL(LY)/CONTINUOUS(LY). The distinction between these words, sometimes overlooked, is useful and therefore worth preserving. When we speak of some politician's "continual lies," we obviously don't mean that he doesn't take time out for eating and sleeping, or even that he doesn't occasionally tell the truth, if only by accident—all of which would be implied by "continuous lies." A "continuous rain," unlike the mendacious politician, continues without a break; if there were intermissions, we'd say something like "continual (or repeated) showers." In some tropical regions, it rains continually, but not continuously, for much of the year.

"Human beings are continually changing" is arguably true, if we're talking about their personalities. But "Human beings are continuously changing" (which Simon dislikes) is unquestionably true, if you're talking about *physical* changes: we are not composed of precisely the same molecules as we were a minute ago. As always, the key question is "What—exactly—do you mean?"

COP/OFFICER/POLICEMAN. Cops call cops "cops" but don't care much for noncops calling them "cops." If you're addressing a cop, say "officer"; if you're likely to be read or overheard by one, say "policeman" (or "police officer" if you're trying to avoid the **GENDER** gap). As for "fuzz" and "pig," they are dated and, if used to a cop, both rude and risky. When you're dealing with somebody armed with a gun and a heavy club, common politeness is simple prudence.

COPE. Many authorities object to sentences like "She can't cope" and "The man who gets the job must be able to cope" *(HDCU)*, at least in writing. Their reason is that you don't just "cope," you cope *with* something or someone. They're right —and wrong. The first sentence is meaningless as it stands, but its context should make clear what it was she couldn't cope with—whether some specific problem or life in general.

The second sentence, by contrast, is likely to be meaningless in any context: it amounts to saying "The man who gets the job must be able to handle the job"—eleven words' worth of nothing. To cope with "cope," watch your context.

COULD(N'T) CARE LESS. "I couldn't care less" has been in the language for generations, and means exactly what it says: my concern with the matter is zero. (Mathematically, of course, negative numbers are even less than zero—but let's not open *that* can of worms.) Over the past twenty-five years, many people have begun to say "I could care less," with the same meaning. Setting aside the overheated comments in *HDCU* ("vulgar," "stupid," "I wince," "Kill! Kill!"), I'd call the new phrase questionable. Used with a clearly ironic tone, in the sense of "I could care less—but just barely," it's clear enough; used "straight" (which it usually is), it's likely to be confusing. The original version may be somewhat tired, but better a cliché than an ambiguity.

CRAFT (verb). Bernstein considers it a creation of "the advertising fraternity" and therefore (of course) to be shunned. The facts are a little more complicated. The verb actually came into English some centuries ago, dropped out of use and then was revived in the 1960s *(OED Supp.)*. Its first recorded modern use was *not* in advertising but in the *Listener,* published by that model of propriety the British Broadcasting Corporation.

Nor is the word used only (or even, I think, predominantly) in advertisements. Thus a few years ago the *New York Times,* another bastion of propriety, referred in its editorial columns to "a well crafted foreign policy." Having said this, however,

I'll add that at present (early 1986) the word *is* being overused, and should perhaps be avoided on that ground.

CRESCENDO. Musicians know that this technically means a gradual increase in volume; recently it has acquired a broader meaning of a gradual increase in other stirring (or alarming) things—excitement, violence and the like. Some people, however, have taken to using it as a synonym for **CLIMAX,** which is almost guaranteed to confuse any musicians (and many nonmusicians) in the audience. Moreover, to misuse the term in this way deprives us of a useful word for what leads up to a climax—literal or figurative. Just remember that in Italian (from which we borrowed it) *crescendo* literally means "growing"—not "full-grown."

D

DECIMATE. Roman generals, a notably hard-nosed lot, sometimes disciplined mutinous troops by decimating them: lining them up and beheading every tenth man. (The "deci-" is the same root we find in "decimal system"—counting by tens.) For some centuries, however, the word has been used in the broader sense of destroying or otherwise inactivating a large proportion (usually well over one-tenth) of a group of people, or even things. So far, so good.

Nowadays, however, it is sometimes used to mean simply "destroy," as in "The building was decimated by the wrecker's ball" (Bryant). This is both muddy and overblown: if destroyed is what you mean, say so. Or you could try "smashed" or "obliterated."

DEDUCE/DEDUCT. A confusing pair of verbs, for the rather odd reason that they have given birth to identical-twin nouns. "Deductions" are what you try to apply to your taxable income—but also what Sherlock Holmes was continually making, to the perennial amazement of Dr. Watson. And there's the catch: you *deduct* interest and taxes on your IRS form—but Holmes, on his first meeting with Watson, *deduced* that the good doctor had recently been in Afghanistan. As a friend of mine remarked, it's a rather taxing distinction.

DEPRECATE/DEPRECIATE. Another confusing pair—and the distinction is made no clearer by some of the examples given in usage manuals. "Deprecate" originally meant to protest against; "depreciate," to reduce in value, hence, to belittle. But "deprecate" is now quite widely used in the second sense, especially in such compounds as "self-deprecating" (= self-belittling) and "self-deprecatory."

Granting that the two words are—or were—different, what can we say of *HDCU*'s ". . . he *depreciated* the importance of his contribution . . ."? The usage is certainly correct ("He belittled the importance of . . .")—but "deprecate" would be a near-miss ("He protested against the [supposed] importance of . . .").

The confusion has arisen partly because the words are somewhat similar in meaning and very similar in sound. Equally important, I suspect, is that nowadays most people are accustomed to think of "depreciate" and its relative, "depreciation," in their original (lowered value) sense, whence the economist's "depreciating currency" or the tax accountant's "depreciation allowances." As a result, "depreciate" in the sense of "belittle" may sound wrong—as "deprecate" in the same sense sounds wrong to traditionalists.

For maximum clarity, stick with the original meaning of both "depreciate" (lower or drop in value) and "deprecate" (protest against); if you mean "belittle," say so. However, "self-deprecating" for "self-belittling" should do well enough. I must add that I deprecate the importance given to this controversy—and depreciate its significance.

DESERTS/DESSERTS. How much of the confusion between these phonetically identical words (not to be confused with deserts like the Sahara) is due to ignorance and how much to simple misspelling is hard to say. Your deserts are what you deserve—which may or may not include desserts (in the case of obstreperous children, definitely not). Confusion apart, "deserts" is rather musty, and "just deserts" (its most common use) is a cliché, so give the word its deserts: avoid it.

DIFFERENT FROM/TO/THAN. "Different from" is Standard American, "different to," Standard English, and both are logical—or as logical as language ever gets. "Different to" follows the pattern of "similar to," while "different from" contrasts the separation of different things to the closeness of similar ones (compare "far *from*" and "close *to*"). "Different than" is nonstandard in both countries, but is becoming standard in such constructions as "Is your address different than it was?" *(HDCU),* which eliminates a word from the purists' "different from what it was." So far as clarity goes, none of them is very different from, to or than the others.

DILEMMA. The situation of being forced to choose one of two unpleasant alternatives (occasionally—despite the purists but according to the *OED*—one of several such). For example, during the 1950s a number of Americans faced the dilemma of becoming political informers or going to jail. However, as a synonym for "problem" ("Conglomerates are a major dilemma confronting the American people"), the word is both confusing and pompous.

DISASSOCIATE/DISSOCIATE. Both words date from the early sixteenth century, so they're equally legitimate—if you're talking about people ("I want to disassociate/dissociate myself from that statement"). "Dissociate" saves you a syllable, but "disassociate" is easier to remember, since it pairs with "associate" as, for example, "disaffiliate" does with "affiliate." In nonpersonal (especially scientific) senses, "dissociate" is preferable ("dissociate the compound into its elements"; "a series of dissociated ideas"). And when it comes to the associated nouns, I completely dissociate myself from "disassociation." Unless you have an absolute passion for six-syllable words, make it "dissociation."

DISCREET/DISCRETE. Another case where typographical error has compounded phonetic confusion. Since their meanings are quite discrete, consult the dictionary discreetly if you're not sure which to use.

DISINTERESTED/UNINTERESTED. A first-class semantic muddle, which is made no clearer by the many experts who either aren't aware of its complexities or prefer to ignore them. Taking it from the top, "disinterested" entered the language early in the seventeenth century, with the meaning "unconcerned" ("How dis-interested they are in all worldly matters"—*OED*). Soon afterward, "uninterested" arrived, with the meaning of "unbiased"—that is, their meanings then were precisely the reverse of their standard meanings today.

Now the plot thickens. In less than a century, "disinterested" had picked up a second meaning, "having no personal stake" (in the outcome)—hence, "unbiased." In another century, "uninterested" had come to mean also "unconcerned." Eventually, both words lost their original meanings and, in effect, swapped places. But during the past forty years or so, increasing numbers of people have begun using "disinterested" to mean "unconcerned"—thus, ironically (and quite unwittingly), reverting to its original sense.

The change illustrates two interesting things about language: the way in which all of us, on occasion, "reinvent" it (see **BACK FORMATION**), and the fact that changes in one area often force changes somewhere else. Here, the problem began with the noun "interest." This word started out with the meaning of a right or title to something ("an interest in a piece of property"), whence also "a personal stake," but it soon acquired the additional sense of simply "concern." This is now its predominant sense, though the older meaning survives in such phrases as "conflict of interest."

Now, if "interest" means "concern" (as it usually does) and "disinterest" means "unconcern" (as it invariably does), then anyone encountering the word "disinterested" for the first time will assume, quite reasonably, that it means "uninterested" or "unconcerned"—a sensible conclusion, but one that drives many experts wild. Thus the English author Anthony Burgess called this usage "one of the worst American solecisms" *(HDCU).* There'll always be an England —and in it, Englishmen who think they own the English language. (In fact, the usage is becoming increasingly common in Britain.)

If it were simply a matter of the experts vs. the rest of us, the solution would be easy. Unfortunately, the actual situation is more complicated: *both* meanings of "disinterested" are current, and making clear which of them you intend requires careful footwork.

To begin with, *never* use "uninterested" to mean "impartial": it conforms neither to the dictionary nor to current usage. Second, if you use "disinterested" to mean "impartial," make sure the context makes this clear. "A disinterested opinion" does nicely, but "disinterested in the outcome" doesn't: the reader may have to stop and figure out whether the person referred to has no stake in the outcome or simply doesn't give a damn. When in doubt, use a synonym, which in my impartial, unbiased and unswayed opinion shouldn't be hard to find.

Finally, if you're tempted to use "disinterested" in its newest (and oldest) sense of "uninterested," be aware that (1) some people won't be sure what you're trying to say; (2) others will be sure—but will be equally sure you're saying it wrong; (3) still others will be wholly uninterested (or will have a total disinterest) in the whole business.

DO YOUR OWN THING. Either a dated catchphrase or a cliché, or both. "Do your thing," on the other hand, is to my ear perfectly acceptable shorthand for "Do whatever you customarily or frequently do." One of *my* things is writing about the English language—and I'm doing it right now.

DON'T/DOESN'T. *HDCU* claims that "I don't" and "you don't" are considered suspect by some people. I don't know any such people, but agree with the editors that the suspicion makes no sense. "He don't," on the other hand, is unquestionably blue-collar English, so nobody should use it if he don't want to be labeled.

DOPE. A term whose intricate history, as traced in the *OED Supp.*, is well worth a look by any word lover. It comes from the Dutch *doopen,* to dip, whence *doop* (pronounced "dope") —a sauce you dip things into. Dutch sailors voyaging to the Orient transferred the word to the gooey mass that opium forms when it is melted for smoking.

Gradually, "dope" expanded to include not just opium but also its derivatives (laudanum, morphine, heroin), and eventually cocaine and various other "recreational" drugs. (In some parts of the United States, it even came to mean Coca-Cola, whose formula originally included extract of coca leaves.) It also begot a verb, as in "doping a horse." Subsequently, the noun picked up the additional meaning of a dopey person—one who acted as if he'd been doped.

All these meanings were more or less slangy. But the term also was soon applied to various legitimate kinds of goo—a mixture of tallow and other things which, applied to the soles of boots, enabled the wearer to slide over snow; a type of paint used on the canvas wings of early aircraft, and so on. Nearly all these meanings are now obsolete or obsolescent.

"Dope" survives today mainly in three slang senses: a stupid person, a drug (often specifically marijuana) and information ("the straight dope"). "Dope fiend" is obsolete except as irony—and was always misleading when applied to someone under the influence of opium or opiates, which tranquilize rather than excite. (The only time an opiate addict is likely to be fiendish is when he's *not* under the influence—i.e., when he's suffering withdrawal symptoms.) Your real "dope fiend" is a coke-hound or speed freak, since both cocaine and the amphetamines can definitely produce paranoid behavior. As the jazz musician Mezz Mezzrow said of cocaine, if you're not crazy before you use it you will be afterward.

DOUBT IF/THAT/WHETHER. Many experts object to one or another of these phrases when used in certain constructions, but few of them agree on which phrases should be used in which. Since I doubt that your meaning will be obscured, whichever one you use, I also doubt whether (that) the distinction is worth wasting time over—indeed, I doubt if (that) anyone cares much.

DROWNED/WAS DROWNED. Some usage manuals will tell you that "was drowned" implies not just death from submergence but actual killing, as by holding the victim's head under water—that is, you don't say that someone "fell overboard and was drowned." A better reason for not using "was drowned" here is that it adds an extra word; a good reason for not using it anywhere is that it is in the **PASSIVE VOICE.**

DRUNK/DRUNKEN. Trying to distinguish between these two words is enough to drive you to drink. If the driver of a car is drunk, he's a drunken (or drunk) driver, guilty of drunk (or drunken) driving; the only important thing to remember is— don't drive with him. Note, however, that "drunken" in certain contexts implies not just drunkenness but alcoholism: a drunk bum simply happens to be drunk, while a drunken bum is implicitly that way all or most of the time.

DUE TO/BECAUSE OF/OWING TO. When I was in high school, my teachers insisted that "due" was an adjective, and therefore had to modify a noun or pronoun somewhere in the sentence. You couldn't say "I fell due to ice on the sidewalk," since "due" obviously didn't modify "I"—or "ice" or "sidewalk." The correct usage would be "My *fall* was due to ice . . ."—or "I fell *because of* ice . . ." since "because of" is not an adjective but a prepositional phrase. Yet it was perfectly O.K. to say "I fell *owing to* ice on the sidewalk" *(OED)*, though "owing to" looked remarkably like the tabooed "due to." Forty years ago, the purists were still fighting to preserve these confusing distinctions, and a few still are. For practical purposes, however, "due to," "owing to" and "because of" are now interchangeable. The proof? In 1957, Queen Elizabeth II, in a speech to the Canadian Parliament, declared "Due to inability to market their grain, prairie farmers have been faced . . ." *(HDCU)*. That was the Queen's English in every sense—and what was good enough for Her Majesty surely ought to be good enough for the rest of us.

DUMB. Purists object to using this word in the sense of "stupid," claiming that it "really" means speechless. Any good dictionary, however, would have told them that these are two different words: the first harks back to Old English; the second was borrowed into American English (from the Dutch *dom* = stupid) over a century ago. Anyone who can't tell from the context which word is being used must be pretty dumb.

E

EACH/EITHER. A room has fireplaces on opposite walls. Does it have a fireplace at *each* end, at *either* end—or at *both* ends? Here's one place you can take your pick: any one of the three is correct. But be careful: "either" (usually) and "both" (always) imply that you're dealing with only two things, as with the two ends of the room. If, improbably, the room had fireplaces on all four walls, they would be "on each wall"—though "on every wall" would be still better.

EACH OTHER/ONE ANOTHER. Some purists distinguish between these, insisting that the first can refer only to two things; the second, only to more than two. The distinction is long out of date, if indeed it ever existed: under "each other" the *OED* says, succinctly, *"=one another."*

ECOLOGY/ENVIRONMENT. A pair confusing enough to stump even some experts. "Ecology" originally meant the science or study of organisms in relation to their environment —that is, to the conditions surrounding them—and to one another. But for over eighty years it has also been used to mean a particular set of such relationships, as in "the ecology of a glacial lake." (Here, "ecosystem" would be more precise, though less familiar.) More recently, "ecology" has acquired various figurative meanings, most of which strike me as either trendy or blurry, and on either count to be avoided.

The state of confusion generated by these various meanings can be judged from an example cited in *HDCU:* "Even so simple an undertaking as maintaining a lawn affects the ecology," which (according to the Associated Press Writing and Editing Committee) should have been ". . . affects the environment." In fact, *either* could have been right. Maintaining a lawn certainly affects the environment—surroundings—of nearby homes. But it also affects the ecology (or ecosystem) of that particular plot of ground—and even, to a degree, of the neighborhood. That is, maintaining a lawn produces one kind of ecosystem; letting the land go back to wildflowers (weeds), a quite different one.

Likewise, the problem of acid rain, which some politicians have worked so hard to dodge, is an environmental problem, in that it concerns the surroundings in which we live. But it's a problem partly because it can alter the ecology over wide areas, destroying aquatic life in mountain lakes and stunting the growth of some trees. That is, it's an ecological problem too. If, then, you're going to talk about ecology, make damn sure you know what you're talking about—which, come to think of it, is a good idea whatever you're talking about.

EFFETE. A word unknown to most Americans until the 1972 Presidential campaign, when Vice-President Spiro Agnew denounced critics of the administration as "an effete corps of impudent snobs." The word actually means "worn out" or "decadent," but I'd give odds that Agnew, like some other people, thought it had something to do with "effeminate." (I'd also bet that his speechwriter picked the word for that reason.) If you don't know the difference between machismo and masculinity, it's logical to suggest, ever so slyly, that people who dislike your machismo are deficient in masculinity. Since the word itself is by now both effete and ambiguous, avoid it.

EMOTE. Often considered an "illegitimate" **BACK FORMA-
TION** (from "emotion," of course), but not by me. As I've
used it, and heard it used, it means something much more
specific than its "literal" meaning (to express emotion). To
say that an actor or actress emotes means that (s)he expresses
emotion in an overblown and artificial style—hams it up, in
fact. If I'm right, then the word is a useful addition to the
language. See also **ORATE.**

END RESULT. *HDCU* calls this a redundancy, and it is—sometimes. If you're talking about a single consequence of something, or even several more or less simultaneous consequences, "result(s)" alone will do nicely. But if you're
speaking of the last and most important of several consequences, then "end result" is clearer. Hitler's racism produced systematic discrimination and frequent brutality
against German Jews; its end result was the Holocaust.

ENORMITY/ENORMOUSNESS. "Enormity" (enormous
moral deficiency) once meant "enormousness" (enormous
size) and vice versa; then the words changed places (compare
DISINTERESTED/UNINTERESTED). For generations the
experts have insisted that using the first for the second is
wrong—and people have kept doing it. "Enormousness," in
fact, seems to be dropping out of the language, perhaps because it's rather hard to pronounce. Since *some* word was
needed to express the quality of being enormous, "enormity"
has been drafted to fill the job.
  This is no doubt deplorable, but probably irreversible.
Note, however, that using "enormity" to mean size will always
get you into trouble with the purists—and may get you into
other kinds of trouble as well. If you speak of the "enormity"
of a tycoon's financial operations, you may be right in both
senses (i.e., they were both enormous and grossly immoral)
—but don't be surprised if you hear from his lawyers.

ENTHUSE. Like **EMOTE,** a **BACK FORMATION,** but one with little or no excuse for existence. "Enthuse over" says nothing more than "praise"—and takes three extra syllables to say it. In short, it's a word I can neither praise nor enthuse over. I could say the same, however, of some of the shrill comments in *HDCU* ("Ugh!" "illiterate," "terrible"). To quote a famous *New Yorker* caption, "A simple yes or no will suffice!"

EROTIC/ESOTERIC/EXOTIC. Nowadays, every adult—and plenty of kids—knows what "erotic" means. To some people, "exotic" is a sort of **EUPHEMISM** for "erotic," thanks to the show-biz usage of "exotic dancer" to mean "stripper." Personally, I don't much care for euphemisms (see next entry), and especially not this one, since "exotic" has two perfectly respectable meanings of its own. The first is "foreign": the common dandelion is an exotic plant in North America, since it originated in Europe. This fact is rather esoteric—meaning "known only to a few."

"Exotic" also has the figurative meaning of "(fascinatingly) unfamiliar" (as exotic plants and animals often are), though I personally prefer to stick with the original sense.

EUPHEMISMS. The practice of coining pleasant or neutral expressions for unpleasant, disgusting or frightening things probably began shortly after the invention of language; it shows no signs of diminishing. Its function is to "talk around" words and phrases that deal with things we, or our readers, find disgusting or frightening: thus people don't die, they "pass away"; and don't shit, but "defecate."

Euphenisms are often sexual; these reached a high (or low) point during the Victorian era. Trousers were called "unmentionables" (because of the unmentionable regions they covered), women's legs were called "limbs" (presumably because "legs" would lead the mind to higher—to the Victorians, lower—things) and cockroaches were called roaches because the older term contained the dreadful word "c--k." Likewise, the barnyard c--k became a rooster.

Nowadays, sexual euphemisms are considerably less pervasive than they were a century ago, but another major category of euphemism—the political—has been proliferating like poison ivy. To the Pentagon, invasion has become "forcible entry operation"—if "we" do it, that is; if "they" do it, it's a brutal act of aggression. During World War II, the Allies systematically circulated lies to mislead the enemy; these were called "black propaganda," and probably still are—if "we" do it. If "they" do it, it's *desinformatsaya,* or "disinformation." Similarly, "official" burglaries become "black-bag jobs" and assassination becomes "neutralization" or "termination with extreme prejudice." See also **BUREAUCRATESE**.

How you feel about euphemisms depends pretty much on your feelings about the concept being euphemized—and, naturally, on the feelings of whoever you're talking to. Personally, I prefer to avoid sexual euphemisms, but I also know they'll remain current so long as some people find sex frightening or disgusting. On the other hand, I deeply distrust people who use political euphemisms and flatly refuse to use them myself. To me, lies are lies and murder is murder, even when they are undertaken in what some official (often anonymous) claims is a good cause.

Note that sexual euphemisms are used to protect other people's feelings, while political euphemisms are used to protect the user's own interests—to pretty up policies or situations that, if called by their right names, would alarm or anger the electorate. When (for example) the U.S. State Department decides that its reports on human rights in various countries will no longer speak of "killing" but rather of "unlawful or arbitrary deprivation of life," it's obviously eliminating a blunt, brutal word in order to disguise a blunt, brutal fact. Similarly, "atmospheric deposition of anthropogenically derived acid substances" uses seven words, many of them polysyllabic, to avoid saying "acid rain."

Some political euphemisms are useful mainly among the euphemizers themselves. For example, an American law enforcement official can hardly tell a subordinate to carry out a burglary, which both parties would know perfectly well was criminal; instead he orders a "black-bag job."

Bureaucratic euphemisms are bad enough when the bureaucrats use them; they're even worse when the rest of us pick them up, because they encourage us to embrace the bureaucrat's moral neutralism (to put it no lower)—to "think about the unthinkable" with equanimity.

Bureaucrats who use euphemisms to mask the dirty tricks they or their subordinates are engaged in would probably say (if you could get a straight answer out of them) that a certain amount of burglary, blackmail and murder is regrettably essential to preserve **NATIONAL SECURITY;** since "they" do it, so must we. I find this argument something less than overwhelming, since I prefer to believe (perhaps foolishly) that there are moral differences between "us" (or some of us) and "them." But even accepting the argument, I'd still reject the euphemisms because they encourage us to kid ourselves about what is being done in our name. To me, self-deception is the worst kind of deception: if I kill someone, for whatever reason, good or bad, then dammit I killed him—I didn't terminate him with extreme prejudice. See also the next entry.

EXECUTION. In the sense of "killing," this word has for some years been applied by journalists to gangland murders ("a **MAFIA**-style execution") and, more recently, to various sorts of political murders. The usage does violence to the facts as well as to the victim. Since the fourteenth century, "execution" in this sort of context has meant killing someone *legally* for some criminal offense, real or alleged. Whatever you think of capital punishment, it's imposed by a judge, not a godfather or a terrorist.

Even the Nazis didn't have the face to call their mass murders of Jews, Poles, Russians, Gypsies and so on "executions." Since the Mob and the terrorists do retail what the Nazis did wholesale, let's call it by its right name: murder.

EXPECT. Widely used, and widely objected to, as a synonym for "guess" or "suppose." Given that its standard meanings all refer to future events ("I expect to get a raise next year"), I'd say that using it to refer to something in the past or present ("I expect I got a raise") is at least mildly confusing. But there's nothing wrong with "expecting" (supposing) that something *will* happen ("I expect I'll go to Mexico next month")—which isn't the same as saying "I expect *to* go to Mexico next month," which implies that you're definitely planning to do it. I also expect that this past-future distinction won't outlast the century.

F

FACTS, REAL or TRUE. Both expressions are often called redundant, on the ground that a fact is, by definition, both real and true. This is a fact. A further fact, however, is that public figures of all stripes are constantly citing facts that are by no means factual. Some simply make up whatever "facts" support their argument; others—the most dangerous—really believe their fake facts are real facts. (As Will Rogers is supposed to have said of President Calvin Coolidge, "It's not what he doesn't know that bothers me; it's what he knows for sure that isn't so.")

I'd say that if you're citing facts to refute somebody else's "facts," it's perfectly legitimate to call your facts "real" or "true" facts—though "actual" facts would do just as well.

FAD WORDS. Often called "vogue words," though both expressions encompass phrases as well as words. They are popular among politicians: to announce that you've appointed a *task force* to devise a *crash program* that will *target* some problem or other and produce a *breakthrough* tells—or is supposed to tell —the voters that you've got a winning *game plan.* They are even more popular among disc jockeys and talk-show hosts, for whom trendy language is as much a professional necessity as trendy clothes and a trendy haircut. Like **CLICHÉS** (which most of them rapidly become), fad words are often hard to identify and almost always good to avoid. At best they are usually tired, tiresome or both; at worst, they are dated, and therefore will date *you*. Call something "grody to the max" and you're out of date; call it "groovy" and you're practically prehistoric. Note, too, that the overuse of fad words tends to give them multiple meanings, and therefore confusing ones. Thus "hang-up," as *HDCU* accurately notes, can mean a problem (usually emotional), a sense of irritation or a fixation, obsession or phobia. Saying all these things, it says none of them clearly.

As with clichés, however, personal taste plays a part: your fad word may be my useful expression. Thus "image" (in the public relations sense), which some people object to, has certainly been overused at times, yet I still find it valuable. It reminds us that what we see of public figures is all too often merely a carefully crafted illusion—an image that only dimly portrays the real person. See also **HIGH-TECH LANGUAGE.**

Often lumped together with fad words are "nonce words" —literally, words coined "for the nonce" (i.e., for a particular occasion), but clearly implying a word with a brief life span. Evidently, then, labeling something a "nonce word" is risky unless the word has already come and gone. To use it on first hearing amounts to saying that the expression *will have* a very brief life span—and such predictions have a way of coming back to haunt their makers. When Lewis Carroll coined "chortle" in 1872, neither he nor anyone else expected it to pass into the language, but it did.

Two more-recent examples are "glottochronology" and "lexicostatistics," which the editors of *HDCU* call nonce words because they find them "ugly." In fact, both are technical terms (which I won't attempt to define), used in historical linguistics. As such, they are more accurately classed as **JARGON.** As for their alleged ugliness—that is both irrelevant and, like beauty, lies in the eye of the beholder.

FAMOUSLY. In the sense of "excellently" ("We got along famously"), it is somewhat archaic and also often confusing, since it has no apparent connection with its much more famous relative, "famous." On either count, avoid it.

FANNY. One of the few words where the difference between British and American usage can produce not merely misunderstanding but indignation. In this country, it's a somewhat dated **EUPHEMISM** for "bottom" or "buttocks"; in England, it refers to a considerably more intimate part of a woman's anatomy. If you're among Britishers and speak of someone's "fanny," you could get your, uh, fanny in a sling.

FARTHER/FURTHER. These two stump even the experts, as the comments in *HDCU* make clear. And not surprisingly: their meanings have overlapped for nearly a thousand years. The traditional distinction is that "farther means distance, further means degree"—but does "distance" refer only to physical space ("How much farther do we have to go?") or also to metaphorical space ("He wandered farther and farther from the point")—and perhaps to time as well ("farther back in history")?

The farther (or further) you dig into the question, the more bewildering it gets—see both entries in the *OED*. About the only place you can be sure which is which is when you mean "additional" or "in addition" ("He made the further [not "farther"] point that . . .") For all other senses, I suspect, the distinction between the two words, already blurred, will vanish completely in another twenty or thirty years. Why, then, carry the argument further—or farther?

FASCIST. Like **COMMUNIST,** a frequently misused word, though the two are misused by different people. "Fascist" is loosely used of any very repressive right-wing government; more loosely, of anyone who has a good word to say for such a government or, still more loosely, of *any* government that deals in repression (meaning, of course, any government)— provided that the speaker disapproves of it.

The main source of the confusion is that while all fascist governments are (or were) intensely repressive, not all intensely repressive governments are fascist. Fascism is not merely repressive, it is terrorism in power, its frequently murderous activities unrestrained by law or anything else. And even terrorist governments aren't necessarily fascist. Stalin certainly ruled by terror, but calling him a fascist obscures some important differences between him and Hitler, in both ostensible aims and actual results. Stalinism supposedly aimed to benefit the "proletariat"; Hitlerism, the "Aryan race." Stalinism benefited only Stalin himself and a few of his henchmen (those who survived the purges); Hitlerism benefited not only the Nazis but also German industrialists and financiers.

In the real world, of course, many governments don't fit neatly into categories. Hitler's Germany and Mussolini's Italy were obviously fascist; Pinochet's Chile and some Central American governments, under which opponents simply "disappear," are near-fascist, while the South African government is not fascist in the strict sense, since its vicious repressions are occasionally limited by the courts.

The U.S. government, as practically everyone knows, is not and never has been fascist or anything like it—though there was a time when some of our Southern states were near-fascist so far as their black citizens were concerned. People who talk of "fascists" in Washington merely reveal their own ignorance: under a real fascist government, they'd be talking through bars—if at all.

FAULT (verb). Though *HDCU* calls it a vogue word, the usage (in the sense of "blame" or "find fault with") is four centuries old, and has been common for at least thirty years. *HDCU*'s characterization is therefore faulty—and few people will fault you for ignoring it.

FEARFUL/FEARSOME. From its first appearance in English (fourteenth century), "fearful" has meant exactly what you would expect—full of fear—but also, unexpectedly, fear causing—that is, horrible or terrible. "Fearsome," a more recent word, means *only* the latter, for which reason I prefer it if I'm describing something terrifying.

The double meaning of "fearful" sometimes produces ambiguity and even unintended humor, as in "His fearful family would count in agony the hours of his absence" *(OED).* Read as a whole, the sentence clearly means that his family was frightened, but the first three words suggest, at least momentarily, that they were horrible people, so that the reader may be brought up short by what follows. To avoid contretemps of this sort, watch your context with "fearful" or avoid it entirely: if you mean "full of fear," say "nervous," "anxious," "frightened" or "terrified," depending on how much fear the person is full of.

FLAMMABLE/INFLAMMABLE. Technically, they mean exactly the same thing: easily set on fire. "Flammable"—not a new word, though some people think so—has gained in popularity despite some purists, and for good reason. In English, the commonest (though not the only) meaning of "in-" is "not" (in-dependent, in-divisible, in-flexible, in-sensitive and so on)—meaning that people of limited education could easily take "inflammable" to mean "fireproof."

Ordinarily this sort of confusion would be trivial; here it could be a matter literally of life or death: we surely don't want anybody treating inflammable materials as if they were fireproof. And to say, as did one of *HDCU*'s contributors, that "inflammable" might be confusing "but it . . . doesn't confuse me" is completely off the point: the whole idea of language-as-communication is precisely *not* to confuse other people. If, then, you insist on describing some substance as "inflammable," make damn sure *everybody* you're addressing knows what it means—otherwise your prose is a fire hazard. Figurative uses are another story: both you and your readers will be quite safe if you say (for example) that Middle Eastern politics are inflammable.

FLAUNT/FLOUT. Purists flaunt their knowledge that the two words mean very different things; many other people—some of them highly educated—unwittingly flout the distinction. Since "flout" in its original sense strikes me as rather pompous, I'd recommend dropping it from your vocabulary and substituting "dismiss" or "sneer at." Just remember that "flaunt" means to display proudly or boastfully—which sometimes involves flouting other people's opinions or feelings.

FORCED/FORCEFUL/FORCIBLE. The differences between these three words—especially between the last two—are sometimes confusing, but seldom important: the context will make clear what you mean nearly all the time. If, like me, you prefer to be precise, remember that the standard sense of "forcible" is actual physical force ("a forcible arrest of the suspect"); "forceful" means metaphorical force ("a forceful speech"), and "forced," usually, something *resulting from* force or compulsion, physical or otherwise ("a forced landing"). A burglarious break-in may be called either a forcible entry or a forced entry—but not a forceful one.

FORMER and LATTER. Most usage manuals make a great to-do about the importance of using these terms *only* when you're dealing with two things. Bernstein deserves a posthumous "Bravo!" for making the rather more important point that the terms are often confusing, because they compel the reader "to shift into reverse and look back" to see what they referred to. His example is brilliant: "Although many a gifted leader adorns history, and the skein of history's crises is endless, it is only when the former is tested in the fires of the latter that true greatness gets its opportunity to rise." Try figuring out what was being tested in the fires of which and you'll see why I avoid both words whenever possible.

Some people even insist that you can't say "of his two plays, the first was more popular"; it should be "the former was more popular." This is nonsense: an author's first play is his first play, whether he wrote two or a dozen.

FORTUNATE/FORTUITOUS. The not uncommon confusion between these two words results, I suspect, from their relationship to luck. As originally used, by gamblers, "luck" meant (and often still means) the chance—fortuitous—fall of the cards or dice, good or bad. But almost from the beginning the word was also used to mean specifically *good* luck and, eventually, any fortunate occurrence, whether or not due to chance.

The Rockefellers are certainly fortunate to have inherited the large fortune amassed by their piratical ancestor, John D., Sr., but there was nothing fortuitous about their inheritance. On the other hand, finding money in the street is both fortuitous and fortunate—and having your pocket picked is a fortuitous misfortune.

FOURTEEN KARAT. As a synonym for "pure" or "unadulterated" ("He's a fourteen karat bastard"), it's a cliché, and an inaccurate one at that: fourteen karat gold is far from pure, since it's only a little more than half gold. A more accurate—and also fresher—expression would be "twenty-four karat bastard." But calling someone a "twenty-four karat phony" mixes images: pure gold isn't phony!

FRANKENSTEIN. If you have any doubts about whether usage really does determine meaning, reflect on the fact that the original Frankenstein (from Mary Shelley's 1818 novel of that name) was a scientist who created an artificial man. In a mere twenty years, however, the word was being used to mean a man-made monster, not the man who made it. Today, thanks to Hollywood (and despite *HDCU*'s view), the "error" has become standard usage; call somebody or something a "Frankenstein" and obviously you mean Boris Karloff.

FREE ENTERPRISE. As used to describe the U.S. and similar economic systems, the phrase is something between a **CLICHÉ** and a **EUPHEMISM.** Literally, it implies that anybody is free to start a business enterprise, using their "individual initiative"—another cliché of economic discourse. The phrase should be avoided because it muddles (often deliberately) the distinction between theoretical and actual freedom. In theory, I'm "free" to launch a major publishing company; all I lack in practice is a few million dollars. Also worth recalling here is Anatole France's classic comment on economic freedom: "The rich and the poor have an equal right to sleep under bridges." If you need a term for the U.S. economy, call it "capitalism," or "private enterprise" or "the profit system," all of which are both accurate and nonjudgmental.

FROM . . . TO/FROM . . . THROUGH/BETWEEN . . . AND. When used with dates, both the first and the last of these are less than precise. When you say, for instance, "Between 1980 and 1984, the federal deficit increased by $500 billion" (or whatever the figure was), are you comparing the deficits at the beginning of each year, the end of each year—or the beginning of 1980 and the end of 1984? Better would be "During the years 1980 *through* 1984 . . ." (if that's what you mean). Again, to say "He worked from May 1 to May 15" leaves some doubt as to whether he worked fourteen or fifteen days; "May 1 through May 14" (or 15) removes the ambiguity. However, it's perfectly reasonable to say that something happened "between 1980 and 1984" if you're merely describing a general period of time.

FROM WHENCE. As the example of the King James Bible makes clear ("I will lift up mine eyes unto the hills, from whence cometh my help"), the phrase has been fairly common for a long time. Nowadays, however, it is almost certain to evoke a chuckle, as did Frank Loesser's famous line "Take back your mink to from whence it came." As currently used, "whence" means "from which"—meaning that an extra "from" is redundant.

FULSOME. Originally (thirteenth century), "abundant, plentiful," but this and related meanings were soon joined by the general sense of "overabundant," thereby reflecting the common human experience that enough is not only enough but sometimes too much. Eventually the original group of meanings dropped away; today, the predominant sense is "overabundant, overdone, exaggerated," with strongly negative connotations. "Fulsome praise" is the kind that, as Shakespeare put it, "was laid on with a trowel."

Recently, however, some people have begun using the word in its original sense. This, I suspect, involves a sort of **BACK FORMATION,** from "full"—from which the word was indeed derived. Whichever way you use it, you'll probably confuse somebody—meaning that the safest course is to avoid it. It certainly is not one of the "common words that are daily used" recommended by Caxton (see the Introduction).

FUNNY. A statement that something is "funny" may invite the venerable catchphrase "Funny peculiar, or funny ha ha?" Since the word can mean either one, watch your context.

G

GAMUT/GANTLET/GAUNTLET. You can run the first two, but in very different ways; the third you either wear or throw down. "Gamut" originally meant the lowest note of the musical scale, then the scale itself, whence its modern, figurative meaning: the entire range of something. If you run the gamut, that's what you're running through. "Running the gamut from A to Z" is rather tired; hardly less so is running the gamut of emotions "from A to B"—once said of Katharine Hepburn.

Miss Hepburn, like other theatrical folk, had to run the *gantlet* of criticism—meaning, take whatever punishment the critics saw fit to hand out. (The original sense was to run between two lines of soldiers armed with sticks; the consequences were always painful and sometimes fatal.)

And now for something completely different: a gauntlet is (or was) a heavy, over-the-wrist glove, often part of a suit of armor. In days of old, a knight threw down the gauntlet if he wanted to pick a fight with an equal (knights didn't fight with commoners; they just killed them). Nowadays, when both gauntlets and duels are out of fashion, people sometimes confuse them with gantlets ("run the gauntlet"). The mistake isn't important—the context will tell which you mean—but you might as well get it right.

GAY. Used for fifty years, first by criminals, then by homosexuals, most recently by the general public, to refer to (male) homosexuality (lesbians, for some reason, prefer to call themselves "lesbians"). "Gay" began as an adjective ("a gay boy") but has become a noun as well. Simon, in his usual restrained language, protests against "the wanton and shocking destruction of the good and necessary English word *gay.*" My own feeling is if that's what gays want to call themselves, so be it (compare **BLACK**).

Has the original sense of the word has been "destroyed," wantonly or otherwise? When *I* read of someone "whistling a gay tune," I don't assume it was written by that unabashedly gay composer Noel Coward, though people familiar mainly with the "modern" meaning of the word might do so. But if there is indeed a problem here, I see no remedy for it: there's no other polite term for "homosexual" except "homosexual" —which is cumbersome.

GENDER. Until very recently, this was a purely grammatical term, having to do with the classification of nouns and pronouns as masculine or feminine (in some languages, also neuter). Gender is important in French, German and many other languages, since both adjectives and articles (a, the) change their form depending on the gender of the noun they refer to. The classification is largely arbitrary—that is, it has no necessary connection with whether the thing under discussion is male, female or sexless (in French, for instance, the word for "pants" is masculine—but so is that for "panties"). It is also largely unnecessary, since it almost never affects meaning.

We know this because English has gotten along without grammatical gender very comfortably for centuries. A thousand years ago, the language employed gender routinely, but it survives only in our pronouns (he, she, it, etc.), and a handful of nouns (e.g., actor, actress). More important, it has evolved into "natural" gender: people (and sometimes animals) are "he" or "she," other things are "it."

Worth emphasizing is that "gender," in its original sense, is not—despite some dictionaries (e.g., *AHD*)—a substitute for "sex" (but then, as Bernstein remarks, what is?): to refer to a woman as a person of the "feminine gender" is both pretentious and wordy.

With the rise of the modern feminist movement, the word has taken on another, often ill-defined, sociopolitical meaning, centering on the identity and social roles of male and female people. As such, it has had repercussions in the field of language, since many English expressions involving or implying gender distinctions are felt by feminists to carry loaded overtones. Chief among these are "man" (or "-man") and "he," when used to refer to a person of either sex; a few feminists even object to "women" (see **LADY/WOMAN**).

The problem is that English, like many languages, is short of "gender neutral" expressions. This was not always so. Originally (ca. A.D. 700) "man" meant simply "human being"; a male human being was a *wer,* a female one, a *wyf* or a *cwene.* Over the next few centuries, this neat set of terms became badly muddled. *Wer* dropped out of the language completely except in the word "werewolf" (man-wolf); *cwene* radically changed its meaning, both up-market ("queen") and down-market ("quean"). Meanwhile, "man" took on a double meaning: both "human being" and "male human being" and *wyf* (or "wife") evolved its own double meaning: both "woman" and "woman married to a man." (As noted in the Introduction, Chaucer still used it in both senses.)

Thus using "man" to mean "human being(s)" ("the Family of Man") simply conforms to the original sense of the word; it isn't some sort of male chauvinist conspiracy. However, it's just as easy to say "the Human Family" or "the Family of Humanity."

Which still leaves us, unfortunately, with a number of expressions like "chairman" and "congressman" that many feminists, with or without reason, find offensive. Quite a lot of other people—including me—find the substitute, "-person," cumbersome or self-conscious or both, and I for one will go to great lengths to avoid it. Most of the time the lengths aren't very great. So long as I'm talking about a real person, he or she is obviously either male or female, and is described as such: if I'm presiding at a meeting, I'm the chairman; if my wife is, she's the chairwoman; Tip O'Neill is a congressman, Gerry Ferraro was a congresswoman. The only excuse I can see for using "sexually neutral" terms is in talking about mixed groups ("members of Congress" or "representatives"), or about someone whose identity (and therefore sex) has not yet been determined. If a mixed group has to pick a presiding officer, it's electing a chair—but once elected, he'll be a chairman, or she'll be a chairwoman. (When it comes to pronouns, we often have an even simpler out: using "they" instead of "he or she"—see **AGREEMENT, INDEFINITE PRONOUNS.**) Likewise, someone issuing a statement on behalf of an organization or government is either a spokesman or spokeswoman.

But what about those firmly anonymous corporate and governmental mouthpieces sometimes called "spokespersons"? Personally, I see little excuse for this usage; the people in question may be anonymous but they aren't sexless. An even better solution, I think, would be to simply avoid quoting them. The usual function of the anonymous spokesperson is to publicize information, or a point of view, that nobody is willing to put their name to—meaning that it's quite possibly false and almost certainly self-serving. If some "spokesperson" chooses to tell us that the island of Amnesia, population 230,000, is a threat to the United States, population 230,000,000, I think that journalists can and should demand that he or she put his or her name where his or her mouth is.

Having said all this, let me emphasize that there is simply no way of eliminating *all* supposedly sexist terms from English without doing violence to either our style or our meaning. This applies with special force, I think, to "man" as used in some compound words. It's sensible enough to say "worker" instead of "workman," if some or all of the workers are female—but if you're talking about workmanship (say, of a piece of furniture), no other word will do. "Workpersonship" is grotesque, and other possibilities (skill, refinement ,etc.) don't say the same thing. The same applies to "craftsmanship."

No less recalcitrant is "gamesmanship." Bobbye D. Sorrels, in her often useful but sometimes heavy-handed book *The Nonsexist Communicator,* proposed to replace "The participants used shrewd gamesmanship" with "The participants played the game shrewdly"—but it doesn't work. "Gamesmanship" (according to Stephen Potter, who invented the word) means "the art of winning at games without actually cheating"— clearly something more (or less) than playing shrewdly. Sorrels also considers "freshman" a sexist noun; does anyone nowadays seriously think that it refers to men only?

In this and similar situations, it's worth reminding ourselves that "man" meant "person" or "human being" long before it meant "male person"—and the English language can't help but reflect that fact. Women face many problems in our society, including unequal pay for equal work, violence from their husbands and other men, and many other forms of sexism—of which linguistic sexism, I'd say, is well down on the list of priorities. I hope that someday we'll reach the point where the most serious thing women have to worry about is whether they're called Mrs. or **MS.**

GENIUS (adjective). The brief discussion of this word in *HDCU* is a neat example of how to be right for the wrong reason. The editors condemn the statement that some officeholder did a "genius job," on the ground that "genius" is a noun "and cannot be used as an adjective." And this in a *usage* (noun) manual! English, of course, constantly uses nouns as adjectives (*space* shuttle, *radio* telescope, *cable* television), though grammarians pretend it isn't so by labeling these adjectives "attributive" nouns. See **INTERCHANGEABLE PARTS.**

The real problem with the phrase—aside from the fact that it was almost certainly bunk—is its unclarity. If the speaker was trying to indicate that the jobholder was a genius, why not say so? If, on the other hand, he was saying that the man wasn't a genius but had performed like one, he was talking nonsense: it just doesn't happen. He'd have done better to say that the man had done a superb, marvelous or brilliant job.

GIFT (verb). Another case of "Ask a loaded question and you get a predictable answer" (see **AGGRAVATE**). The editors of *HDCU,* conceding that the word has long been used as a verb, ascribe its recent vogue to gossip columnists and advertising. This disgraceful alleged pedigree naturally inspired such comments as "dreadful," "vulgar" and even "one of the reasons America is in such terrible shape today" (!).

Editors and panelists alike managed to thoroughly muddle three somewhat different meanings of the verb: (1) "Make a gift *of*" ("The Regent Murray gifted all the Church Property to Lord Sempill"—*OED,* 1878); (2) "Make a gift *to,*" as in the *HDCU*'s alleged modern example, "So-and-so gifted her with a twenty-carat diamond" (note the implication that so-and-so was a pretty vulgar fellow!); (3) "Endow with (unspecified) gifts" ("Gift mother well at Christmas time"—another *HDCU* example).

All three senses date from the sixteenth or seventeenth century. (1) is obsolete, having been replaced by the more concise "gave"; (2) and (3) were obsolete until their recent revival. Both are self-conscious, and (2) is also wordy: it takes two words and three syllables to say "gave." As for (3)—anyone who has to be *told* to "gift mother" at Christmas probably won't do it anyway. Note, however, that there's nothing wrong with such phrases as "gifted child" or "gifted with many talents," though in the second case you could as easily say "endowed."

GOLDBRICK GENERALITIES. One of the commonest tricks of literary gamesmanship. When somebody tells you "Everybody knows that . . ." you can safely offer six to one that everybody *doesn't* know it. What the speaker is really saying is "I think this is true—and if you disagree, you're obviously an ignoramus."

Equally spurious are statements beginning "America believes . . ." or "The people think. . . ." America, whether you consider it a piece of real estate, a government or a collection of people, is quite incapable of believing: only people believe, and they do it as individuals, not as a group. True, groups of people may all believe the same thing—but when you're talking about groups numbering millions, the odds are overwhelming that some of them *don't* believe it.

Only a trifle less obvious are goldbricks like "Homosexuality is destroying the American family." To begin with, there is no such thing as "the American family," though there are, of course, some millions of American families. To strip the glitter off goldbricks of this type, all you need do is ask "Whose family?" (or whatever it is). When it comes to homosexuality, for instance, my wife and I agree that it's not destroying *our* American family, or any other American family we know of. I also doubt very much that it's destroying yours —or, for that matter, the families of the politicos and preachers who are peddling this goldbrick.

If you happen to be hustling goldbricks yourself, I can't stop you. But if somebody tries to sell you one, make sure you scratch the surface before you buy it!

GOT/GOTTEN. In England, the standard form is "I've got"; in the United States, both forms are used, but with a shade of difference. "I've got twenty dollars" means "I have twenty dollars," with no implications as to when I got it; "I've gotten twenty dollars" means "I have recently obtained twenty dollars." In the first sentence, the emphasis is on the having; in the second, on the getting. We also use "gotten," of course, to mean "become" ("It's gotten warmer").

Some people object to "I've got" on the ground that it's redundant, saying no more than "I have"; on similar grounds, they reject "I've got to" in favor of "I have to" or "I must." Technically they're right, yet many educated people continue to use both expressions, probably because they consider "have" a rather pallid verb—a view that I've got to agree with (see **MUST**). Note, however, that "I got" (= I have) and "I got to" (= I must) are blue-collar, not educated, usage.

GRADUATED/GRADUATED FROM/WAS GRADUATED FROM. A few ultra-purists still insist that "graduated from" is incorrect, on the ground that it's the college, not the student, that does the graduating—hence one should say "was graduated from." This is pure nostalgia. Note, however, that the simple "graduated" ("He graduated high school in 1963") is blue-collar; if you graduated from college, avoid it.

GRAFFITI/GRAFFITO. Is "graffiti" singular, plural or both? In Italian (whence we borrowed the word) *un graffito* is an informal inscription on a wall, fence or one of the other public places where one often finds fools' names and fools' faces; *graffiti* are more than one such inscription. In American English, however, the current tendency is to treat "graffiti" as both singular and plural, like "sheep" and a few other native words.

The predictable result is that writers are sometimes uncertain which is which—for example, in a sentence I recently culled from the *New York Times*, which described how, on some new subway cars, "graffiti was removed before it could dry." Somebody obviously goofed: if the car really had only one inscription (which, as a regular subway rider, I don't believe for a minute), it should have been "*a* graffito [or a graffiti] was removed. . . ." If there were several graffiti, then ". . . graffiti *were* removed before *they* could dry."

Eventually, I suspect, the word will follow the path of other imported nouns such as "pizza," and acquire a regular plural —"graffitos" or, perhaps, "graffitis" (though the latter will certainly grate on Italian-speakers). Since there is still no real agreement on how the word should be inflected (if at all), I myself will continue to treat "graffiti" as plural only, using "graffito" as the singular. If, however, you prefer to consider "graffiti" as both singular and plural, just remember that it can't be both at once. That is, the rest of your sentence (notably, the verb) must make clear whether you mean one inscription or several.

GRIEVE. In recent years, this old English word has acquired a specialized meaning in trade-union and labor-relations **JARGON**: to file, process or be treated as a grievance ("The shop steward's suspension is being grieved"). The editors of *HDCU* professed themselves horrified by this **BACK FORMATION;** I can't see why. Like many "inside" terms, it sounds odd to outsiders and should therefore be used cautiously, if at all, among them. But among the insiders who mostly use it, it's a clear and concise way of saying what they mean.

GROOM/BRIDEGROOM. When horses were a lot commoner than they are now, a groom was the man who looked after them; the male lead in a wedding was a *bride*groom. Nowadays, when most horse owners do their own grooming, a groom stands next to a bride—probably because "bride and bridegroom" sounds redundant even though, technically, it isn't. Unless you belong to a very horsey set, stick with "bride and groom."

GUESS/SUPPOSE. "I guess" in the sense of "I think" or "I suppose" goes back to the fourteenth century (*Of twenty yeer of age he was, I gesse*—Chaucer). Later it dropped out of educated use in England, but was carried across the Atlantic by English colonists, most of them pretty uncultivated types. Eventually, English writers began using it whenever they tried to write "American" dialogue—and English critics cited it as one of the ways in which Americans were "corrupting" English. Nonetheless, it has become standard in this country, as well as in Canada and Australia. See also **EXPECT.**

H

HANGED/HUNG. "Hung" is the standard, indeed the only form in all senses except the judicial, where both forms are correct ("The murderer was hanged/hung"). I prefer "hanged" in this context—among other reasons because it's possible for a murderer (or any other man) to be both hanged and hung.

HIGH-TECH LANGUAGE. Something like four thousand years ago, the techniques of metalworking spread to the region of northern Europe inhabited by people speaking a language ancestral to English. It was then, as near as we can guess, that the ancestors of the words "smith," "anvil" and "tongs" appeared, and for an obvious reason: when you start talking about new things, you need new words. New technologies have been generating special vocabularies ever since, and not a few such technical terms have acquired figurative meanings that have brought them into general use (see **JARGON**).

In the years since World War II, the explosive expansion of technology in such fields as computers has brought dozens of new words into English (and other languages). And some of these have been yanked into the general vocabulary, not (as in the past) because they filled a need, but as a way of displaying the supposed sophistication of the speaker. Instead of saying "I'd like your ideas on this," the up-to-the-minute executive will say "I'd like some input from you"; people don't talk or confer but "interact." (I once actually got a letter, from a man I'd interviewed in—where else?—California, telling me that it had been "a pleasure to interact with you.") Recently, my son-in-law overheard the proposal (or perhaps proposition) "Let's interface over lunch."

As these examples suggest, I take a dim view of high-tech language, not because it's unclear (it seldom is), and certainly not because it's new, but because, like other **FAD WORDS,** it's used to show off rather than communicate. Trendiness, in words or anything else, is partly a matter of personal taste— but if your taste happens to run that way, bear in mind that today's fashionable headpiece may be tomorrow's old hat. To stick with a trend only as long as it's trendy requires a sharp ear and fast footwork; myself, I seldom bother.

HISSELF/THEIRSELVES. When people "reinvent" the language, as they constantly do (see **BACK FORMATION**), they tend at the same time to "regularize" it. That is, when constructing past tenses and similar **INFLECTIONS,** they are likely to use regular rather than irregular forms—"knowed" instead of "knew," for example.

Most of the "-self" (reflexive) pronouns are based on the possessive pronouns—my(self), her(self), your(self), our(-selves). Hence "hisself" and "theirselves" are perfectly logical. But since English, as we've noted several times already, is not constructed logically, both are considered dialect, not Standard English: stick with "himself" and "themselves."

HISTORIC/HISTORICAL. Often confused, and the distinction in meaning is important enough to keep in mind. "Historic" means important from the standpoint of history, either actually or prospectively; "historical" means merely based on or pertaining to history.

I'd guess there are several hundred historical novels published each year in this country; few if any them are historic novels. James Joyce's *Ulysses,* by contrast, was not a historical novel—it was based on life in the Dublin he knew—but might be fairly described as historic, because of its extraordinary innovations in both style and substance.

Even academicians sometimes lose sight of this difference. For example, I have before me an ad for a book by a Columbia professor, *Illustrated Dictionary of Historic Architecture.* The brief description of the book, however, makes clear that though some of the buildings illustrated are indeed historic (e.g., the Roman Colosseum), the book aims to depict "the entire history of architecture." A better title would have been *Illustrated Historical Dictionary of Architecture.*

Differences in meaning aside, "historic," used of current events, is usually nonsensical on its face; judging the historical importance of anything close up is almost never possible. I have in my lifetime been exposed to several hundred "historic" speeches, changes of policy, etc.; most of them were important only to the people concerned—or their press agents. (A notable exception was the explosion of the first atomic bomb. Of the few dozen people who saw that mushroom cloud over the New Mexico desert, every one knew very well that it was historic—and, God help us, they were right.)

A footnote: many Britishers and some Americans say "an historic" rather than "a historic." Which you favor depends, I'd say, on whether you pronounce the word as "(a) historic" or "(an) istoric." But when it comes to "history," stick with "a"—unless you're a member of the British working class and pronounce it "istory."

HOI POLLOI. This phrase, borrowed from Greek, originally meant "the many." Over the generations, it has acquired overtones of "those not like us"—"us" being the highly educated minority. A tiny minority of this minority (Simon is one) uses the phrase without a "the" in front of it, on the ground that the added word is redundant. If most of the people who use the phrase knew its literal meaning, Simon might have a point. However, most people don't, so follow the rules of English syntax and keep the "the"; otherwise it'll be Greek to most of your readers.

HOPEFULLY. As examples of rhetorical overkill, it would be hard to improve on some of the *HDCU* panelists' comments on this word. The author and columnist Hal Borland pretty well summed up the majority view when he called it "barbaric, illiterate, offensive, damnable, and inexcusable"; the educator Harold Taylor claimed (not for the first time) to be "physically ill" (did he *really* throw up?), while Prof. T. Harry Williams called it "the most horrible usage of our time."

Frankly (= speaking frankly), these comments are not only shrill but nonsensical, and hopefully (= speaking hopefully) the experts will eventually recognize this. But realistically (= speaking realistically), I'm not holding my breath.

What bothers the purists is that "hopefully" is an adverb, yet is commonly used without any verb or adjective to modify —whence the terms "bastard adverb," "ungrammatical" and the like. But adverbs, like some other words, can be used elliptically—that is, as a sort of syntactic shorthand in which one or more words are omitted but understood, as with "speaking" in the examples above. How do we know this? Because neither "frankly" nor "realistically," as used above, applies to any word actually in the sentence: to say "I'm not realistically holding my breath" is nonsense (can you imagine holding *anything* realistically?). That is, they too are "bastard" adverbs—yet are used by the most puristical purists.

For people who insist on grammatical chapter and verse, then, "hopefully" is an ellipsis, a type of construction that has been good English at least since the sixteenth century ("hopefully" itself has been used in this way since 1932). Bernstein was among the very few experts with the wit to recognize that the word is no bastard but absolutely legitimate. Though in 1965 he viewed it dimly, ten years later he very sensibly called it "useful, nay necessary." Moreover, as he pointed out, even if you "translate" it as "it is to be hoped that," the usage is paralleled by such wholly acceptable expressions as "regrettably" (= it is to be regretted that).

Having said all this, I'll add that "hopefully" is probably overused these days, and sometimes, I'm told, misused as a synonym for "probably" ("Hopefully, the new federal budget will be published next week"). Don't, in other words, use it unless you really *hope* that whatever-it-is will happen, or is true ("Hopefully, the new budget will allot less money to nuclear weapons"). As for the purists: to borrow a remark of Jim Quinn's, hopefully they'll shut up. But truthfully, I don't think they will.

I

I/ME. English nouns have lost nearly all their **INFLECTIONS,** but English pronouns haven't—to the frequent confusion of experts and nonexperts alike. And the most confusing pair of inflections, possibly excepting **WHO/WHOM,** is I/me.

For example, *HDCU* says that "Nobody was there but me" is right, but "Nobody but me was there" is wrong. The reason, they say, is that in the first case, "but" is a preposition; in the second, a conjunction. I'm not sure they're right; indeed Bernstein concedes that opinions on the point have historically been marked by "nothing but vacillation." To me, that's a good reason for ignoring the distinction. So unless you get a kick out of splitting hairs, stick with "but me" no matter where it falls in the sentence.

Both *HDCU* and Bernstein are considerably more permissive when it comes to "It's me," and high time, too. The expression, condemned by generations of schoolteachers, is standard among virtually all native English-speakers, and the notion that it's wrong is pure invention. Back in the seventeenth or eighteenth century, some grammarian reasoned that since in Latin one said *Ego est,* then its literal English translation ("It is I") must be right. But there is nothing either eternal or universal about Latin syntax (see **INFINITIVES, SPLIT**). Indeed, the French, whose Latin-derived language gives them far more excuse for following Latin rules, say *C'est moi*—"It's me."

Unfortunately, many Americans have been so traumatized by the "It's me/It's I" hassle that they overcompensate and avoid "me" under almost any circumstances—for example, "between you and I" instead of "between you and me." Simon, with his usual overkill, calls this "a grammatical error of *unsurpassable* grossness" (his emphasis); myself, I can think of several grosser ones—that is, errors that aren't just inelegant, as this is, but unclear to boot. Yet Simon himself admits to having had trouble with the two words: when he was asked to write a column on language, he first thought "Why me?" —but then wondered if it shouldn't have been "Why I?"

The simplest way of dealing with the I/me problem, and its siblings he/him, she/her, they/them and we/us, is to use "I" (or "he," "she," etc.) *only* when it's clearly the subject of a verb. Otherwise, stick with "me" and you'll be right at least 95 percent of the time. (If anybody asks you who said so, tell 'em it was me.)

For example, Simon's first thought, "Why me?" was obviously correct, since he was wondering "Why [did they ask] me?"—with "they," not "me," the subject of "ask." Sometimes, of course, spotting the subject requires some thought. Bernstein gives the example "Four years of hard work are required for he who seeks a degree." Here "he" seems at first glance to be the subject of "seeks"; in fact, the subject is "who," meaning that the sentence should read ". . . him who seeks. . . ."

But note, too, that changing the pronoun still leaves an overblown, verbose sentence; the writer could have bypassed the he/him problem (and made the statement applicable to both sexes) by simply dropping three words: "Four years of hard work are required for a degree." Or, still better, "Getting a degree requires four years of hard work," which eliminates another word and avoids the **PASSIVE VOICE** to boot.

The most confusing usage problems tend to show up in convoluted sentences, meaning that restructuring the whole thing will often eliminate the problem—and will certainly improve the sentence.

IDENTIFY (ONESELF) WITH. *HDCU* claims that this expression *must* be used with a reflexive pronoun: not "I identify with . . ." but "I identify *myself* with. . . ." I call this overcareful and out of date; more than half the *AHD* usage panel concurs. I also think the expression is a bit overused, but that apart, it's both current and clear.

IDENTITY CRISIS. This one *is* overused, with no ifs or buts. People occasionally do have identity crises, but the phrase should be saved for real ones. Don't use it if you're uncertain about what job to take or who to marry: a real identity crisis involves not just deciding between A and B but reexamining the basic assumptions about yourself that you've been using to make decisions. I don't envy you the job.

I.E./E.G. These two abbreviations are not infrequently confused, since few people today have enough Latin to know what they stand for. "I.e." stands for *id est*—"that is"; "e.g.," for *exempli gratia*—"for the sake of example." I.e., you use the first to explain what you've just said, the second to give a "for instance" illustrating what you've just said—e.g., a sentence embodying a usage you've been discussing. Both are best avoided unless you're trying to conserve space: Say "that is" and "for example" (or "for instance") instead.

IF/WHETHER/THAT/THOUGH. "If" is irreplacable in conditional statements: ("If you move, I'll shoot!"); in most other situations, either "if" or "whether" will do. "If" is preferable in "iffy" situations, when doubt or uncertainty is involved ("See if you can get him on the phone"); "whether," when alternatives are involved ("I don't know whether he's crooked or just dumb").

Bernstein warns against using "if" to introduce a noun clause at the beginning of a sentence, but his example is grotesque: "If we were coming to dinner was the object of his inquiry." I can't believe that anyone ever said this (rather than "He inquired if we were coming for dinner"). Here, as with an earlier example (see **I/ME**), recasting the sentence both improves it and ducks the usage problem.

After negative verbs, "that" can substitute for "if," but with a shade of difference. "I don't know that he's a crook" suggests that that the speaker is willing to give him the benefit of the doubt; "I don't know if he's a crook" leaves the question wide open. (To make things even more confusing, "I don't *know* that he's a crook" indicates that the speaker thinks he is, but can't prove it.)

Neither "if" nor "whether" can substitute for "though." To say "Diamonds, if expensive, are a girl's best friend" may be true, but means something different from "Diamonds, though expensive, are. . . ." In the first case, only expensive diamonds are friendly; in the second, all diamonds are considered expensive—and all are friendly.

ILLEGAL/ILLEGITIMATE/ILLICIT. *HDCU* claims that all three words mean, in way or another, outside the law. Technically they're right—but the words also mean other (and different) things, and using them interchangeably can generate confusion.

An illegal action means, ninety-nine times out of a hundred, one that breaks the law of the land; that is, you can be fined or jailed for it. Occasionally, however, the "law" may be the rules of a game; thus chess players speak of "an illegal move." Something that's illicit may or may not be illegal, but is in some sense *not permitted* (its original, Latin meaning), by custom or community moral standards. Thus adultery is illicit, but is not illegal in most places outside the Muslin world. Selling heroin is both illicit and illegal, selling weapons to the government is neither, yet both can generate illicit profits. "Illegitimate," finally, should be reserved—*AHD* to the contrary—for bastards and for things that violate the laws of evidence or logic ("an illegitimate conclusion"). Don't use it interchangeably with "illegal": it's no crime to be wrong.

ILLITERATE. Since the sixteenth century, when it came into English, this word has meant what it still means: without a knowledge of letters—and there's the rub. For the "letters" in question could and can mean either the letters of the ABC ("the population was 90 percent illiterate") or "letters" in the sense of literature or book learning ("an illiterate usage"). In the last sense, the word is widely used by literary critics and usage experts.

In theory, "illiterate" in the second sense is a neutral, descriptive term; in practice, it has acquired strong negative vibrations. The probable reason is that many of the people who use it believe, consciously or otherwise, that being men or women of letters marks them as superior to less fortunate folk. Being something of a man of letters myself, I can give a wholly disinterested opinion: it doesn't.

Thus "illiterate" has become a snob word, except when used in the sense of "unable to read and write." As such, it should be banned from books on usage, except as a horrible example; if you think a particular usage is characteristic of people with a limited education, call it "uneducated" or "nonstandard" or "blue-collar"—terms that are both accurate and nonjudgmental.

A not uncommon term nowadays is "functional illiterate." Some people dislike it—for example, the editors of *HDCU*, who call it a "bureaucratic euphemism for 'an uneducated person.' " This just isn't so—and the fact that they think it's so perhaps tells us something about their own attitudes toward uneducated people.

Many, probably most people of limited education are *not* functional illiterates. They may not be at home with philosophical treatises or the World's Great Books, but can still read and write well enough to make a decent living and raise a family. Functional illiterates can't: they can read street signs and write their names, but (as *Newsweek* recently put it) they can't make sense of the instructions on a bottle of medicine or the warning on a can of Drāno. Meaning, of course, that their ability to function in today's America is very limited.

A small fraction of this unfortunate group is mentally subnormal; a larger fraction had little education, at least in English (that is, some were educated in Spanish, Chinese, Vietnamese, etc.). Most functional illiterates, however, attended American schools for years but, as the Irish say, got no good of them. Indeed, one of the most serious criticisms of our schools is that they turn out too many functional illiterates: kids who know their letters, and even groped their way through the "Dick and Jane" books, yet who, when it comes to coping with the modern world, might as well have dropped out in third grade.

IMMIGRANT/EMIGRANT/MIGRANT. You can keep the first two straight if you remember that "im-" comes from "in-" (= into) and "em-" from "ex-" (= out of). Out-migrants (emigrants), obviously, are bound to become in-migrants (immigrants), unless they die on the way (as not a few nineteenth-century emigrants did en route to the United States). In the first case, however, you're talking about where they came from, in the second, where they went. Most of my own ancestors emigrated from various parts of the United Kingdom—

and, days or weeks later, immigrated to the American colonies or the United States.

Logically, "migrant" ought to encompass both the preceding terms, but it doesn't. As applied to people, it means those who move about more or less regularly, and generally within the boundaries of a particular nation ("migrant workers"). Many birds are migrants in a similar sense, but of course their seasonal wanderings ignore national boundaries.

IMPLY/INFER. This pair can befuddle even the experts—see their comments in *HDCU*—but the distinction is worth knowing if you care about clarity. "Imply" comes from Latin via French, and originally meant "fold in" (we find the same root in "du*pli*cate," a double or two-fold document). An implied meaning or implication, then, is one "folded in" with a statement—what the speaker suggested without actually saying it.

"Infer," by contrast, means to draw an inference or conclusion—often from someone else's implication; as Bernstein neatly put it, the implier pitches, the inferrer catches. I'm not implying that this distinction is a life-or-death matter, but if you infer that I observe it myself, and advise you to, your inference will be correct.

IMPRACTICABLE/IMPRACTICAL. When applied to things, the two words overlap in meaning: their principle sense is "impossible to carry out in practice." However, "impracticable" means *only* that, whereas "impractical" can also mean possible, but foolish or otherwise undesirable. Thus an "impracticable" business scheme simply can't be carried out—for example, because the capital or the technology isn't available; an "impractical" one can be carried out—but will lose money.

For clarity, then, stick with "impracticable" if you mean impossible, with "impractical" if you mean possible but unwise. And note that while *things* may be either impracticable or impractical, people can *only* be impractical—meaning that they may have brains but don't have sense.

INDEFINITELY. For more than three centuries, this has been used in the sense of "for an indefinite (long) time," or even "forever"—and the two senses can blur your meaning. Frozen foods, for instance, will keep indefinitely (for a long time), but nowhere near forever, and nobody would say "I'll love you indefinitely." If you want to be indefinite, say "indefinitely"; if you mean "forever," say so.

Note also that qualifying "indefinitely" can get you into trouble. "Almost indefinitely" is passable, though "almost forever" is better, but "more or less indefinitely," is indefinitely indefinite—that is, almost meaningless.

INFINITIVES, SPLIT. The principle that it's wrong to ever split an infinitive was made up out of whole cloth by some eighteenth-century grammarian. His logic—if you want to call it that—was that Latin infinitives were single words (*amare* = to love) that couldn't be split; hence our two-word infinitives *shouldn't* be split. He got away with this non sequitur because the British upper classes saw Latin syntax as a set of eternal truths; I doubt that even the Romans were that naive.

The "rule" against splitting infinitives violates both common English usage and a fundamental principle of English sentence structure: a modifying word should be placed as closely as possible to the word it modifies (see **MISPLACED MODIFIERS**). In the first sentence of this entry, "ever" modifies "split," and is therefore exactly where it belongs; to say "It's wrong ever to split" would split modifier from modified, while "to split ever" isn't English at all.

My own view can be summed up by a remark ascribed to the writer Raymond Chandler. Writing on a proof that had been "improved" by some officious editor, he declared: "When I split an infinitive, it's going to damn well stay split." Which is not to say, of course, that I split on principle—only when it sounds right. In short, when in Rome, by all means do as the Romans do, or did, but don't feel compelled to do it elsewhere.

INFLECTIONS. When you use words to make a statement, you obviously don't just toss them together like a salad and hope they'll make sense. The rules of *syntax* tell you how to combine words into meaningful sentences—that is, how to indicate their relationship to one another: who's doing what to whom.

Broadly speaking, there are three ways that languages do this. One is by placing the words in a particular order; the second is by adding other words to the sentence (in English, most of these are what we call prepositions and conjunctions); the third is by changing the word itself, a device called inflection. Many languages use more than one of these methods; English, as it happens, uses all three.

In English there are only two ways of inflecting a word: either you add something to it or you change one of its vowels. For example, consider "sing." Usually, this is a verb (occasionally, a noun, as in "community sing"). "Sing-ing" turns it into the adjective-like present participle ("a singing commercial") or the noun-like gerund ("singing is good for the soul")—see **PARTICIPLES a.k.a. GERUNDS.** Changing the vowel gives us the past participle "sung," while another vowel change gives us the noun "song."

All these words deal with the same basic idea, but each of them has—must have—a different relationship to the other words in the sentence. That is, each serves a different syntactic function.

Some other common syntactic inflections in English are the "-d" or "-ed" used to convert most verbs into their past participles ("love-d," "kill-ed"), the "-'s" that indicates possession and similar relationships ("the farmer's daughter"), the "-y" that turns a noun into an adjective ("dirt-y"), the

"-ly" that turns an adjective into an adverb ("hopeful-ly") and the **-IZE** that turns nouns, and sometimes adjectives, into verbs.

A few English inflections are not syntactic but *semantic:* they change the meaning of a word without altering its syntactic function. Thus "sang" is a verb like "sing," but of course deals with the past, not the present, while "-s" or "-es" turns singular nouns into plurals ("song-s," "class-es").

Occasionally you will run into some musty text which tells you that Modern English is "basically" an inflected language. This just isn't so: English syntax depends overwhelmingly on word order. "Dog bite man" omits the inflection of "bite," but clearly means the same thing as "Dog bite*s* man," whereas "Man bite dog" just as clearly means something else. Matters are very different in a heavily inflected language such as Latin, in which *Canis mordit hominem* means "Dog bites man," whereas *Canem mordit homo,* with identical word order but different inflections, means "Man bites dog."

A thousand years ago, English was inflected almost as elaborately as Latin. In theory (though not always in practice), nouns and pronouns had eight different inflections (four singular, four plural), adjectives had sixteen and verbs had six different forms (three singular, three plural) for the present and six more for the past.

For the last thousand years, English has been losing its syntactic inflections, for reasons I have discussed elsewhere (see *OMNT*). Nouns have only four, two singular (farmer, farmer's) and two plural (farmers, farmers'), and three of them are pronounced identically. Verbs (except for "to be") have only two different forms in the present (I/we/you/they go, he/she/it goes) and only one in the past, while adjectives are not syntactically inflected at all (some undergo *semantic* inflection—e.g., "strong, -er, -est"). The only place where anything approaching the Old English inflectional system survives is in pronouns (I/me/my, they/them/their, etc.).

The loss of inflections in English has several important implications for modern usage. First, some of our surviving inflections contribute nothing to meaning and can therefore become sources of confusion (see **I/ME**); a few are dropping out of use entirely (see **WHO/WHOM** and **SUBJUNCTIVES**). Second, the loss of distinctive inflections for nouns, verbs and adjectives means that these words are no longer "frozen" into their syntactic categories, but can shift from one to another (see **INTERCHANGEABLE PARTS**).

Finally, and most important, the loss of nearly all the inflections that once helped to define relationships among our words puts an even heavier burden on word order. Using "who" instead of "whom" may get you in trouble with the purists, but neither they nor anyone else will wonder who (or whom) you're talking about; placing a word wrongly in a sentence can do anything from muddying your meaning to completely garbling it (see **INVERSION**).

INFRASTRUCTURE. Not a new word, though many people think so; it was first recorded in 1927. Since it is often considered a fad word (Winston Churchill attacked it in 1950), it should be handled with care. In its original sense, it meant the fixed installations, such as barracks and airfields, required by a military organization, as contrasted with the men and weapons of the organization itself. More recently, it has taken on a similar sense in economics: the fixed installations, such as roads, port facilities and water and sewage systems, required by a modern economy, as contrasted with the factories, machines and workers that make up the economy itself. In either of these senses it's clear; in any other, it's muddy.

INTERCHANGEABLE PARTS. Some usage experts insist that a noun can't be used as a verb (see **CONTACT**), or as an adjective (see **GENIUS**). These and similar "rules" have no foundation in English grammar or usage, now or in the past.

Nouns have been used as adjectives (i.e., to modify other nouns) for as long as there has been an English language. In Old English, whose earliest documents date from around A.D. 700, *gar* meant "spear," *beam* meant "shaft," and *garbeam*, of course, spear-shaft. That is, the noun "spear" modified the noun "shaft," and thus became an adjective. English has been using such noun-adjectives (technically called "attributive nouns") ever since. Another compound, "spear-shaped," reminds us that nouns can also serve as adverbs; other common examples include "penny pinching" and "girl crazy." Here, too, there are precedents in Old English.

Adjectives frequently become nouns. Blacks, whites and reds know this; so do doctors, with their sedatives, anesthetics and antibiotics. Armies have privates and generals and conduct offensives; you can find highs and lows on the weather map, or tune your TV to serials, documentaries—and, of course, commercials. All these expressions are shorthand: "general (officer)," "analgesic (drug)," "high (pressure area)," "documentary (program)" and so on.

Some adjectives double as verbs—a dull day can dull thought—others, as adverbs (see **ADVERBS AND HOW TO SPOT 'EM**). Prepositions double as adverbs more often than not (see any dictionary).

In recent centuries, nouns have increasingly doubled as verbs, and vice versa. In Old English, this was impossible, since the two classes of words had quite different **INFLEC-TIONS**. Thus "love" (the noun) was *lufu*, if it was the subject of a sentence (the F was pronounced V); "to love" was *lufian*. The wholesale loss of inflections during the Middle Ages changed all that: most nouns became indistinguishable from their related verbs, except by context. The natural result was that people began coining new verbs out of old nouns and vice versa; they've been doing so ever since.

To sum up: a sizable part of the English vocabulary consists of "interchangeable parts"—words that serve or can serve more than one syntactic function. The probable record holder is "in," which (check your dictionary) can serve as preposition, adverb, adjective, and even—for those who like to have an in with the right people—a noun. And, as we've seen, there's nothing in the least new, abnormal or outrageous about this; it's the way English syntax works.

Of course there are limitations on this principle. For example, nouns and verbs don't become prepositions and conjunctions, or (with a handful of exceptions) vice versa. You can't, that is, use just any word for any purpose.

The important thing to remember is that any dictum about usage based on the supposed principle that "a noun is a noun is a noun" is shaky at best. The usage itself may, indeed, be bad for some other reason: it may be unclear (though most noun-verb and noun-adjective interchanges are not), or self-consciously trendy (see **FAD WORDS**), or simply pretentious, any of which are good grounds for rejecting it. For instance, I've never *authored* a book, though I've written a dozen. And of course some usages will label you as **ILLITER-ATE**—for example, if you *loan* someone money in hopes of getting an *invite* to his home.

A good question to ask about any unfamiliar or dubious interchange is "Is it necessary?" To talk of money "bequested" to a college (quoted in *HDCU*) is silly when we already have "bequeathed"—or simply "willed." *Time* magazine once spoke of "efforting to get into Czechoslovakia"; the writer should have efforted a little harder.

Equally superfluous are "fragmentize" for the verb "fragment," "thefted" for "stole" and "hosting" a party rather than "giving" or "throwing" it. On the other hand, I see nothing wrong with saying that A and B "cohosted" a talk show; certainly it's better than the cumbersome "acted as cohosts of." Nor do I have any problems when I hear that a play or a movie has "premiered," which is crisper than "had its premiere."

Whenever you confront the question "To interchange or not to interchange," remember Caxton's advice to favor the common words that are in daily use. In usage as in other things, it's a good idea, before trying something new, to ask yourself why—and if you can't think of a plausible reason, don't do it.

INTERNATIONAL COMMUNIST CONSPIRACY. A phrase heard less often today than thirty years ago, but still often enough to sow a certain amount of confusion. It implies that all **COMMUNIST** movements and governments (plus other individuals and groups that only a paranoid would call communist), all over the world, are united in their aims and tactics, which (of course) center on the destruction of the United States.

Forty or fifty years ago, when virtually all communist parties were intellectual captives of Moscow, one could have talked fairly reasonably about an "international communist conspiracy"—though its supposed influence was as inflated then as it is now. Today, things are very different. Considering only governments, we find that the Soviet communists are on very cool terms with the Chinese communists, while the latter are on even cooler terms with the Vietnamese communists (only a few years ago, the two were at war). The Vietnamese positively detested the Khmer Rouge communists of Cambodia (as did almost everyone else in the world) and eventually chased them out of that country.

The Romanian communists are cool, and the Albanian communists positively frigid, toward both the Soviets and the Chinese; the Yugoslav communists are on less-than-amiable terms with all of these. And the communist Nagy government of Hungary and the communist Dubcek government of Czechoslovakia were both overturned by the communist Red Army. Thus even ignoring the dozens of mutually distrustful (and often mutually abusive) communist parties and sects, we are clearly confronted by a "conspiracy" whose supposed members probably couldn't agree on what to have for dinner.

Long ago, Karl Marx intimated that socialism, or communism, would abolish national antagonisms, turning humanity into one big happy family. The last forty years have proved this to be one of his worst predictions—yet, ironically, its substance has been taken up by some of the world's most devout anti-Marxists. (Equally ironically, the Soviets often act as if they believed in an "international capitalist conspiracy" —though so far as I know they don't use the phrase.)

Be aware, then, that if you refer to an international communist conspiracy, you're talking about something that doesn't exist. And if you read the phrase, you can put the author down as (1) ignorant, (2) paranoid, (3) a con artist, (4) any of the above.

INVERSION. The normal word order of an English sentence is subject (including any modifiers), verb (including *its* modifiers) and the object(s) of the verb, if any, and *its* modifiers ("The crazy man/viciously bit/a helpless dog").

This is no universal linguistic principle—the Germans, among others, don't always follow it—but it's what we're all used to. To change this order without good reason is therefore a bad idea: at best, it will distract your readers; at worst, confuse them.

The commonest reason for using abnormal word order— and it's a good reason—is emphasis. For instance, we can separate the verb-modifier from the verb and put it ahead of the subject ("Again and again he denied it"). That is, by putting the important point (here, that he *kept on* denying whatever-it-was) at the beginning of the sentence, we give it added weight. Often the effect of such inversions is consciously dramatic, or melodramatic, as in "Slowly he drew her to him"—meaning that a little of it goes a long way.

For the same reason—emphasis—we sometimes put the

object ahead of the subject and verb, as in the punch line of the old joke about the honeymooners: "*This* I've got to see!" This particular construction may be a **YIDDISHISM,** but whatever its source, it does the job.

Another variety of sentence inversion was invented in the late 1920s by the editors of *Time* magazine. Here the *verb* was shifted to the beginning of the sentence ("Convicted last week of income-tax evasion was gang-boss Al Capone"). This was supposed to sound snappy and up-to-date, and so it did—briefly; thereafter, it became merely tiresome.

"Timestyle" (as it was called) was unforgettably skewered by Wolcott Gibbs, in his famous parody in the *New Yorker:* "Backward ran sentences until reeled the mind." Henry Luce was livid—but *Time* soon abandoned this particular gimmick. Trendy syntax, like trendy words, has little staying power.

IRREGARDLESS. Incorrectly ascribed to the one-time New York columnist Dan Parker or to Amos 'n' Andy, it is rejected by practically everybody. I concur, when it's used as a substitute for "regardless (of)," since it adds an unnecessary syllable. But I retain a lingering fondness for the word as a forceful bit of shorthand for "regardless of the consequences" or "no matter what," or "and try and stop me!"—for which reason I will continue to use it occasionally, irregardless. For the record, the word goes back at least to 1910—long before anyone had heard of either Dan Parker or Amos 'n' Andy.

-IZE. An inflection-suffix that has been turning nouns and adjectives into verbs for centuries. The earliest known "-ize" word is the thirteenth-century "baptize," which, like many ecclesiastical words of the time, came ultimately from Greek *(baptizein)*. Many later examples came from French coinages —verbs constructed on the pattern of NOUN or ADJECTIVE + *-iser* (e.g., *humaniser,* which begot our "humanize").

By the late sixteenth century, English had acquired so many

words of this type that writers began using the suffix to coin new words. Purists criticized the practice then, and still do, but the coinages have continued unabated; some nineteenth-century examples are "insignificantize," "Joe Millerize" (make a joke of), "nakedize" (!) and "antisepticize."

As these examples suggest, "-ize" coinages seldom last long, at least outside the sciences, where "oxidize," "alkalize," "sterilize" and scores of others are part of the normal vocabulary. It follows that new, nonscientific coinages should be handled with care as probable **FAD WORDS.** But don't criticize or satirize such words without scrutinizing them to make sure they *are* new, or you may have to apologize.

A very popular recent target of the purists, for some reason, is "finalize." I think their dislike of the word makes some sense, but not their reasons. To begin with, the word is not, as some think, a very new coinage: it dates from the 1920s. Second, it did not originate, as some claim, either on Madison Avenue or among government bureaucrats, but among Australian businessmen.

Myself, I think the word has a legitimate place in English— but only with a precise meaning: "put into final form" ("We need to finalize our strategy"), since there's no concise alternative. "Approve in final form" ("Let's finalize the contract"), given by the *OED,* is barely possible, though I'd be inclined just to sign it. But saying "Let's finalize this discussion" is merely a hokey way of saying "Let's wind it up," or "Let's end it," or "It's time for a drink."

J-K

JARGON. A word of many meanings; the one discussed here is "the specialized or technical language of a trade, profession, class or fellowship" *(AHD)*. All such groups develop jargons, for several reasons. One is to strengthen the group's solidarity—its members' sense of belonging—by creating a special language that outsiders don't understand. That's why, for example, a New York City cop calls a criminal a "perp"(etrator) and an arrest a "collar."

But jargon also serves a very practical function: it supplies concise expressions for the specialized tools and concepts that the group deals with, things that can be described only cumbersomely, if at all, in ordinary language. For this reason oil-field workers say "Christmas tree" instead of "collection of valves and pipes on top of a well," and computer owners talk knowledgeably of "bytes," "modems" and "RAM."

Jargon terms, almost by definition, are unclear to outsiders, but there's nothing wrong with that: they're clear to those who have a "need to know." Equally clear are those jargon terms that have seeped into the general vocabulary in a figurative sense: we still speak of something as being "between the hammer and the anvil" (Lebanon vs. Israel and Syria, for instance). Likewise, a person who is "backing and filling" (moving back and forth but getting nowhere) is doing exactly what an old-time sailing ship did in light and shifting winds;

we "bail out" of a dangerous situation as an aviator does from a crippled plane.

Since World War II, however, the headlong advance of technology and the sciences has multiplied both jargon terms and their figurative use in Standard English. All too often, their use outside their proper environment is merely pretentious—a way of showing that the speaker is up on the latest lingo (see **HIGH-TECH LANGUAGE**). Technical jargon is O.K. when used between consenting technicians but, like other harmless perversions, should be practiced in private.

JOB ACTION. Objected to by many purists on the ground that it's "a euphemism for an illegal strike," "a semantic cop-out," etc. *(HDCU).* The editors themselves load the dice by referring to job actions by "our so-called public servants," and indeed one gets the impression that most of the objectors aren't crazy about *any* strike.

Some labor leaders certainly call illegal strikes "job actions"—but from their standpoint the euphemism is essential: if the strike is illegal, to call it by that name invites jail. However, the rest of us, even if we sympathize with their problem (as I sometimes do), don't have their excuse and should avoid the usage: a strike, legal or otherwise, is still a strike.

On the other hand, "job action" is also employed to encompass various kinds of union pressure tactics short of a walkout —slowdowns, "sick-outs" and so on. In this sense, it's a useful term, always provided the context makes the sense clear.

KILT(S). Most Americans, to the despair of the experts, use the word in the plural, probably by analogy with "pants"; the English and Scots use the singular, as in "He wore the kilt" (not usually *a* kilt"). The distinction strikes me as a good thing not to worry about, but if it matters to you, just remember the old jingle "Oh, what does a Scotsman have under his *kilt?*"

KIND OF or SORT OF (= **"rather"** or **"somewhat"**). A very common informal usage, though highly distressing to a small minority. I think worrying about it is kind of silly.

KIND OF A or SORT OF A. Another popular locution deplored by critics. Technically, they're right: the "a" is superfluous, for which reason I don't use it—but it's not the kind of (a) thing you need to lose sleep over.

KIND(S) OF THING(S) IS/ARE. The distinction between "This kind of thing is . . . ," "These kind of things are . . ." and "These *kinds* of things are . . ." can trip up even some experts, but is still important. If you're talking about one kind of thing, then say "this kind of thing"; if you mean two or more different kinds of things, it's "these kinds of things"; saying "these *kind* of things" is likely to leave the reader confused as to how many kinds of things you're talking about—which is the kind of thing you should avoid.

KNOTS PER HOUR. A usage that will evoke the scorn of any sailors in the audience. "Knots" means "nautical miles per hour" ("the new destroyer has a top speed of thirty-eight knots"). "Knots per hour," then, literally means "miles per hour per hour"; stick with "knots" alone and you save two words. Note, too, that sailors measure distance at sea in nautical miles or in kilometers, never in knots.

A curious literary note: Kipling, one of the few authors of his day who found technology and its lingo interesting, almost invariably got this bit of jargon wrong, saying "knots per hour" instead of "knots." Even more curiously, none of his many naval friends seem to have bothered to set him right.

L

LADY/WOMAN. Both these words have long and complicated histories, involving attitudes toward both class and **GENDER.** The original, literal meaning of "lady" was "loaf-kneader," as "lord" meant "loaf-keeper," both testifying to the central importance of bread in family life a thousand years ago.

Even then, however, a lady seldom if ever engaged in actual bread making. Rather, as the female head of an upper-class household, she supervised the domestic staff who actually produced food and clothing, as her husband, the lord, supervised the plowmen, shepherds and cowherds who supplied the raw materials. For centuries afterward, "lady" remained the standard term for a woman of the nobility or gentry.

In the Victorian era, when millions of Britishers and Americans were moving up the social scale, or trying to, "lady" became almost the normal term for any "respectable" woman. Even the "lower classes" normally used it, as in the first line of the old Pat and Mike joke, "Who was that lady I seen you with?" To call someone a "woman" was considered rather insulting—though the elite used it routinely to refer to the **HOI POLLOI,** female division.

Some fifteen years ago, feminists began objecting to "lady"; their reason, apparently, was its inclusion in such expressions as "ladylike," which to them implied the sort of stereotyped, passive image of femininity they were crusading against. Personally, I don't see it that way: to me, a lady is simply a polite, considerate woman, meaning that I use the word rather as a compliment than as an insult. (For the same reason, I have no problems with being called a gentleman.) But on the general principle that people are entitled to be called what they choose to be called (see **BLACK** and **GAY**), I'm willing to call any lady a woman, if that's what she prefers.

Yet even "woman" bothers a few feminists. They believe that the "-man" in it "defines women in terms of men," and therefore insist on spelling it "wummon" (plural, "wimmin"). Here I draw the line, since their view has nothing to do with the facts. "Woman" goes back to Old English *wyfman,* in which "-man" had its original sense of "human being." *Wyfman,* then, meant "female human being," which is what "woman" still means; spelling it any other way proves nothing except that the spellers don't understand their own language.

"Girl," applied to an adult woman, is widely considered insulting, for which reason I avoid it—and think the worse of an executive if he refers to his secretary as "my girl." Here too, however, some women insist on carrying the matter to extremes: any human female past the age of puberty is a "woman" or a "young woman," though most of us find it hard to think of fourteen-year-old kids as either "women" or "men." I remember once referring to such a "girl" and being told sharply by a feminist in the room that she was a "woman"; I told her, just as sharply, that the "woman" in question was twelve years old.

Of course "girls" is often used by women of a certain age to refer to themselves and their friends, as their husbands use "boys" ("a night out with the boys"). This has nothing to do with sexism, but reflects the widespread, rather pathetic desire to seem younger than one is.

A final point: "girl" applied to an adult black female is insulting, with no ifs or buts, and the same applies to "boy" applied to a black man.

LATE. In the sense of "recently deceased," it's standard—always assuming that the decease *was* recent; one doesn't speak of "the late President Roosevelt," either Franklin or Teddy. In the sense of "recent but not at present" ("John Jones, late Professor of Physics at . . .") it's confusing—unless, of course, the professor in question died recently; otherwise say "former." And to call someone "the widow of the late so-and-so" is redundant: if she's his widow, he's dead, no?

LAUNDER (money). A usage violently objected to by most *HDCU* panelists, apparently because they consider it a euphemism (see **WATERGATE ENGLISH**). To me, it's no such thing, but a valuable addition to the language: there's simply no other word to describe the manipulation of dirty money to eliminate ring-around-the-bankroll. I have no doubt that the word will remain in English as long as people engage in the financial finagling it so vividly describes—and that, alas, promises to be a long, long time.

LAY/LIE. Millions of people naturally say "I was lying on the bed"; millions of others just as naturally say "I was laying on the bed," and in neither case will anyone be in doubt as to what the speaker was doing. Nonetheless, many educated people consider "laying" blue-collar, and condemn it.

One source of the confusion is the fact that the verbs "overlap"; that is, it's perfectly proper to say either "I lay (place) it on the bed" or "I lay (reclined) on the bed." If the distinction matters to you, just remember that lie/lay/lain is intransitive, while lay/laid/laid is transitive, meaning that it's something you do *to* something—or somebody. A good way of remembering the difference is the old tombstone inscription: HERE LIES (not LAYS) so-and-so.

A historical note: right through the eighteenth century, plenty of educated people used the two words interchangeably—and, I'm told, not a few educated people have begun to do so today. Once in a long while, this produces unintentional humor, as in the following, written by a graduate student in English (!). He describes a Spanish market with "fat-gutted rabbits hanging by their feet and strangled chickens laying in large heaps. . . ." With birds, or other egg layers, make sure you say they're *lying*—unless they're actually laying.

LEARN/TEACH. A distinction not unlike the last. In educated English, learning is "input" while teaching is "output"— which the teacher hopes will become input to the learner. Thus you learn something *from* somebody—or from experience—but you teach *somebody*, or something *to* somebody; saying that you're going to "learn" somebody is blue-collar.

I must confess, however, to a certain sympathy with Mr. Badger in *The Wind in the Willows,* who evidently considered "teach" a rather feeble verb. Preparing for a confrontation with the Bad Guys, he announced that he and his friends were going to "learn 'em," and when the Water Rat suggested that "teach 'em" was better, snapped "But we're not going to teach 'em, we're going to *learn* 'em!"

LEAVE/LET. Another case of verbal overlap, this one semantic. You can, quite properly, say either "Leave him alone!" or "Let him alone!" Bernstein suggests that using them interchangeably may cause confusion, but I must say I don't find his examples very persuasive.

If you want to avoid even the tiniest chance of confusion, say "leave alone" only if you mean leaving someone in solitude, "let alone" if you mean refrain from interfering with. And to say "leave us" do so-and-so is blue-collar—though I suspect that most of those who use it nowadays are educated people trying for a laugh. Leave us avoid this tired joke.

LENGTHY/LONG. Some authorities (e.g., Fowler) claim that while "long" means merely long, "lengthy" implies tedious-ness as well as mere length; however, it's not always used that way. Since the word's exact meaning has become blurred, better avoid it entirely; if you mean long, say so; if you mean tedious, say that—or "tiresome" or "boring."

LESS/FEWER. "Many careful users of language," says *HDCU,* "draw a distinction between *less* and *fewer,* restricting *less* to quantities that can be measured . . . and *fewer* to things that can be counted." Given such a loaded question (who wants to be considered a careless user?), the panelists of course voted overwhelmingly to preserve the distinction; even those who admitted ignoring it promised to reform.

If the distinction was really clear, I'd go along with them— but it isn't. As Bernstein points out, it often depends on whether you're considering the countable things individually or collectively; thus you don't say that someone makes fewer than $20,000 a year, or that a building is fewer than thirty years old, though both the years and the dollars can certainly be counted. Nor can you say that a political party won "one fewer seat," though you *can* say "three fewer seats," or "three seats less"—or "one seat fewer."

Given this thoroughly muddled state of affairs, it's not surprising to read in the *OED Supp.* that the distinction between the two words has been dwindling away for at least a century. (Do you say there were "less than five" or "fewer than five" people in the room"? What about "less than a dozen" vs. "fewer than a dozen"?) Using "less" consistently certainly won't confuse the reader, while trying to decide when and where to substitute "fewer" is likely to confuse the writer.

LIBEL/SLANDER. Though many people use them interchangeably for any false, defamatory statement, lawyers will tell you that "slander" applies only to actual word of mouth; libel, to any other such statement, whether in print or on the radio or TV. Unless you're a lawyer, the distinction isn't worth bother-

ing about—just remember that engaging in either one may
land you in court.

LIBERAL. The rise of hard-core conservatism has turned this
formerly neutral word into a political epithet. "Liberals," in
the eyes of the Radical Right, are people who favor crime in
the streets, **PERMISSIVE(NESS)** in education and sex (not to
mention English usage), pornography, **SECULAR HUMAN-
ISM** and various other unspeakable things. Indeed, some
"liberals" are seen as disguised agents of the **INTERNA-
TIONAL COMMUNIST CONSPIRACY.** The Radical Left
has also gotten in its licks at "liberals," claiming that they are
really disguised agents of the establishment.

The widespread misuse of "liberal" reflects two common
fallacies. The first is that people who are opposed to prohibiting something by law must be in favor of it. This is nonsense,
of course. For example, I (and, I think, nearly all Americans)
would fight against any law prohibiting the practice of Roman
Catholicism, yet I certainly don't favor either the church or its
doctrines.

The second fallacy is that if you question the value of a
proposed remedy, you must be in favor of the disease. That
is, if you believe that "getting tough" on street crime isn't
likely to reduce it much unless something is also done about
its causes—notably, unemployment—you must love street
criminals. Which makes about as much sense as saying that
doctors who criticize a dubious cancer cure must love cancer.

As currently used, then, "liberal" is a Humpty-Dumpty
word: it means whatever the speaker chooses. As such it
should be avoided, except where the context makes the sense
absolutely clear—or in political mudslinging.

LIKE/AS. Grammarians who go by the book have long insisted
that "like" is a preposition, hence must be attached to a noun
or pronoun ("He writes like Hemingway"—*HDCU*). It can-

not, that is, be used as a conjunction meaning "in the way that," for which only "as" is correct ("He writes *as* Hemingway wrote"). If you find this distinction confusing, you're in good company: so did Charles Darwin, T. S. Eliot and William Faulkner.

Purists were particularly enraged when the American public was told, some years back, that "Winstons taste good, like a cigarette should." The slogan was seen not as the synthetic folkiness common in **ADVERTISINGESE** but as "advertising corruption of the language" (Earl Ubell), "a deliberate vulgarism by hucksters" (David Schoenbrun) and so on.

Whatever the grammarians say about the alleged misuse of "like," most people talk like that. Whether you choose to go along with popular usage depends pretty much on how much you want to stay in the grammarians' good graces. If you do, stick with "as"; if not—tell it like it is.

LIKE/SUCH AS. For over a thousand years, the basic idea of "like" has been similarity of one thing to some *other* thing ("My love is like a red, red rose"). By this reasoning, the phrase "preachers like Jerry Falwell" would not include the Reverend Falwell himself, but only those other preachers who resemble him. To include him in the group, one would have to say "preachers *such as* Jerry Falwell."

So much for theory; in practice, "like" has been used to mean "such as" for a century—yet I still feel rather uneasy about using it that way. I can't reasonably insist that you share my feelings; I do suggest that when using "like" in this sense you watch your context. Are you talking about Falwell *and* his clones, or only the clones—and will the reader be certain which you mean? To avoid any chance of confusion, use "such as" in the first case, "like" in the second.

LIKELY (adverb). "Likely" as an adjective (= probable) raises no problems for anyone, and neither, for centuries, did "likely" as an adverb (= probably). Around 1900, however, educated people, for unknown reasons, began abandoning "likely" as an adverb—*unless* it was preceded by "very," "most" or some similar modifier.

For the past twenty years, the pendulum has begun swinging back in the United States and Canada (though not, apparently, in England). I therefore feel free to recommend that you do what I've been doing for some years: use "likely" as an adverb, with or without modifiers. To approve "He will very likely do it" but reject "He will likely do it" will likely confuse people, as it certainly does me.

LINE, IN/ON. In most parts of the United States, you stand *in* line for a bus; in New York City, most people stand *on* line, and the usage seems to be spreading. A major reason, I suspect, is the widespread catch phrase "Get on line!"—meaning "Your sentiment is shared by many!" ("I'd like to slug that s.o.b.!" "Get on line!"). As a New Yorker, I have no objection to standing either in line or on line, provided the line isn't too long. (Britishers, incidentally, do neither, but queue up instead; their equivalent of "Get on line!" is "Join the queue!")

LOOSE(N)/UNLOOSE(N). As the editors of *HDCU* point out, "unloosen" should logically mean the opposite of "loosen" —but language isn't logical. Unfortunately, in their haste to make this sensible point, they fall into the error of saying that the two words mean precisely the same thing. They don't.

"Loosen" means to make looser—that is, less tight; "unloosen" almost always means "unloose" (= unfasten or set free, as in the misquotation "Cry havoc, and unloose the dogs of war"). A cop may loosen the handcuffs on a perpetrator, but the man will still be cuffed; if the cuffs are unloosed or unloosened, his hands will be free. "Unloosen," then, should be avoided in either situation: it adds an extra syllable and subtracts from clarity.

M

MAFIA. A term often used to refer to the Mob, the Syndicate or the Outfit—that is, organized crime. The word, and its synonym "(La) Cosa Nostra," is disliked by some Italian-Americans, who feel that it reflects unfavorably on them.

Before considering these feelings, let's briefly examine the facts. To begin with, most American criminals aren't Italians and most Italian-Americans aren't criminals. In fact, "crime," in its broadest sense, extends right across the ethnic spectrum. Thus "big-business crime"—price-fixing, rigged bidding and fraud in defense contracts, illegal pollution and the like—is naturally dominated by the same ethnics who dominate big business: the WASPs.

"Street crime" (mugging, robbery and the like) is a form of unskilled labor, a field that has always been dominated by whatever ethnic group happened to be at the bottom of the economic totem pole. A century and a half ago, it was the Irish; currently, the blacks and Hispanics. Like other kinds of unskilled labor, it doesn't pay very well.

"Organized crime"—illegal gambling, extortion and the narcotics trade—involves members of all ethnic groups, but its top figures are mostly Italians. This wasn't always true, and probably won't always be true, but it's true today.

If you don't like "Mafia," you can say the same thing just as clearly with "Mob" or "Syndicate." I use all three; I feel that if some people are fool enough to think that "Mafia" implies something about Italians generally, or the "Italian character" (whatever that is), nothing I say or don't say is likely to change their minds. However, I also restrict the word to gangsters; such phrases as President Kennedy's "Irish Mafia" or President Nixon's "California Mafia" were witty when they were coined, but the joke has gone stale.

MAJORITY/PLURALITY. Sometimes confused, probably because a majority (more than half the votes or whatever) is automatically a plurality (the largest number). But a majority should never be *called* a plurality, because a plurality is not necessarily a majority; as generally used, it never is.

Plurality, that is, should be reserved for situations where you're talking about something divided into three or more groups. The largest of these groups is a plurality, *provided it's less than half the total;* otherwise, it's a (or the) majority.

Also worth noting is that while "majority" technically means anything over half of what you're discussing, it generally implies not much more than half—say, between 50 and 60 percent, if you're talking about votes or an opinion poll. Over 60 percent would be a "large" majority; over 75 or 80 percent, an "overwhelming" majority.

If you're talking about something else, the numbers may be a little different. In many medical studies, for example, the researchers assume that a sizable proportion of the patients will improve with or without treatment. In this situation, saying that "a large majority" of patients benefited from the treatment implies something like 80 percent or better; while an "overwhelming" majority would suggest at least 90 percent.

Pluralities are never "large," let alone "overwhelming." If what you want to say is that candidate A got nearly half the vote (the largest possible plurality), while his opponents B, C and D split up the remainder, don't say that A got "a large plurality," but rather, "a near majority." You can, however, speak of a large *minority* (40 percent or so), a sizable minority (25 percent or so) or a small minority (10 percent or so). Below 5 percent it's a tiny minority.

MASTERFUL/MASTERLY. Another confusing pair—especially since they obviously derive from the same word. "Masterful" conveys the idea of domination ("She's a very masterful person"), and therefore applies only to people. "Masterly," on the other hand, does not apply directly to people but rather to what they produce or create ("A masterly piece of criticism"—though some critics are pretty masterful at that).

"Masterly" is one of those words that make **GENDER** such a tricky linguistic problem. You can say that the writer Jane Austen was a mistress of her craft, but hardly that her portrayal of English country life was mistressly—though it was certainly masterly.

MAY/MIGHT. Like **CAN,** a "defective verb," with no infinitive, participles or future. Technically, "May" is present, "might" is past, as in "He *says* he *may* go" vs. "He *said* he *might* go," but most usages of the two have nothing to do with tense. That is, both are normally used in the present tense but referring to future time: "I may go to Europe"or "I might go to Europe." Here, the sense (uncertainty) is almost identical, but "might" is just a bit *more* uncertain than "may."

In certain past constructions, "might" is, or has the force of, a **SUBJUNCTIVE;** it implies a possibility that didn't come off ("Of all the words of tongue or pen/The saddest are 'It might have been' ")—thereby, ironically, indicating certainty rather than uncertainty.

MEANINGFUL. Another case of card stacking by *HDCU.* To determine whether this word was acceptable, the editors cited "*meaningful* relationship" and "*meaningful* dialogue," then asked the panelists whether *they* used the word. Not surprisingly, given the clichéd context in which it was presented, nearly two-thirds denied using it in speech and an even larger majority, in writing.

I'd give odds that many of the panelists were kidding themselves: they were reacting to the phrases, not the word itself. This was conspicuously true of Leo Rosten, who described it as "Student cant of the 1960s. Baloney." Rosten is a lot more reliable on Yiddish than on English: "meaningful relationship" may date from the 1960s, but "meaningful" itself appeared in the 1850s. Another panelist insisted that "*anything* uttered or written is *meaningful*"; his acquaintance with political speeches must have been slight.

As I've already noted, "meaningful relationship" and "meaningful dialogue" are clichés—that is, neither is now very meaningful. But there's nothing clichéd about saying that she gave him a meaningful glance, or that it took the scientists a long time to get meaningful results. (*Any* scientific experiment yields results, but not all of these, alas, add up to anything—that is, are meaningful.) However, in either of these contexts, "significant" says the same thing.

MEET UP WITH. *HDCU* insists this is a redundeancy—that is, "meet" alone will do the job. It won't. While "meet," "meet with" and "meet up with" are obviously related, they convey distinctly different shades of meaning.

To meet someone means either to encounter them for the first time ("Pleased to meet you") or to get together with them at a specific time or place ("I'll meet you at the theater"). If you meet *with* someone, however, you're not encountering them but conferring with them for a more or less prolonged period: "I met with him yesterday" doesn't mean the same as "I met him yesterday."

"Meet up with," finally, implies an element of chance or

uncertainty; it's equivalent to "run into." Moreover, it generally does *not* apply to a first meeting: "I'm glad I met up with you" means something different from "I'm glad I met you." Note also that of the three expressions only "meet" can be used of things as well as people: you can meet a demand, or a deadline, but not meet with, or up with, either one.

Conciseness in language is important—but preciseness is more important (see also **STUDY UP ON**).

MIGHTY (= very). According to *HDCU, acceptable* in informal speech but not in writing; according to Bryant it *occurs* "in standard speech and in informal written English." Here we have a good example of the prescriptive vs. the descriptive approach to language: *HDCU* tells you what it thinks ought to happen; Bryant, merely what does happen.

Those who look askance at "mighty" do so, I think, because they see it as a rural or regional (Southern) term and therefore to be avoided. Since my own family came from Virginia, I consider this a mighty provincial point of view, but the fact that the word comes naturally to me doesn't mean that it will, or should, come naturally to you.

MINIMIZE. Its predominant (and obvious) meaning is "reduce to a minimum"; some people, however, employ it in the weakened sense of "reduce," in such expressions as "greatly minimize." Saying "minimize" instead of "reduce" is confusing and pretentious, uses three syllables where two will do and blurs the logical connection between "minimize" and "minimum." English, like every other language, has its illogical elements, but we should minimize them.

MISPLACED MODIFIERS. The usual way of introducing this subject is to quote some amusing but imaginary example: "For sale: Large sideboard by relocating couple with mahogany trim." Misplaced modifiers are seldom that funny, but almost invariably confusing. Bernstein cites as an example "The new facilities will make it possible for babies to be born in Roosevelt Hospital for the first time." Here, "for the first time" seems to modify "born," which is ridiculous; nobody is born twice, except, perhaps, spiritually.

Putting "for the first time" directly after the word it modifies, "possible," makes the sentence clearer (" . . . makes it possible for the first time for babies to be born . . .")—and also shows it up as silly. There was never a time when it wasn't "possible" for babies to be born at Roosevelt Hospital; they can be born anywhere, including in taxis en route to the hospital. What the inept writer was trying to say was that the hospital's new maternity wing would make it possible for babies to be born there with the full trappings of modern medicine—something that was obvious without his saying so. Clarifying what you're saying sometimes reveals that you shouldn't have said it.

The general rule governing the placement of modifiers is a simple one: put them as close as possible to what they modify. The more words that intervene between modifier and modified, the greater the odds that the reader will be confused about what modifies what. (A frequent exception to this rule is **ONLY**.)

More specifically, adjectives should come immediately before the noun or pronoun they refer to ("my *best* girl"); adjectival phrases, after it ("the girl *that I married*"). Adverbs or adverbial phrases that modify a verb generally come immediately after it ("Go *gently* into that good night"), or after its object, if it has one ("Beat the drum *slowly*"). If they modify an adjective or another adverb, however, they come before it ("Beat the drum *very* slowly"). Occasionally, however, adverbs or adverbial phrases are shifted to the beginning of the sentence for emphasis (see **INVERSION**).

Particularly prone to misplacement are clauses at the beginning of a sentence that modify a later noun or pronoun. The rule here is that once you've stated your clause, the noun or pronoun it modifies must follow it *immediately*. That is, the reader will be "set" to apply the clause to whatever noun or pronoun comes next—and if that isn't the right one, the result is trouble; Bernstein cites "Lying astride the Quebec-Labrador boundary, a prospector looking for gold found the ore in what is known as the Labrador Trough." His discussion of these and other misplaced modifiers, which he calls "danglers," is both amusing and instructive.

What might be called the ultimate dangler is a modifying clause with nothing to modify. An example (also from Bernstein): "Although sixty-one years old when he wore the original suit, his waist was only thirty-five." Here "sixty-one years old" apparently refers to "waist"; its actual referent—the owner of the suit—is nowhere specified (presumably it's "he" —but presumably isn't good enough). As with Roosevelt Hospital, however, clarifying the sentence reveals a double whammy: "Although *he was* sixty-one years old when he wore the suit, his waist was only thirty-five" leaves the sixty-one-year-old man with a thirty-five-year-old waist; to avoid a snicker, you have to add "inches" at the end.

If your sentence includes two clauses modifying the same thing, you must pick your way very carefully. A recent example, from some World War II memoirs that I never finished: "George Duncan . . . gave us all the information about the larger operation of which *Whynot* was a minute part that his superiors had thought fit to give him." The last clause, beginning with "that his," is a real dangler that brought me up short when I read it.

The problem is that the clause seems to refer to "part," which immediately precedes it, yet obviously doesn't. The solution is to put it right after the word it modifies, "information." The sentence then reads ". . . all the information that his superiors had thought fit to give him about the larger operation . . . ," which is clear if a bit cumbersome.

Some alleged experts on reading believe that complex sentences such as the one we've been talking about should be avoided on principle, because they're hard to read. I don't agree. Or rather, I do agree, but only "other things being equal"—which they seldom are. Saying something in a few complex sentences may make more demands on the reader than using a long series of simple, short ones, but a long string of the latter can get awfully dull—see any of the "Dick and Jane" books. And if that happens, the writer may lose the reader's attention—and with it, his or her comprehension. A better practice is to use both kinds of sentences, interspersing long ones with short, punchy ones. Like this.

However, there's no doubt at all that the more complicated the sentence, the more chance for messing up the structure—meaning, the more demands on the writer's skill. So if you're not really sure of your skills, stick to relatively simple sentences; if you *are* sure—watch your step anyway.

To close this section, consider "The first two runners to finish" vs. "The two first runners to finish." The editors of *HDCU* say that just a few years ago, "grammarians" insisted that only the second phrase was correct. I don't know who these grammarians were, but am happy to agree with a large majority of the panelists that "the two first runners" is wrong, unless you're talking about a dead heat. (If you don't see this, try "The ten first runners. . . .")

The really interesting thing about this example is the fact that almost a fifth of the panelists still clung to "The two first" —in one case, "even though I don't bother to say it that way" (!). Such reactions, I think, illustrate the almost hypnotic effect that "grammar" has on some writers, leading them to ignore not only clarity but plain common sense.

MISQUOTATIONS. If you refer to something as a **FRANKEN-STEIN,** ninety-nine readers out of a hundred will assume you mean a machine or a man-made monster that has escaped from its maker's control, though the original Dr. Frankenstein was the maker, not the monster. As I've already noted many times, a word means what it means now, not what it meant then.

People sensitive to misquotations (Bernstein was one) wince at such statements as "Pride goeth before a fall" (the original was "Pride goeth before destruction, and an haughty spirit before a fall"), "gild the lily" (Shakespeare said "to gild refined gold, to paint the lily") and so on. I myself have an aversion to the misuse (*not* the misquotation) of **MORE HONORED IN THE BREACH.**

There are really two problems here. "More honored in the breach . . ." and "Frankenstein" are not really misquotations, since the words haven't been changed, just the sense. In real misquotations, the problem—if that's what it is—is that popular usage, over the generations, has condensed, modernized or otherwise "improved" the wording of the original; often the streamlined version has become an idiom in its own right —and sometimes a cliché as well.

As usual, my main interest is clarity: will sticking to the original wording make the sense clearer, or less clear? In the case of "paint the lily," I'd say less clear: to us, painting something doesn't automatically mean fancying it up, whereas gilding does.

Often, too, it's a good idea to ask yourself what the phrase, misquoted or not, really means. Thus whether you paint the lily or gild it, you're obviously trying to improve something that needs no improvement. Yet I've seen "lily-gilding" used to mean "whitewashing," which means something very different: "improving" something that badly needs it.

Sometimes the "misquotation" results merely from modernized syntax. The film of *The Maltese Falcon* ended with Sam Spade describing the Black Bird as "the stuff that dreams are made of"; surely neither Spade nor anyone else nowadays would use Shakespeare's exact words: "such stuff as dreams are made on." As a general principle, "misquotation" should perhaps be avoided—but in any particular instance, it's likely to be a judgment call.

MOBILE/MOVABLE. Not often confused, in my experience, but if there's any uncertainty in your mind, remember that mobile things move but movable things are not, strictly speaking, mobile. Literally, of course, "movable" means "capable of being moved"—but it should not be applied to things specifically designed to be easily moved, whose mobility, so to speak, goes with the territory. The couches in my living room are movable but not mobile, while a missile launcher mounted on a truck, though certainly movable, is better called "mobile."

MONGOLISM. An offensive term, because it implies—and was intended to imply—that there is some connection between the physical abnormalities in this tragic genetic disease and the characteristics of the so-called Mongolian **RACE.** Dr. Charles Down, who first described the condition, evolved an elaborate theory whereby certain diseases in whites were supposedly caused by "reversion" to the characteristics of other —and, need I say, inferior—races.

Geneticists and doctors have known for years that the condition has nothing to do with the Mongolian or any other "race" (it occurs in all ethnic groups) but is caused by the presence of an extra chromosome; that is, sufferers have three copies of chromosome 21 instead of the normal two. To the geneticist, the condition is "trisomy 21"; to anyone else, it should be "Down's [or Down] syndrome."

MOOT. A real befuddler because its two meanings are almost directly opposed. In general use, the word means "arguable"; if you say "That's a moot point," you're saying that you're not ready to accept it without further discussion—if then.

As used by lawyers, however, the word means "not worth arguing about" or "of academic interest." For example, a woman claims she was fired from her job for protesting the low salaries paid women workers, and sues for reinstatement. The court gives a verdict in her favor; the employer appeals. While the appeal is pending, she dies. The appeals court may then dismiss the case as moot, meaning that there's now no point in deciding whether the firing was illegal, since nothing can be done about it.

Unfortunately, the legal sense of "moot" has seeped into general usage, meaning that people can take it as meaning either "arguable"—and therefore, presumably, worth arguing about—or "not worth arguing about." Avoid it—unless you're a lawyer talking to lawyers.

MORE HONORED IN THE BREACH THAN IN THE OB-SERVANCE. One of the great literary solecisms in English— and a vivid illustration of the principle that usage governs meaning. Hamlet's original remark concerned the Danes' predilection for boozing, which he called "a custom more honored in the breach than in the observance." He meant that the more honorable course was to breach the custom, and stay sober, rather than observe it, and get stinking drunk.

Today, as for several generations past, the phrase is used in a very different sense: a custom more often broken than observed. The result is that if you stick with Shakespeare's original meaning, almost nobody will know what you're trying to say—yet using the phrase in the modern sense amounts to rewriting Shakespeare. Since I refuse to do either, I don't use it at all. Anyway, it's pretty tired.

MOST ALL. In some parts of the country, most everybody says "most all" instead of "almost all." If you're talking to your neighbors in one of these regions, there's no reason not to use it; if you're addressing a more extended audience, you'll label yourself as either uneducated or self-consciously folksy.

MS. Though this expression was introduced some fifteen years ago, it is still controversial (for example, the good, gray *New York Times* still refuses to use it). On the *HDCU* usage panel, 70 percent preferred the traditional forms "Mrs." and "Miss" —not as bad as might have been expected, perhaps, considering that the panel was 93 percent male.

A good deal of the hassle can be avoided by simply dropping *all* forms of address, male or female. Letters can be addressed simply to JOHN or JANE DOE. This not only saves space but avoids the practice—which I personally detest—of addressing the married Jane Doe as "Mrs. John Doe." The letter itself can begin "Dear Jane (or John) Doe." If you feel that addressing a woman you don't know in this way is a bit too informal, then use "Miss" or "Mrs." if you known her marital status, "Ms." if you don't.

Having said this, I'll just add that I think the importance of "Ms." has been considerably overblown. Some feminists see it as a symbol of liberation (but does calling a woman "Ms." really diminish the inequalities she suffers?), while to some antifeminists (in or out of the closet) it is a symbolic threat to the old, comfortable system where men were men and women were allegedly glad of it. Either way, it's an awfully big ideological load for two letters to carry.

A related, and much less tractable, problem is how to address the anonymous members of a corporation or a government bureau. "Gentlemen" and "Dear Sirs" are arguably sexist, "Ladies" is equally so and "Persons" is ridiculous. "Dear Friends" is impossible—at least *I* refuse to address my bank, or the IRS, in this affectionate manner. Any suggestions?

MUST/HAVE TO/HAVE GOT TO/GOT TO. All of these expressions, of course, imply compulsion or obligation of some sort. The first two are completely interchangeable; the third is often described (e.g., by *HDCU*) as a redundancy. I think things aren't quite that simple. Rather, I believe we're dealing with one of the rare cases where phonetics has influenced usage.

It is a linguistic truism that the sounds of words have nothing to do with their sense, apart from such obvious exceptions as "crash," "boom" and "chickadee." Yet when we listen to "have" and "got," the latter, with its explosive G and snapping T, clearly sounds more forceful. In addition, "have" is a rather colorless verb, because of its very common use as an auxiliary. It is for these reasons, I think, that many people feel the need to add "got," even though it isn't, strictly speaking, necessary. And I've got to admit that I don't find this reprehensible.

Using "got" alone for "must" ("When you got to go, you got to go") is blue-collar. See also **GOT/GOTTEN.**

MUTUAL/COMMON. The word doctors disagree over this pair: *HDCU* says that "mutual" can refer only to two people; Bernstein says two or more. On the historical evidence, Bernstein is right. The earliest (and still current) sense of "mutual" is "reciprocal"; to say that a husband and wife show mutual affection means that each feels affectionate toward the other. But the couple and their three children can all five of them show mutual affection—though combined, usually, with some mutual hostility.

Everyone agrees, however, that "common" can refer to two or more people or things: specifically, to something they share or are related to in the same way ("their common [not 'mutual'] interest in football"). With "mutual," that is, we're talking about people's relationships to one another; with "common," about their relationships to something else. The U.S. and the Soviet governments are conspicuously devoid of mutual affection, but they have a common interest in avoiding nuclear war.

The single exception to these principles is "mutual friend" (or "acquaintance"), meaning, of course, "friend in common." A few purists still object to this expression, but it has by now been sanctified by more than a century's use, and it would be in our common interest to quit arguing about it.

N

NATIONAL SECURITY. One of the most-used and most-abused expressions of our time: everybody's for it, but—just what is it? Its obvious meaning is security against attack (by the Russians, of course; who else is powerful enough?). But its meaning has been broadened to cover "security" against any nation, however feeble, that is, or is supposed to be, under Soviet influence. If you think about it, this definition implies that Soviet influence can work miracles, converting economic and military weakness into menacing strength. Personally, I don't see the Soviets as either miracle workers or supermen.

In a still broader sense, "national security" means security against anything threatening the "national interest"—a phrase that is even muddier, if possible. Doubtless we Americans—all 230-odd million of us—do have a few interests in common, but I'd want specifics before deciding whether a particular "national" interest was really *my* interest (see also **SPECIAL INTEREST GROUP**).

For instance, some people, in and out of the Pentagon, seem to consider it in "our" interest to be the strongest military power on earth, *everywhere* on earth—and in space as well. I certainly don't consider this in *my* interest as a taxpayer, or even as a citizen. The British pursued this goal, quite successfully, for more than a century—and ended up with the moribund economy we see today. The Soviets spend even more of their GNP on "national security" than we do—and look at *their* economy; the Japanese spend much less—and look at theirs!

"National security," by implication, refers to things immensely important to all Americans. Yet it's also used of things so important that—they can't be talked about. In such cases, it's worth asking whether talking about these things publicly would benefit the Russians or the rest of us; to some officials, our national security equals their job security.

The best way of dealing with this and similar expressions is to treat them as **GOLDBRICK GENERALITIES**: ask for chapter and verse. If somebody tells you such-and-such is important to national security, ask them why—and then ask yourself whether such-and-such will really make *you* feel more secure. The same goes, of course, if you feel moved to use the expression yourself: exactly what do you mean by it—and how do you think "it" will make you, or the rest of us, more secure?

NATURE. Often used as padding; "He is of a generous nature" seldom says anything that "He's generous" doesn't. If you mean that he's generous *by* nature, say that—though I find it hard to imagine any other way he *could* be generous.

NAUSEATED/NAUSEATING/NAUSEOUS. Until fairly recently, the last of these meant only "nauseating," as it still does in England. For at least a generation, however, Americans have used it to mean "nauseated" (as in "I feel nauseous"). Purists find this alarming. The rest of us, given that the word now has two well-established meanings, would do well to avoid it. That is, you feel *nauseated,* while whatever made you feel that way is not nauseous but *nauseating;* it's worth using the extra syllable to be clear.

Note, by the way, that the problem isn't new: in the seventeenth century, "nauseousness" meant both the quality of being nauseat*ing* and the feeling of being nauseat*ed*. English survived this ambiguity, and people who suggest that the current ambiguity of "nauseous" is destroying the language make me—sick.

NEGATIVES, DOUBLE. The grammarians' rule against double negatives ("I don't know nothing") is based on the principle that two negatives equal a positive—that is, "I don't know nothing" equals "I do know something." Which may be true in mathematics, but not necessarily in language; for example, the French equivalent, *Je ne sais rien,* means, literally, "I not know nothing."

Shakespeare used double negatives routinely ("Nothing, neither way"), and Chaucer on at least one occasion packed four negatives into one sentence: *He never yet no vilaynie ne said/In all his life unto no manner wight.* (Translation: "He didn't never say nothing nasty to nobody.") Double negatives are still routine in uneducated or blue-collar English—meaning that if you use them around educated people, they'll think you don't know no better.

Note, however, that it's perfectly O.K. to say "not infrequently" or "not uncommon," even though the two prefixes, "in-" and "un-," mean "not." Here, you've got to look beyond the prefixes and recognize that the words aren't "true" negatives. That is, "infrequently" means "rarely," and there's nothing wrong with saying that something did not happen rarely—that is, it was a not uncommon occurrence. Handle with care, however: some people wrongly take "not infrequent" to mean "frequent," and "not uncommon" to mean "common."

NOISOME/NOISY. *HDCU* claims that these two words, because of their similarity, are "often confused." I doubt it, if only because "noisome" is seldom used nowadays. On the chance that *HDCU* is right, however, just bear in mind that the word is related to "annoy"—and means annoying, in spades: disgusting or (occasionally) dangerous.

"Noise," surprisingly, goes back ultimately to the Latin *nausea* (an English word in its own right, of course). The Latin word passed into French and several other Romance languages, in the process acquiring several different meanings—most of them unpleasant. In English it somehow wound up meaning almost any sound, unpleasant or otherwise, but we find a trace of its original bad vibrations in such expressions as "noisy" and "noise level."

NOT ABOUT TO. "I'm not about to," meaning "I don't intend to" or "I'm not going to," originated in the Southwest, and began moving into general use during the 1960s—partly, perhaps, through the influence of President Lyndon Johnson and his Texas buddies. Fifteen years ago I'd have called it self-consciously folksy; today, it's part of the American language, and I'm not about to criticize it.

NOT (ALL) THAT + adjective. The "all" is technically redundant, and is therefore expendable, and the same *may* apply to the "that." However, the construction often conveys a shade of meaning that can be expressed in no other way. Thus (for example) "I didn't enjoy the party" means "I didn't have any fun," while "I didn't enjoy the party much" means "I didn't have a lot of fun." "I didn't enjoy the party (all) that much" implies a comparison: "not as much fun (as I expected) (as you say *you* had)." Likewise, "He's not that bright" implies (or should imply) "not bright enough to have done whatever-it-is." Like **NOT TOO,** "not all that" can be replaced by "not very"—but to me the difference is not all that important.

NOT (ONLY) . . . BUT (ALSO). A tricky construction, since when and when not to use it aren't always obvious. Bernstein's extended discussion is worth reading.

The simplest case is when you mean either of two things but not both, in which case "only" and "also" aren't needed: "Not A, but B." If you mean *both* things, then it's "Not only A but also B"—usually. The same applies to phrases using equivalents of "only" and "also," as in "Not just A but B as well" and "Not merely A but B too."

The exception is when you're dealing, not with two independent things, but with related things, the second of which intensifies the other: "Not just uninformed, but plain ignorant," "Not just affluent, but rich" and so on. Bernstein's example "not only a painter, but a very good painter" is clear but also verbose; much simpler to say "a painter, and a very good one," or simply "a damn good painter." In short, the rationale of the exceptions is not only subtle but frequently confusing—or, more concisely, subtle, and often confusing.

NOT TOO + adjective. If you say that someone is not too bright, everyone will know what you mean. Recently, however, I read a letter to the *New York Times* that described a wall as "not too thick"—and it took me a moment to realize that the writer meant the wall was too *thin.* Why the confusion?

The reason, I think, is that we seldom if ever describe someone as literally too bright, but it's perfectly possible for a wall (or a sandwich or an overcoat) to be too thick. So the "rule" (which I just invented) is: don't use "not too" to mean "not very" with any adjective whose literal meaning might make sense (too thick, too heavy, too slow, etc.). Which means most adjectives. Even simpler: don't use it at all: "very" says the same thing, and is *always* right.

O

OBLIGED/OBLIGATED. A thoroughly confusing pair—compare Bernstein's and *HDCU*'s discussions. Both words implysome sort of compulsion, yet they're not really interchangeable.

"Obliged" has taken on some of the casualness of the phrase "much obliged," which is hardly ever used in its literal sense. That is, "obligated" is the stronger word, implying a legal or a powerful moral obligation. If I feel indebted to someone, I don't say "I'm obliged to you," which says little more than "Thank you," but rather "I'm obligated to you"—though I'd more likely say "I owe you one."

We find a similar difference in "I'm obliged/obligated to" do something. "Obliged" means merely that you have to do it for one reason or another; "obligated," that you're under an obligation to someone else—that is, you've promised or contracted to do it.

OBLIVIOUS/UNAWARE. Originally, if you were oblivious of something you had forgotten it, whereas if you were unaware of it you had never noticed it in the first place. Nowadays, they mean the same thing—that is, most people are oblivious (in either sense) of the original distinction. Thus if you use "oblivious" in the sense of "forgetful," few will know what you mean; say "forgetful" or "unmindful" instead.

OCULIST/OPHTHALMOLOGIST/OPTICIAN/OPTOMET-RIST. When I was a kid, an oculist (a doctor specializing in diseases of the eye) diagnosed me as being severely near-sighted. I'm still nearsighted, but have not been to an oculist for forty-odd years—though I occasionally consult an oph-thalmologist, which means the same thing. More often, I go to my optometrist, who checks my eyes to make sure my eyeglass prescription is still right. If I need a new pair, he puts on his optician's hat, and makes them.

Oculists became ophthalmologists, I suspect, because "-ologist" is used in other medical specialties ("cardiologist," "radiologist")—and sounds more impressive.

OF, with COULD, SHOULD or WOULD. A "bad usage" much commoner in writing than in speech—and even commoner, I suspect, in usage manuals. Many people, educated and other-wise, say "could've," "should've" and "would've," with the " 've" sounding very like "of"; in few if any cases can the ear distinguish reliably between "could've" and "could of." Mike Jacobs, the fight promoter, was once quoted as saying "I should of stood [stayed] in bed"; I bet what he really said was "I shoulda stood. . . ."

Some uneducated people *spell* the expressions "phoneti-cally," as "should of," for example. And so do some educated people, if they're trying to render the speech of the unedu-cated. This gimmick is sometimes called "eye dialect."

Writing authentic regional dialect is beyond the talents of some authors, since it requires a sharp ear for phonetic nu-ances and for regional variations in syntax and vocab-ulary. The untalented or lazy writer simply spells certain expressions as uneducated people would, or might, spell them ("could of," "wimmen," "likker"). The actual sound of the words is unchanged from their "educated" pronunciation, but the spelling is supposed to suggest that the people in question talk funny as well as spell funny.

Whenever I run into eye dialect, I mark its author down as inept.

OFF OF. The "of" is unnecessary; KEEP *OFF* THE GRASS!

OLDER/ELDER. The distinctions between the two are trivial; if you stick with "older" you'll always be right. If you insist on being pernickity and using "elder," remember it applies to people, not things, and usually to people in the same family ("My elder brother's car is older").

ON ACCOUNT OF. Standard if it's followed by a noun or noun clause ("on account of his poverty"), regional if it isn't ("on account of he was poor"). But why bother splitting these hairs? "Because" says the same thing in one word, and is right either way ("because of his poverty," "because he was poor").

ON TO/ONTO. Both words are prepositions, but "on" is also an adverb. And if the adverb is followed by "to," they should be separated ("From Chicago, I'll go on to Milwaukee"). "Onto" is always a preposition ("walk onto the stage"). I'm not sure that it was worthwhile getting onto this subject, but in any case let's move on to more important matters.

ONE (impersonal). When one begins a sentence with "one," one must continue as one began—but if one does so, one sounds prissy and pedantic. One should therefore avoid the impersonal "one" unless one is absolutely compelled to use it. Usually "we" says the same thing better.

ONE OF THOSE THINGS. The debate over "one of those things that happen" vs. "one of those things that happens," as in *HDCU,* is a real teapot tempest. Technically, "things that happen" is correct—but nine times out of ten you can say, with Cole Porter, "just one of those things."

ONLY. A "problem" word, in part because it's both an adjective ("only a bird in a gilded cage") and an adverb ("I only work here"). The other reason is that even educated people frequently put it in the "wrong" place in the sentence—and in language, if enough people are wrong, they're right.

Consider the very common phrase "I only said that. . . ." Almost invariably the "only" refers not to the saying but to what was said—that is, it has been misplaced (see **MISPLACED MODIFIERS**). Technically, the phrase should run "I said only that . . ."—but you'll seldom find anyone actually using the construction today. Indeed, more than a century ago, Lewis Carroll wrote "He only does it to annoy," which technicaly should have been "He does it only to annoy"—that is, only for the purpose of annoying.

In most cases, it makes no difference where you put "only" —but sometimes it does: there's obviously a difference between "I only work here" (= All I do here is work) and "I work only here" (= Here is the only place I work).

ORAL/VERBAL. Another technicality that has been obliterated by idiomatic usage. In its original sense, "verbal" referred to words of any kind, "oral," to (among other things) *spoken* words, especially when contrasted with written ones. Thus an "oral examination" meant what it still means: examinees are questioned face-to-face and reply the same way, instead of writing down the answers as in most exams.

Since the sixteenth century, however, "verbal" has also been used to mean something conveyed by speech rather than writing. Thus a passage dated 1591 refers to "His Majestys verball answer to . . . Her Majestys letters." Today, if you refer to a "verbal agreement" nobody will suppose you mean an agreement put into words (what agreement isn't?), but rather, an unwritten one—the kind that, according to the legendary Sam Goldwyn, "isn't worth the paper it's written on."

ORATE, verb. A **BACK FORMATION** disliked by some people, but which, like **EMOTE,** can serve a useful purpose. If I read that Senator Bullheaver "orated," rather than "spoke," I assume that his oration was pretentious hokum.

ORCHESTRATE. Literally, of course, it means to arrange a musical composition for orchestra, but it has taken on the figurative sense of "carefully and elaborately arranged"— usually with overtones of phoniness ("Nixon's carefully orchestrated renomination"). On the other hand, when (then) Senator Tower of Texas wrote that President Kennedy "orchestrated the force that brought down" a South Vietnamese politician, he was using it as an elaborate hedge. That is, he was carefully not saying that Kennedy actually gave the orders, while implying that the President was still in some way responsible.

Tower was also using the word ineptly; you can, conceivably, orchestrate forces, but not a force. Since the word tends to be overused, avoid it unless the arrangements you're talking about were indeed elaborate and somewhat phonied up.

OUTSIDE (OF). "Outside" is a notable **INTERCHANGEABLE PART.** When it's a noun ("on the outside of the box"), the "of" is required; used as an adjective ("an outside chance") or an adverb ("Let's go outside"), the "of" is unnecessary, and indeed few if any people use it. The problem comes when "outside" is used as a preposition ("outside the house") Here "of" is unnecessary—but a lot of people still say "outside of the house." When "outside of" is used to mean "except for," it bothers some people, but not many outside of the purists, or outside the academic world.

OVER (= more than). Some pedants, and authors of stylebooks, still insist that "over" must be used only in its literal sense— physically above ("the horseshoe over the door"). Everyone else routinely uses it to mean "above" in various figurative senses, notably "more than"; over half the *HDCU* panelists "admitted" doing this in speech. I'd guess that well over 90 percent of the rest of us use it this way, in both speech and writing.

P

PALM OFF/PAWN OFF. The second of these phrases is occasionally substituted for the first. Since "palm off" means to pass off by deception ("palming off fake jewelry"), it obviously has nothing to do with "pawn" (as in "hock your watch"); that is, "pawn off" should be avoided.

PANT(S). One of those singular but apparently plural nouns that have been "singularized"; other examples include "pea" (originally "pease") and "sherry" (originally "sherris"). "Pant" originated not (as I'd thought) with the L. L. Bean catalogue during the 1960s but with people in a similar line of business—men's clothing—during the 1890s. Their logic was presumably that if a pile of trousers is a pile of pants, one such garment must be a pant. The word is clear enough, but sounds a bit eccentric.

PARTIALLY/PARTLY. Though some dictionaries distinguish between these two, the distinctions are too fine-drawn to be very useful. I'd say save a syllable and use "partly." The author Walter Lord claims, indeed, that "the [football] kick was partly blocked" is wrong; it should be "partially." Maybe I don't watch enough football, but I'm damned if I can see any difference. If (as I suspect), the idea was that the kick was *deflected,* rather than simply blocked, then that—not "partly" *or* "partially"—would have been the right word.

PARTICIPLES, a.k.a. GERUNDS. An outstanding example of **INTERCHANGEABLE PARTS.** Present participles (all of them end in "-ing") and past participles (most of them end in "-d" or "-ed") are verbs, in the sense that they're used to make "compound" verb forms with the auxiliary verbs "have" and "be" ("As I was *saying* . . ." and "You have *said* enough").

But both participles can also be used to modify nouns and pronouns—that is, as adjectives (" 'Curses!' the *baffled* villain snarled"; "*Smiling,* the boy fell dead"). Yet the present (though not the past) participle, even when used as an adjective, remains enough of a verb to take an object, as of course no true adjective does ("*Slamming* another clip into his machine gun, Rambo blasted . . .").

Finally, the present participle can also do duty as a noun ("*Wishing* will make it so"), in which case it changes its name and becomes a gerund. Like other nouns, gerunds can serve both as objects and as subjects of verbs ("I like *skiing*"), but they can also take objects of their own ("Stealing *a thousand bucks* will put you in jail; stealing *a million* won't").

Participles used in compound verb forms aren't likely to give anyone trouble. But if you use them as adjectives or nouns, make sure their placement clearly shows which they are. A participial adjective (plus its object, if it has one) usually goes where ordinary adjectives go: immediately before the noun or pronoun it modifies ("The smiling boy fell dead"). Alternatively, it can go after the verb ("The boy fell dead, smiling"). If, however, the verb has an object—watch out! "The boy shot his mother smiling" fails to make clear who was smiling, while "The boy shot his smiling mother" indicates that she, not he, was smiling—which I doubt was the case. Participial nouns (gerunds) go where any other noun goes, depending on their function within the sentence.

PASSIVE VOICE. A way of, as it were, backing into a statement, sometimes for good reason, often not. Scientists are particularly addicted to this construction: "It was found that . . . ," "It has previously been shown that . . ." and so drearily on. I suppose there are reasons for this (see next paragraph)—but the endless string of passive-voice constructions found in the typical scientific paper can become tedious, to say the least. Surely they could say, once in a while, "*I* found that" or "*We* concluded that."

As Bryant points out, there *are* good reasons for using the passive voice—broadly speaking, when who done it is less important than who or what got done: thus "The child was hit by the car" reflects the obvious fact that the hit was far more important to the child than to the car. Sometimes who done it is too obvious to mention ("Reagan was elected President" —by the voters, who else?), or unknown ("My house was robbed last week"), or unimportant ("My car's being repaired").

Which is to say that the passive voice can be considered a form of **INVERSION:** using it allows you to put the object of the action up front, while the actor comes later, if at all. As with other kinds of inversion, the purpose is emphasis—or deemphasis.

Sometimes the deemphasis is a deliberate ploy, to *conceal* the author of the action, whom the writer for some reason prefers not to identify; elsewhere, I've called this device "the plausible passive." A writer who tells you simply that "wilderness areas are being destroyed" neatly ducks the question of who—developers, mining interests, lumber companies or whoever—is or are destroying them.

In general, the passive voice should be avoided *except* for purposes of emphasis—or, of course, if you'd rather not say who's doing what to whom.

PATRIOTISM. When Samuel Johnson defined patriotism in his dictionary as "the last refuge of a scoundrel," he may have been putting it a bit strongly. But there's no doubt whatever that it's the first refuge of the political hustler, and often of the undercover manipulator as well; the novelist Stan Lee has called it "the ultimate cover story." Waving the flag and making the eagle scream have been standard political gimmicks since our Republic was founded, and their patriotic equivalents were used by politicians in ancient Greece (for all I know, in Egypt and Babylon too).

Like so many overused terms, "patriotism" eludes precise definition. To most people it means "love of country"—but does this mean love of the land, love of its people (all 230 million of them?), love of its government, love of all three, or none of the above? And—if it means love of the government, does that mean *any* government, or merely governments of which the speaker approves?

Mark Twain's Connecticut Yankee, from whom as a boy I learned a great deal about patriotism, defined it as "loyalty to one's country, not to its institutions or its officeholders. The country is the real thing, the substantial thing, the eternal thing; it is the thing to watch over, and care for, and be loyal to; institutions are . . . its mere clothing, and clothing can become ragged. . . . The citizen who thinks he sees that the commonwealth's political clothes are worn out, and yet holds his peace and does not agitate for a new suit, is disloyal; he is a traitor."

Whether or not you agree with this definition, it's worth thinking about. And whatever definition you choose for "patriotism," make sure the context makes it clear—and that it's *your* definition, not that of some political hack whose chief loyalty is to his paycheck.

PEACEFUL/PEACEABLE. Almost but not quite interchangeable. The primary meaning of "peaceful" is "full of peace"— that is, undisturbed by violence, natural or man-made ("a peaceful landscape"). It is seldom if ever used to characterize people; they may lead peaceful lives—but (illogically) that doesn't make them peaceful people.

If we want to describe someone or something as inclined toward or promoting peace, the usual term is "peaceable"— generally. However, *HDCU*'s example (". . . peaceable means of settling the dispute") is a poor one: for more than a century, "peaceful" has been the normal word in this particular context—that is, to describe methods or actions that are not violent or warlike. Probably the best solution, though not a perfect one, is to describe people as peaceable (if they are), but their actions as peaceful (if *they* are).

PEOPLE/PERSONS. Another gray area. "People" is best if you're talking about an unspecified number of individuals ("several people," "millions of people" and so on)—that is, "persons" applies only to an exact number. But in most such cases, "people" will do just as well, and sometimes better; would you really want to say "Six persons were seated around the table"?

PERFECT. Purists list this among the uncomparable adjectives (see **ADJECTIVES, UNCOMPARABLE;** most people compare it—including the authors of the U.S. Constitution ("in order to form a more perfect union"). Follett shrewdly notes that since "nothing on earth achieves perfection . . . the degrees of approximation to it deserve to be named."

The purists' wording is illustrated by "The day . . . was the most nearly perfect in the history of the New York Weather

Bureau . . ." (*New Yorker,* 1958, quoted in Bryant). Assuming the sentence was supposed to be read seriously, the wording is false refinement—quite possibly the work of some officious copy editor. It's also nonsense: Weather Bureau records deal with degrees of temperature, not degrees of perfection.

PERMISSIVE(NESS). Yet another all-purpose political word; it implies, or is supposed to imply, that there are some people for whom anything goes—though the only such people I've ever heard of are sociopaths. The vast majority of us are willing to permit some things but not others; the arguments come over what. Usually when A charges B with permissiveness, (s)he's saying that B "permits" things that A doesn't think should be permitted.

For instance, some people would doubtless consider me "permissive" in English usage, where *HDCU* (for example) is not. Yet this book should certainly make clear that there are many usages that I won't permit myself to use, and advise others not to use—just like *HDCU.* Some of the things they'd permit I wouldn't, and vice versa, but that doesn't make either of us "permissive."

Like **LIBERAL,** to which it is close kin, "permissive" frequently muddles several different ideas: (1) what things are undesirable, morally or otherwise; (2) whether, assuming they're undesirable, the government should do anything about them; (3) what (if anything) it should do. If, like me, you believe that government should interfere with individuals as little as possible (meaning, only when needed to protect them against other individuals, or groups) you're probably "permissive" in some people's eyes.

If you think someone is "permissive," you'll be more convincing if you specify what it is they permit—or you think they do. If you don't, many people will feel that you don't really know what you're objecting to, or don't care to say (see also **PERVERSION**).

PERSONALITY (= celebrity). Though certain people dislike the word, their reasons don't make much sense. Some claim that "show business personality" has overtones of press-agentry—but that applies to many things written about showbiz people. The best solution, I'd say, is simply to ignore the personalities—and their press agents.

PERVERSION. Originally, a "turning away" (from morality, righteousness, etc.); later, a debased or corrupted belief or act. When used in nonsexual contexts nowadays, it implies *deliberate* corruption. Thus a miscarriage of justice means merely that an innocent person was convicted or a guilty one got off; a perversion of justice, that the accused was framed, or somebody put in the fix.

About a century ago, "perversion" acquired a sexual sense: according to the *OED Supp.*, sexual satisfaction "through channels [no pun intended] other than those of normal heterosexual intercourse." Which is, of course, something less than precise: what's "normal"—and who says so? Some people consider anything but straight "missionary position" sex a perversion—which, I suspect, would make most Americans at least part-time perverts.

AHD is no more helpful: "A sexual practice or act considered deviant." Considered by whom, and deviant from what? As most people use it, it means either "a sexual practice I don't like" or (occasionally) "a sexual practice I do like, but don't think I ought to." For this reason I don't use the word; my perversion could well be your diversion.

If what you're talking about is a kind of sex you consider immoral or sinful or psychologically destructive, then say that. Calling it a "perversion" says merely that you don't approve of it, and neither should anybody else—if they know what's good for them.

Note, by the way, that perversion is *not* the same thing as perversity. David Mamet made this point rather neatly when he titled one of his plays "Sexual Perversity in Chicago"; it had nothing to do with perversion, in any sense, but a great deal to do with obstinate persistence in error—one meaning of perversity.

PIGGYBACK MODIFIERS. At almost the beginning of this guide (see **AGGRAVATE**), I drew attention to the sentence "Aggravate originally simply meant to make worse." Two piggyback modifiers, both ending in "-ly," sound peculiar. But note, too, that "simply" is also a **MISPLACED MODIFIER**: it doesn't modify "meant" (as its position implies) but "to make worse," and should have been placed before "to."

A more common form of piggybacking jams together three or more modifiers (adjectives, adverbs or attributive nouns) with no "air" between them: "The quick, clever, brown fox jumped. . . ." Here one of the three should have been either omitted or moved: "The quick, brown fox jumped . . ." or "The clever, brown fox quickly jumped . . . ," or "The brown fox, quick and clever, jumped . . . ." Limiting or separating your modifiers in this way makes it easier for the reader to get the full impact of all of them. A good rule of thumb is no more than two piggybacked modifiers to a customer; no more than one, if both end in "-ly."

Once in a long while, piggybacking three modifiers together can make a point. In the Introduction, for example, I said that many nineteenth-century Britishers viewed the young United States as some Americans today view Cuba, as a "small, uppity, subversive country." By piling on the adjectives, I was trying to suggest that the people in question were somewhat overwrought.

PITEOUS/PITIABLE/PITIFUL. Despite what *HDCU* says, all three often mean the same thing—"exciting pity" (their original sense, "full of pity," is obsolete). The last two *may* also mean "contemptible," as in "The candidate made a pitiful showing," but this usually refers to things, not people. Watch your context.

PLAN (AHEAD). Both "plan ahead" and "advance planning" are often described as redundancies, on the ground that *all* planning, by definition, is done ahead of time. I think the premise is faulty: in my experience, a fair number of plans are improvised on the spur of the moment, and some of them even work.

In some situations, however, it's clearly necessary to plan ahead—or engage in advance planning—and I see nothing wrong with saying so. Obviously "ahead" and "advance" should be omitted unless they're needed to distinguish between improvisation and careful preparation. But if they *are* needed—use them in good health!

PLAN TO/PLAN ON/TRY TO/TRY AND. According to both *AHD* and *HDCU,* "plan to" and "try to" are preferable to "plan on" and "try and," except in informal contexts. Both distinctions strike me as not worth worrying about: I plan on using the allegedly informal versions any time I feel like it; just try and stop me! ("Try and," incidentally, was good enough for both Coleridge and Matthew Arnold.) Note, by the way, that "plan to" and "plan on" are not interchangeable in their syntactic context: you plan *to do* something, but plan *on doing* it.

PLUMBER (political). Another example of **WATERGATE EN-GLISH,** and as such deplored by *HDCU.* To me, a useful word, because it concisely describes a person assigned to stop up political "leaks"—that is, the spread of information embarrassing to people in power. (Some "leaks," of course, are deliberately contrived to *benefit* people in power—but then nobody worries about stopping them.) Political plumbers are often pretty unsavory types, but what else would you call them

—"people assigned to stop the spread of confidential information"?

PRACTICABLE/PRACTICAL. The distinction here parallels that in **IMPRACTICABLE/IMPRACTICAL.** If something can be done at all, it's practicable; if it can be done but shouldn't be (it's not needed, too costly, etc.), it's practicable but not practical. And of course *people* can be practical, but not practicable.

PRACTICALLY/VIRTUALLY. Used to mean "almost," they're interchangeable; used to mean "for all practical purposes," only the first will do. In the latter case, however, it's well to emphasize the nuance in meaning by putting "practically" at the beginning of the sentence or clause. "Practically, the new arms-control agreement is in effect" means that it's operational even though a few formalities remain to be completed. "The new agreement is practically (or virtually) completed" implies that the parties are still arguing about some minor points. But you can save yourself trouble, and syllables, by using "almost" or "nearly" if that's what you mean.

PRECIPITATE/PRECIPITOUS. At one time, both these words meant the same thing; people still confuse them. Both derive ultimately from the Latin *caput,* head; a "precipitate" action is one you rush into *head*long, while a "precipitous" slope resembles a *preci*pice—you can fall down it *head* first. The common phrase "a precipitous retreat" offends purists, on the ground that such retreats are properly precipitate, not precipitous. It offends me because it's a cliché; say "hasty" or "disorderly" or "headlong" or "panicky" retreat.

PREMODIFICATION. When publishing tycoon Henry Luce and his associates invented "Timestyle" (see **INVERSION**), one of their gimmicks was to clip the "the" from descriptive nouns and phrases preceding proper names: "gangster Al Capone" rather than "the gangster Al Capone" or "Al Capone, the gangster." Unlike most Timestyle devices, this one has survived and is used fairly often by journalists, though editor Ted Bernstein didn't care for it and critic John Simon detests it.

The British author Kenneth Hudson has gone further, blaming the construction on non-English-speaking American immigrants, whose "literal, but illiterate translation from [their] own language . . . strikes roots in the country of [their] adoption." British critics not infrequently blame un-"English" features of American syntax on immigrants—sometimes, specifically on Jewish immigrants, for reasons that hardly need spelling out—see **SLOW(LY)**.

For the record, immigrant contributions even to the American vocabulary are minor (most of our borrowed words came not from immigrants but from "foreigners" already in residence: Native Americans, Mexicans, French and New York Dutch). Their contributions to American syntax are virtually nil (see *OMNT* and **YIDDISHISMS**). And there were, believe me, no immigrants, and few if any sons of immigrants (or daughters of anybody), among the WASPy editors who invented Timestyle some sixty years ago.

Premodification is normal with titles ("Supreme Court Justice Brennan"), and seems to me unobjectionable with single descriptive words ("columnist William Safire," though you can disarm critics by saying "the columnist"). But jamming two titles (or other modifying expressions) into one premodifying phrase is at least questionable, while three can easily become grotesque ("columnist, word maven and former Nixon speech writer William Safire")—see **PIGGYBACK MODIFIERS**.

PREPOSITIONS (ending sentences with). Late in the seventeenth century, some critics invented the "rule" that prepositions are bad things to end sentences with. (I suspect this was part of the drive to jam English usage into the procrustean bed of Latin grammar—see **INFINITIVES, SPLIT**.) Happily, almost everyone now realizes that the rule was ridiculous. The coup-de-grace was probably delivered by Winston Churchill; when a sentence in one of his memos, ending with a preposition, was "corrected" by a zealous secretary, he scribbled on it the acid comment "This is the sort of nonsense up with which I will not put!"

PRESENTLY. Originally, this meant "immediately" or "at present", subsequently, its predominant sense became "in the immediate future." For nearly fifty years, however, the original sense has been moving back into use; I suspect that it's presently the commoner of the two. The context will make clear which you mean: with a present verb, as in the preceding sentence, it means "now" or "currently"; with a future verb, "soon." In either case, however, the shorter synonyms are preferable; to describe someone as "presently unemployed" is **BUREAUCRATESE**.

PRIORITY. *HDCU* describes this as a *"vogue* word of *yesteryear"* (my emphasis); they're wrong on both counts. The word itself goes back to the fourteenth century, and its commonest current sense, "what has a right to be considered before something else," has been current from World War I to the present —surely one of the longest "vogues" in history. Worrying about this word is not on *my* list of priorities.

PRONOUNS AND THEIR ANTECEDENTS. A pronoun must always refer to a specific noun—and one located not far away. There are several ways of making sure that the pronoun hooks up with the right noun. If they are in different sentences, put them in the same place in both: "The President again denounced the Soviets' 'evil empire.' He also. . . ." If in the same sentence, bear in mind that a pronoun has an "affinity" for the *nearest* noun; thus "The building was sold by the corporation when it was five years old" leaves the reader in doubt about whether "it" means the building or the corporation. Turning the sentence around ("The corporation sold the building when it . . .") cures the problem.

The writer in a hurry will sometimes forget to put in the noun at all, as in "They expressed their views to business executives. It was one of several meetings. . . ." You have to stop and think before you realize that the views were expressed, not to the executives individually, but to a *meeting* of executives, which is what "it" referred to; not saying so left the "it" twisting slowly in the wind.

PROPAGANDA. Originally a neutral term, having to do with propagating ideas or doctrines; specifically, it derives from the Vatican's Congregation for Propagating (in Latin, *propaganda*) the Faith. Nowadays, of course, it means material that propagates ideas tendentiously or dishonestly. *We* release information; *they* engage in propaganda—or disinformation. See also **CLAIM.**

PROPOSITION (noun and verb). In its narrowest sense, the noun means a well-defined proposal; less specific proposals are best referred to as such, especially since the word is shorter. As a verb, "proposition" started off neutral, but soon acquired a distinctly fishy odor: to proposition someone suggests that you're proposing something illegal, or at least immoral. And if you talk of propositioning a member of the opposite sex, you're obviously proposing you-know-what.

PURIST. According to *HDCU,* someone who is "fastidious," even "excessively precise" in the use of words (either expression would apply to many *HDCU* panelists). As *HDCU* doesn't say, the word also reflects the belief of some literati that the language is degenerating and/or being polluted, and requires energetic action if it is to be kept in its pristine state of purity.

Since I've already discussed this theory at some length in the Introduction, I'll say only that its basic premise is silly: English has never been, isn't now, and never will be "pure." There are plenty of valid grounds for criticizing particular words or usages—unclarity above all—but "impurity" isn't one of them.

R

RACE. When used to refer to some group of people distinguished by their physical characteristics, the word is almost invariably inaccurate or confusing—usually, both. That different groups of people differ physically is obvious, but even the professional anthropologists have never agreed on how many such "races" there are, or how they should be distinguished.

The oldest racial classification is based on the most obvious human characteristic, skin color, giving us the black race, white (or Caucasian) race, yellow race and red or brown race —that is, most Native Americans. Under this scheme, the natives of India, with skins ranging from "white" to near-black, were still classified as Caucasians, since they showed no other physical resemblance to American or African members of the black race.

The black race included not only Africans and Afro-Americans, but also the natives of New Guinea and Melanesia (no relation to the Africans), and, sometimes, those of Australia. Natives of Southeast Asia, on the other hand, were members of the yellow race, though their skins were brown, while the Polynesians were often left in a racial limbo, since their skins ranged from brown to white.

Subsequent schemes of classification have taken into account hair form (straight, wavy, kinky), physical build, facial features, blood groups and almost any other physical characteristic that differs from one geographical area to another. And not one of these schemes, so far as I've been able to discover, tells you anything useful about the peoples concerned, except that they resemble one another in some ways (they also invariably differ from one another in other ways).

In the United States, especially, "race" often has little to do with physical characteristics; rather, it is a social and legal term. The majority of American blacks are actually of mixed "race"—part black, part white and, sometimes, part Native American—yet even those with predominantly white ancestry are still considered "black." (I've known "blacks" with blue eyes and blond hair.)

The ultimate in "racial" nonsense was propagated by (who else?) the Nazis, who classified Slavs, Jews and Gypsies as inferior races and "Aryans" as superior. Not one of these groups is a "race" in any physical sense: "Slav" is a linguistic term (one who speaks a slavonic tongue), Jews and Gypsies are cultural descriptions, while the Aryan race was purely imaginary. "Race" is at best a useless term; at worst, it serves as a rationalization for discrimination, brutality and murder. On either count, avoid it.

RADICAL (noun and adjective). Both words derive from the Latin *radix,* root. The adjective, applied to changes in something (usually a political or social system), means "deep-rooted" or "fundamental"; a "radical" (person) is one who allegedly wants to make such changes.

So long as societies were controlled by rich people (as they were for centuries), radical changes naturally involved curtailing such people's power; that is, "radicals" were what we'd now call leftists. Nowadays, the U.S. and Western European societies are still dominated by the rich, but not controlled by them—meaning that all sorts of **SPECIAL INTEREST**

GROUPS are demanding, or trying to hold on to, a share of power. As a result, we now have radical *conservatives,* who want to put (or keep) these groups in their place, as well as radical *radicals,* who want to further curb the power of the rich or even abolish them—financially, that is, not physically.

As these examples suggest, "radical" has become a Humpty-Dumpty word, usually meaning "somebody (or something) I don't like." Unfortunately there is no neutral word describing someone who wants fundamental changes; "extremist" (for example) has the same bad vibrations as "radical." The best solution, I think, is to say "radical [or extreme] conservative" or "radical leftist"—which at least makes clear that not all conservatives, or leftists, are radicals. And, of course, make sure that the changes such people are committed to really are "radical" (fundamental), not just unpalatable.

RANG/RUNG. Most of us say "I rang the bell"; others say "I rung it"—and the experts can't agree on whether the latter is **SUBSTANDARD.** Frankly, I don't give a damn. If it matters to you, stick with I ring/I rang/I have rung, which follows the pattern of sing/sang/sung and spring/sprang/sprung.

RAVAGE/RAVISH. An army can ravage a town, and/or ravish the women in it—and a great musician can ravish an audience. For maximum clarity, however, the town is *ravaged,* the audience is *enravished*—and the women are *raped.* Perhaps the neatest comment on the misuse of "ravish" was made by a lady who, commenting on the headline ELM BARK BEETLE INFESTATION RAVISHING THOUSANDS OF TREES IN GREENWICH, observed that only God can make a tree (Bernstein).

REALISTIC. *HDCU* objects to both "not realistic" and "unrealistic" when used to mean "impractical" ("The plan isn't realistic"). Since the usage has been common for over a century, I'd say their attempt to turn back the clock just isn't realistic.

REALTOR. Arguably pretentious, though unquestionably shorter than "real estate agent." I'd say take your choice—and remember to read the fine print in the contract.

REASON WHY. As Simon notes, the "why" is unneeded. But as *HDCU* notes, the phrase has become a standard, if technically redundant, idiom. (The ultimate source is probably Tennyson's "Theirs not to reason why" and, much later, Cecil Woodham-Smith's book on the Crimean War, *The Reason Why.*) Standard or not, however, I still prefer to say either "I don't know the reason he did it" or "I don't know why he did it," rather than "I don't know the reason why . . . ." And to say "The reason why is that . . ." sounds weird.

REBELLION/REVOLT/REVOLUTION. A TV announcer once described the Hungarian revolt of 1956 as "the revolution that failed." *HDCU* claims that a rebellion always fails, a revolt sometimes fails and a revolution never fails—that is, if it failed it shouldn't be called a revolution. I rebel against this distinction, and don't think it's grounded in fact. If a revolution is, as *AHD* says, "A sudden political overthrow . . . ," then it's obviously possible to have an attempted but unsuccessful revolution.

Don't, however, confuse a revolution with what used to be called a palace revolution but is now more often called a coup: the overthrow of one small ruling group by another—generally with little or no effect, good or bad, on how the majority of people live. A revolution is a revolt supported, at least passively, by a large part of the population, as were the American, French and Russian revolutions. A revolt or rebellion against a left-of-center government is often called a counter-revolution; I never heard of a "counterrevolt" or "counterrebellion."

REBUT/REFUTE. The first is weaker than the second: a rebuttal merely sets forth counterarguments; whether they actually refute the original argument is a matter of opinion. *I* think that when I rebut other usage experts I also refute them—but I doubt they would agree.

REGIME. Literally, a system of government or a particular government, but often used by politicians or political writers to mean a government they don't like and hope won't last. Thus Washington speaks of the Castro regime and the Sandinista regime; Moscow denounced the Diem regime in Vietnam and deplores the American-dominated regime in El Salvador. The implication, of course, is that a "regime" isn't really a government, and therefore should be done away with. As usual, my regime may be your government, and vice versa.

RELATE. If you talk about things relating to one another, your meaning will generally be clear—though the relationship may not be. But when it comes to people, "relate" has become an all-purpose word: it can mean "like," "love," "become involved with," "understand" or "accept" ("I can't relate to that"). As such, avoid it.

A good example of the misuse of "relate" comes from the *OED Supp.*: "If we only relate to on-campus issues, we run the risk of laying the counterrevolutionary groundwork." Here the writer meant "raise" or "deal with" those issues, and would have done better to have said so. For that matter, I'm not crazy about "counterrevolutionary groundwork," since I doubt that groundwork—a foundation—can be either counterrevolutionary or revolutionary. What the writer meant, and should have said, was "groundwork for counterrevolution."

RELEVANT. A statement can be relevant or irrelevant to the point under discussion; in other senses ("He just isn't relevant") it's a cliché and a blurred one. When college students in the 1960s demanded that their courses be "relevant," it was seldom clear whether they meant relevant to their needs, to their interests, to the current scene or to a particular political philosophy. Also worth noting is that things which seem irrelevant when you're twenty may turn out to be very relevant indeed by the time you're forty.

REPAIRABLE/REPARABLE. They ought to mean the same thing, and they do—sort of. But "repairable" is normally used literally, as of a damaged car, while "reparable" is used figuratively, as of a deteriorating situation. Moreover, "irreparable" is common—probably commoner than "reparable," while "irrepairable" is obsolete. Instead we say "unrepairable" or "not repairable" or—if it's a car—"totaled."

RESIDE. A fancy-schmancy way of saying "live" (in); it's barely tolerable if you're talking about someone's legal residence or domicile ("He lives in Oak Park but resides in Chicago"), but "is domiciled in Chicago" would be clearer—if you *must* talk legalese.

RHETORIC. Originally, the art of speaking or writing eloquently; later, also florid, overblown language. Edwin R. Newman, a prolific writer on words, claims that the second usage is incorrect. In fact, English writers—among them the poets Milton, Cowper and Swinburne—have been using it in the second sense for more than three centuries; Newman didn't do his homework.

RUBBLE/RUINS. Whether rubble is also ruins depends on its source: rough fragments of rock are rubble, but are ruins only if they were were once part of a building. Whether ruins are rubble depends on how ruined they are, and—if you want to be technical—whether they are composed of stone or brick, or of wood. The Acropolis is a ruin but isn't rubble; neither, strictly speaking, is a demolished frame house.

But—*HDCU* to the contrary—I'd be inclined to pass "smouldering rubble" (left by an earthquake, for instance), even though brick and stone can't smoulder. The alternative would be "the smouldering mixture of splintered wood and rubble," which is cumbersome.

RUSSIA(N)/SOVIET/U.S.S.R. Before 1917, it was Russia, or the Russian Empire; since then, it's been the Union of Soviet Socialist Republics (U.S.S.R.) or, more concisely, the Soviet Union or, informally, "the Soviets." "Soviet" is also used as an adjective, of course: it is to U.S.S.R. as "American" is to U.S.A.

However, though an American citizen is an **AMERICAN**, you can't, or anyway shouldn't, call a Soviet citizen a Soviet (I recently saw this term applied to Chairman Gorbachev). Since the original meaning of "soviet" was "council," stretching it to cover individuals seems a bit much. Technically, a citizen of the Soviet Union is a Russian, Ukrainian, Uzbek or any one of the other hundred-odd Soviet nationalities—but is likely to end up as a "Russian" anyway. If you find this a little confusing, you've got company—but I know of no remedy.

I must confess that I'm sometimes tempted to refer to the Soviet government as the Russian government, since it is unquestionably dominated by Russians, and much of the time "tilts" in the direction of that nationality. On the whole, however, it's probably best to stick to "Soviet."

S

SAHARA (DESERT). As *HDCU* indicates, "Sahara desert" is a
redundancy—but not, I think, for the reason given: that *sahara*
is Arabic for "desert." (How many Americans know Arabic?)
Rather more to the point is that "Sahara" means "desert" to
just about everybody—in fact, I'd bet that most of us, asked
to name a desert, would say "Sahara" rather than "Sonora"
or "Atacama" or "Gobi."

Southern Californians or Arizonans often refer to "the
Mojave" since they know it's a desert; the rest of us say
"Mojave desert" because for us its "desertness" doesn't go
without saying. I'm sure we'd do so even if "Mojave" meant
"desert" in some Native American tongue—which for all I
know it does.

For similar reasons, many Americans, not knowing that
yama means "mountain" in Japanese, say "Mount Fujiyama"
—though "Mount Fuji" or (if your audience is fairly sophisticated) plain "Fujiyama" is preferable.

SAME DIFFERENCE. A thoroughly illogical but wholly acceptable idiom. It was originally formed by a fusion of "same
thing" and "no difference"; either way, it's the same difference.

SCENARIO. Hollywood scenarios are an old story, of course.
Much more recent are the "scenarios" contrived by political

and military planners. One of these planners, Herman Kahn (who may have originated the usage), described such scenarios as attempts "to describe [in detail] some hypothetical series of events," such as the probable course of a nuclear war.

Like many new expressions, it began as a **FAD WORD**, and is still so considered by some, but is nonetheless useful. However, using it loosely to mean simply a situation or series of events is both trendy and confusing, and has, as the *OED Supp.* notes, "attracted frequent hostile comment."

Also worth remembering is that in the kind of scenarios Kahn was talking about, "hypothetical" is the operative word; indeed, many of them have as much to do with the real world as your average Hollywood script. A scenario used in Pentagon war games some years ago *started* by assuming that the United States had set up a "pro-American government" in Peking—just like that. The only possible comment on such scenarios is the computernik's **ACRONYM**, GIGO—Garbage In, Garbage Out; in this case, garbage assumptions, garbage conclusions.

SCULP(T), verb. Disliked by some as a **BACK FORMATION** (from "sculptor," of course)—which it isn't, according to the *OED.* Whatever its source, it was a needed word, to describe what a sculptor does. And if a painter paints and a writer writes . . .

"Sculpt" seems to be becoming the "standard" form, though it's not easy to pronounce and "sculpts" is even harder. For this reason, you may want to substitute "carve," which you often can. But note that some sculptors aren't carvers—they model their works in clay and then, perhaps, cast them in metal—and some carvers aren't sculptors. For example, they may carve ornamental designs on furniture—beautiful designs, perhaps, but not really sculpture.

SECULAR HUMANISM. An expression widely used to describe something widely deplored; indeed Congress, apparently in a fit of absentmindedness, has forbidden American schools to teach it—whatever "it" is. On the face of it, definition should be easy: "secular" means "nonreligious," while "humanism" refers to any of several ethical systems based on human needs rather than on theological principles. "Secular humanism," then, should mean a nonreligious, nontheological ethical system—and would therefore be a redundancy (if it's nonreligious it's got to be nontheological).

As commonly used, however, the phrase appears to mean something quite different, since it is somehow connected with all sorts of dire social phenomena: unwed mothers, crime in the streets and the **INTERNATIONAL COMMUNIST CONSPIRACY**. But just *how* it's connected, and what the phrase actually means, are things you'll have to discover for yourself. If you ever do, let me know.

SEMINAL. Long a **FAD WORD** among literary critics, it means seed-like—that is, figuratively, being a "seed" of later significant developments or literary works. Like **HISTORIC**, it shouldn't be used except well after the fact: we cannot, as Shakespeare put it, "look into the seeds of time/And say which grain will grow and which will not. . . ." And it shouldn't be used at all as a trendy synonym for "important." In fact, now that I think of it, I'd recommend avoiding it entirely, since it's either a cliché or the next thing to one.

SENSUAL/SENSUOUS. The first originally meant no more than "pertaining to or related to the senses," but has long had the predominant meaning of "gratifying to, or being concerned with gratification of, the senses." Call somebody a sensualist and you're saying that (s)he goes in heavily for eating, drinking, etc.—especially etc.

The poet Milton seems to have invented "sensuous" be- cause he needed a respectable substitute for "sensual," and so it remained for generations. Recently, however, it has been widely used as a **EUPHEMISM** for "sexy," as in *The Sensuous Woman* and similar self-improvement books—that is, it has taken on some of the raunchy overtones of "sensual." Unless your context makes clear that it *doesn't* mean "sexy," avoid it.

SET/SIT. A confusing pair. In theory, "set" is transitive and is something people do to things, while "sit" is intransitive and is something people, not things, do. But the inanimate sun *sits* on the horizon at sunset and then *sets* intransitively, while an equally inanimate broadcasting antenna *sits* on top of the Empire State Building. To say "I was setting in the living room" is considered uneducated, but is more likely a regional pronunciation: in parts of the South and Southwest, the na- tives not only set in chairs but fasten things with pens (pins).

SHALL/WILL. When I was in school—which was, as they say, longer ago than I care to think about—the rule was that "I shall" and "we shall" expressed the simple future tense ("I shall go to Chicago" = "I'm going to Chicgo"), while "I will" and "we will" conveyed determination ("We will overcome"). But for the second and third persons (you/he/she/they), the reverse was true: "He will go to Chicago" was simple future, while "He shall go to Chicago" meant that he'd damn well better.

This confusing "rule" was actually a grammarian's or schoolteacher's invention. As Follett (and everyone else who's bothered to study the question) notes, it doesn't, and never did, have much to do with the way most people talk and write. The only exceptions are some (not all) educated Brit- ishers, and a few Americans so thoroughly indoctrinated in high school that they've never managed to kick the habit.

Today, "will" is the standard auxiliary verb for all persons, whether you mean futurity or determination. In the latter case, of course, you stress the "will" ("He *will* go to Chicago, by God!"). Substitute "shall" for "will" in the sentence and you'll see how odd it sounds. "I [or we] shall" (simple future) is O.K., however, though to some ears it sounds a bit formal.

The same "rule" was applied to "should" and "would"— and was equally unrelated to actual usage; few people nowadays say "I should like to . . ." rather than "I would [or I'd] like to . . . ." However, unlike "shall," which is obsolescent, "should" remains alive and well, but with the special sense of obligation or necessity ("I should give them some money" or "I should clean out the garage this weekend").

"Should" is also alive, though not really well, as a substitute for the **SUBJUNCTIVE**—that is, to express uncertainty ("If I should die, think only this of me . . ."; the subjunctive would be "If I were to die . . ."). But, like the subjunctive itself, the construction is obsolescent (the quotation is from a poem written in 1914): nearly everyone nowadays would say "If I die . . . ," since the "if" by itself makes the statement "iffy."

Still, old habits die hard. Follett describes the shall/will question as a "confused jungle" (it isn't, really), and then spends twenty-three pages trying to hack his way through the confusion. If you can read him and not end up more confused than when you started, you're a better person than I am, Gunga Din!

SIBLINGS. Originally, and still predominantly, part of the **JAR-GON** of the social sciences—which I think is a pity, since it says in one word that would otherwise take three or four ("brothers and/or sisters"). But usage won't have it: though concise, it sounds pedantic.

SICK/ILL. Another of the handful of cases where British and American usage can lead to serious confusion. Saying "I'm sick" to a Britisher suggests that you're likely to throw up, while "He was sick" means he actually did it. In short, "sick" has become a **EUPHEMISM** for **NAUSEATED** or, as both we and they say, sick at (or to) one's stomach. If you're simply feeling rotten in Britain, say "I'm ill"—and enjoy their system of free medical care.

SIMPLISTIC. A simplistic explanation is an oversimplified or simpleminded one—the sort we often get during political campaigns, in which simplistic solutions to complicated problems are offered routinely. Don't use the word as a substitute for "simple"; it's both pretentious and inaccurate.

SINGULAR PLURALS AND PLURAL SINGULARS. Because English has borrowed so many words from other tongues, it is better equipped than most languages with singular nouns that look plural, and vice versa. For different reasons, it also has a few nouns that don't make the plural normally with "-s" or "-es," such as ox(-en), child(-ren) and goose/geese, or don't make it at all (sheep, deer), or sometimes make it and sometimes don't (fish, both singular and plural, and fishes, plural only).

I've already cited several nouns whose original singular forms looked plural, so that they've been "singularized," formally or informally (see **PANT(S)**). Another one, "shambles," is occasionally, and mistakenly, singularized. Originally, it meant a slaughterhouse, but nowadays is used figuratively, to describe (say) the mess left by energetic vandals; in either case, it's singular. ("Shamble" is a quite different word, meaning to move with a particular kind of gait, or the gait itself.)

Then we have the plural nouns that look singular, such as "criteria," which means "standards" or "measuring rods" and therefore takes a plural verb. (One such measuring rod is a criterion.) Similarly, "phenomena" is plural, its singular being "phenomenon," and "strata" is plural—but its singular is "stratum."

Yet another of this group is "media," which, since it refers to newspapers and broadcasters, is plural. (Occasionally the singular, "medium," is used, as in the famous "The medium is the message"—though I'm still not sure what Marshall McLuhan meant by that.) People who say "the media *is* . . ." are implying, deliberately or otherwise, that "the media" is some sort of monolithic body (which it isn't) and, usually, one up to no good (which is as may be).

When it comes to "data," however, its plurality is withering away. Its original (Latin) meaning was "given" (things), whence its English sense, "facts," which naturally took the plural ("the data are"). But nowadays it's used increasingly to mean "information," which of course takes the singular ("the data is"). This development bothers many academics, especially if they know Latin—so when in Rome . . . Even better, duck the whole issue by substituting "facts" or "findings"; "these findings are" sounds a lot less stilted than "these data are." The same principle applies to "agenda," originally "things to be done" ("the agenda are") but nowadays a *list* of things to be done—hence "the agenda is." "Insignia," too, was once plural, but its original singular ("insigne") is now obsolete, so that we now speak of "insignias."

All these are Latin words borrowed into English. Another such group of borrowings end in "-us" in the singular, "-i" in the plural (hippopotam-us, -i; cact-us, -i; fung-us, -i). Alumn-us, -i, applies if the ex-collegians in question are male or mixed; alumn-a, -ae, if they're female. Some feminists are said to object to "alumni" as applied to a mixed group, preferring "alumnuses," but I can't see that it makes any difference: the "-us-" in "alumnuses" is still masculine. See **GENDER**. "Octopus" sounds as if its plural should be "octopi," but since it's originally Greek, not Latin (*okto-pous* = eight-foot], the classicists say "octopodes," but everyone else says "octopuses."

Then we have a group of words whose singularity or plural-

ity depends on context. "Acoustics" is singular if you're talking about the study of acoustics ("Acoustics *is* as much an art
as a science"), but plural if you're talking about the acoustical
properties of a hall ("Its acoustics *are* superb"). Likewise,
"Gymnastics *is* a very demanding sport"—but "Her gymnastics *were* brilliantly executed." The same principle applies to
"tactics" and "politics": do you mean the science or study
dealing with them (singular), or a series of tactical steps or
political positions ("His politics were unprincipled and his
tactics were sleazy")? In theory, "a tactic" means a single
maneuver or ploy, but since it sounds a little peculiar, I recommend using one of these synonyms.

With "elite" we are on trickier ground. *HDCU* insists that
it's always plural; I'd say so only if it means "members of a
select group." If you mean the group as a whole, then it's
singular ("The Power Elite"). Thus it's perfectly reasonable
to speak of (say) "the elites of Middle Eastern societies"—
meaning, of course, that each society has its own elite.

Three fairly common nouns unquestionably sound plural,
but may be treated as either plural or singular—or so say the
experts. One is "scissors"—though I must say that "The scissors is on the table" sounds odd to me. Likewise, you can say
that "the suspect's whereabouts is unknown," and "NATO
headquarters is in Brussels." Logically this makes sense, since
clearly neither the suspect nor the headquarters can be in
more than one place. But—logic or not, many people, including me, stick with the plural.

Last of all is "fish," which is almost always *both* singular and
plural. "Fishes of the North Atlantic" is considered preferable
to "fish of the North Atlantic," but the latter certainly won't
confuse anyone.

SLANG. In the poor but educated middle-class environment
where I grew up, "slang" was considered something that nice
people didn't use. Much later, I realized that objections to

slang were mostly plain snobbery, conscious or otherwise. Slang was reprehensible not because of what it is (a subject we'll get to in a moment) but because of the "low" people who use or supposedly use it. These feelings are clearly reflected in *HDCU*, which considers slang "best avoided entirely in nonfiction writing and, except in the most casual contexts, in speech." I think the editors are prissy, if not outright **BARMY**.

Before cluing you in on why, let me try to define what we're talking about—which is no cinch. Everyone agrees that slang is "informal" language—but how informal that is, or should be, depends on where you're sitting. Slang terms are often described as imaginative and colorful, and many are—yet (for example) "hit" and "off" (= kill) surely don't fill that particular bill.

Slang terms are often short-lived (many, perhaps most, **FAD WORDS** are slang), yet some hang on, century after century, never quite respectable yet never dying out (e.g., "clap" = venereal disease). "Bones" (= dice) was slang from Chaucer's day down to the 1930s; it would probably still be hanging around if dice were made of bone rather than plastic.

Slang, finally, enriches language; H. L. Mencken called it "the most powerful of all the stimulants that keep language alive and growing." Such now-standard words as "drawers" (the garment), "crony," "mob" and "poppycock" started off as slang; a more recent recruit is "phony" (it comes from "fawney rigging," a nineteenth-century confidence trick involving a fake—phony—gold ring).

A great deal of slang undoubtedly comes from the "lower classes," and a good deal of it stays there. Yet the upper classes have probably always had their own slang, such as the British "indijaggers" (indigestion), used by Lord Peter Wimsey—though most of it, like this example, is rather colorless compared with "low" slang. Nearly all the great British "public schools" (private prep schools) have their own distinctive slang or **JARGON**, often exceedingly elaborate. But of course to the upper classes such terms aren't slang, but simply the way We talk.

Having said all this—what *about* slang? The most obvious point is that it's informal—meaning that when you use it, and how much you use, will depend on how informal you choose to sound. Personally, I dig informality, and have no problems with using slang in much of my nonfiction writing. But I avoid it when (for instance) I'm writing about medicine for doctors, most of whom consider their profession too serious for breeziness or making with the jokes.

The second point is that a great deal of current slang is not long for this world. At a rough guess, I'd say that maybe one slang term in ten is eventually upgraded to Standard (e.g., "crony"), another hangs on indefinitely without becoming respectable (e.g., "clap"), while the remaining eight disappear in a generation or less. Particularly short-lived is teenage slang, whose rapid obsolescence perhaps reflects the short attention span of many teenagers. Before using a slang term, then, ask yourself whether it's really current, or an obsolete **FAD WORD**.

Finally, slang is a condiment or seasoning—which like other seasonings, should be used in moderation. Judicious seasoning can turn a merely nourishing dish into a delicious one; overseasoning can drown out all the other flavors—or, in linguistic terms, distract the reader from the substance of what you're saying: the medium screws up the message. Don't freak out over slang—but handle with care!

SLOW(LY). When *HDCU* asked its panelists whether road signs should read GO SLOW or GO SLOWLY, the vast majority sensibly picked SLOW, for the sake of brevity if nothing else. Yet many nonetheless felt that SLOW was somehow "ungrammatical"—that is, it was really just an adjective, not (as here) an adverb as well. The English writer Anthony Burgess called it an Americanism produced by "the ghost of German usage (undoubtedly via Yiddish)."

I don't know enough Yiddish to say whether it treats the equivalent of "slow" as an adverb—and I doubt that Burgess does either. I do know that "slow" has been an English adverb since 1500, and was so used by Shakespeare (". . . how slow/ This old moon wanes"), Milton, Dryden, Scott, Byron and Thackeray. In compounds, indeed, it's not just legitimate but preferable ("slow-moving traffic").

In short, Mr. Burgess didn't do his homework. His talk about Americanisms and Yiddish tells us nothing useful—except, perhaps, about his feelings toward Americans and Jews.

SMALL(-)BUSINESSMAN. Hyphens don't usually change the meaning; "businessman" and "business-man" are equally clear. But modifiers can sow confusion: a small businessman is not the same as a small-business man, and of course the same goes for "big." Here, the hyphen ensures that "small" will modify "business"; without it, it's the businessman, not the business, that's small.

SPECIAL INTEREST GROUP. A phrase so belabored during the 1984 presidential campaign that it became almost a cliché. But politicians had for generations been accusing their opponents of catering to "special interest groups," or "special interests," or simply "the interests." They themselves, of course, represented "the general public" or "the public interest" or "the nation."

At least 99 percent of the time, statements of this type aren't just self-serving but pure malarkey: the "general public," in the United States or anywhere else, is not, never has been and never will be a uniform, homogenized mass. Certainly there are some things all Americans agree on, such as preventing epidemics or invasion—but the list is a mighty short one. On any other public issue, part of the "general public" will line up on one side, part on the other—often with a third part muttering "A plague on both your houses!"

Even concepts like "liberty," which just about every American accepts in the abstract, become focuses of conflict when translated into actual laws and actions: as Lincoln long ago noted, "The sheep and the wolf are by no means agreed on the meaning of the word liberty." He was referring to the liberty of Southerners to own slaves vs. the liberty of the slaves themselves, but the principle still holds good: A's liberty to do as he pleases is often B's "liberty" to be done to as A pleases.

The real meaning of "special interest group," then, is "a group that pursues *its* interests rather than *my* interests." As the eighteenth-century English bishop William Warburton dryly remarked, when asked to explain the difference between orthodoxy and heterodoxy, "Orthodoxy is my doxy [mistress]; heterodoxy is another man's doxy." The public interest is my interest; special interest is another person's interest.

If you insist on denouncing "special interest groups," I can't stop you. But for your own sake, don't delude yourself that *you* don't have special interests of your own: kidding other people is bad but kidding yourself is worse. And if you read somebody else's denunciation of "special interests," ask yourself what *his* (or her) special interest is—and hold on to your wallet.

SPIRAL/HELIX. To the mathematician, a spiral is a two-dimensional figure: the path of a point moving around another point, while approaching (or receding from) it at some mathematically defined rate. A helix, by contrast, is three-dimensional; a screw thread is a good example, as is the "double helix" of the DNA molecule.

Mathematics apart, however, "spiral" also means "helix"

and vice versa, though the latter is rare outside the sciences. Virtually all of us think of a screw thread as a spiral, which therefore spirals around the screw—and I never heard anyone speak of a "helical staircase." I think the distinction—two-dimensional spiral vs. three-dimensional helix—is (or could be) a useful one, but here, once again, usage has defeated logic.

STUDY UP ON. One of a number of American expressions criticized by some British purists, on the ground that the two adverbs (which some of the critics insist on calling prepositions) are unneeded. The late Professor Gilbert Highet, for example, insisted that "study up on" meant the same as "study." Had Highet merely been English, his mistake would have been understandable, but since he had taught American undergraduates for thirty years, he should have known better.

"Studying" is something you can do at your own pace and for as long as you like; I have been studying the English language for years. "Studying up on" is something you do intensively, to meet a deadline—usually an exam. I'm sure Highet himself studied up on some subjects when he was in college, but—since he was educated in England—called it something else.

SUBJUNCTIVES. An endangered, almost extinct species in English: few people nowadays say "If I were king," or "If this be treason"; indeed, both now have a somewhat old-fashioned flavor. The decline of the subjunctive parallels the decline of most other **INFLECTIONS** in English, and for good reason: it's unnecessary.

The commonest reason for using the subjunctive is (or was) the "condition contrary to fact," as in "If I were king" (obviously, I'm not). But—the "if" has already told us this: if I really was king, there'd be no "if" about it. Another reason is to express doubt or uncertainty. When Patrick Henry, in response to cries of "Treason!" during his famous speech, declared "If this be treason, make the most of it!" he was saying, in modern terms, "This may or may not be treason, but—so what?" Nowadays, the nuance conveyed by "If this be . . ." as against "If this is . . ." will pass right by most people —and some will think you made a mistake.

The gradual disappearance of the subjunctive in English may, for all I know, be a Bad Thing, but nothing can now be done about it. In many people's eyes, indeed, using it marks you as prissy or a pedant; judging from some remarks in one of Raymond Chandler's novels, this was true even fifty years ago. Unless you're in love with the past, feel free to ignore it —with one exception: "If I was king" is Standard, but "If I was you" is blue-collar, and if I were you I'd avoid it.

SUBSTANDARD. Like **ILLITERATE,** it's frequently found in discussions of usage, and is only a little less obnoxious. It means "uneducated" or "blue-collar," of course—but the "sub-" clearly implies that such people speak an inferior grade of English; that is, they don't talk like the superior, educated folks who issue pronouncements on usage.

In fact, as we've seen many times already, "substandard" English can be just as clear—or just as unclear—as Standard (educated) English. Using it will unquestionably label you as "sub" in some people's minds, but that's their problem. (If the label troubles you, of course, then it's your problem too.) Just remember that whether or not you choose to use "substandard" English, "nonstandard" says the same thing without the snobbery.

T

TAUT SHIP/TIGHT SHIP. In the great days of sailing ships, a "taut ship" was one in which all the dozens of different ropes making up the rigging were hauled taut, rather than left hanging in sloppy festoons—hence, a ship with a well-disciplined, efficient crew. Nowadays, it more often means an efficient, well-disciplined organization, as in "The boss runs a taut ship."

The widespread figurative use of the phrase, now a near-cliché, dates from the end of World War II, when it was picked up by men who had served—or wanted people to think they had served—as naval officers. (They also introduced an even more clichéd greeting to new employees or associates, "Welcome aboard!")

The expression is tired enough to deserve a rest, unless you're talking about an actual ship rather than an organization. (*Never* say that an officer in the U.S. Army "runs a taut ship," however efficient his organization. To many Army men, the Navy, including its jargon, is an enemy at least as menacing as the Russians—and the Navy, of course, feels much the same about the Army.) Even more to be avoided is the variant "run a *tight* ship," which, because of the many meanings of "tight," could have unfortunate connotations. Aboard ship, a tight crew is by no means a taut crew.

TEMPERATURE (sick with a). Some people object to the phrase "sick with a temperature," on the ground that our bodies always have a "temperature"—normal or otherwise *(HDCU).* This is pedantry: everybody knows that "sick with a temperature" means having a temperature somewhat greater than 98.6° F (37° C)—that is, a slight fever. Substituting "sick with a fever" doesn't quite work, since to most of us a "fever" sounds more serious than a "temperature." But if "sick with a temperature" raises *your* temperature, try "sick with a low fever."

The same objections have been made, for the same pedantic reasons, to "sick with a virus" or "sick with sinus." The first phrase is, of course, shorthand for "sick with a viral infection," which—if you want to be technical—means anything from a mild cold to AIDS. However, to everyone but doctors and virologists, it means an infection of unknown origin with unpleasant but not serious or prolonged effects. Likewise, "sinus" in this context is simply shorthand for "sinus trouble" or, as the doctors say, "sinusitis." Don't, however, say "sick with *a* sinus"—unless you're sure that only one of the patient's half-dozen sinus cavities is affected.

TENSES, SEQUENCE OF. One of the most complicated aspects of usage: *HDCU*'s discussion is brief and misleading; Bernstein's is comprehensive but confusing. I'll try to hit some of the high spots.

Normally—that is, "other things being equal"—the rule is that the verb in a subordinate clause takes the same tense as that of the main clause: "He *says* he *is* hungry," but "He *said* he *was* hungry." Alas, more often than not other things aren't equal—for example, in "He says [present] he robbed [past] the store because he was [past] hungry." The reason for the shift in tense is that he's saying it now, but was hungry and robbed the store earlier on.

You can also reverse this "abnormal" sequence, as in "She

warned [past] him that drinking and driving don't [present] mix." Again the reason should be clear: it's not just that they didn't mix when she warned him; they still don't, and never will. But, as Bernstein points out, there are exceptions to the exceptions: we normally say "I didn't know you played the piano," even though the person in question presumably still plays it.

So far, the rules for sequence are reasonably clear. But what happens when the second clause deals with a future event? Here, paradoxically, the normal sequence is not, as you might expect, past-future, but past-present. The reason, or part of it, is that English has half a dozen ways of expressing future time, and some of them are identical with present forms. "I go to Chicago next week" = "I'm going to Chicago next week" = "I'll go to Chicago next week"; will the real future tense please stand up?

A good example of how this past-present (= past-future) sequence works is one of Bernstein's sentences: "Some believed that the same issue would be raised again when the name of Japan was presented this year." He points out, correctly, that it should be "is presented this year," since it clearly hasn't been presented yet.

I'd be inclined to amend the sentence further, saying "will be raised" instead of "would be raised" (the raising, like the presentation, is a coming attraction). An even better solution would be to change all the tenses: "Some *believe* that the same issue *will be* raised again when the name of Japan *is* presented this year." The people in question, after all, not only believed it but presumably still do (otherwise, why quote them?).

Come to think of it, a lot of time, trouble and confusion could be avoided if newspapers used the present tense oftener than they do: not only "The administration believes . . ." but also "An administration spokesman *says* . . . ," "The task force *reports* . . . ," "The Republican leadership *claims* . . . ," and so on. But I'm not holding my breath: when it comes to style and usage, newspaper editors, whatever their politics, are mostly hard-nosed conservatives.

Infinitives and participles raise still other problems. The present infinitive is the normal form, whether it follows a present or a past verb: either "He *is* the first pitcher *to win* twenty games this year" or "He *was* the first pitcher *to win* twenty-five games in a season." In fact, I can think of few cases where the perfect infinitive ("to have won") would be an improvement. Bernstein cites ". . . the first woman ever *to have completed* the Channel swim before reaching the age of twenty-five," his point being that the completion occurred before the birthday. I think this is cumbersome: "to complete" says the same thing, since the subsequent "before" makes the sequence of events clear. Indeed, the sentence would be further improved by striking out several more words: ". . . the first woman to swim the Channel before the age of twenty-five." In the original sentence, "ever" means "at any time," and if you substitute those words you'll see that it's redundant.

The present participle ("*Locking* the door, she went out") vs. the perfect participle ("*Having locked* the door . . .") is another tricky distinction—tricky enough to trip up the usually meticulous Bernstein. He prefers the first sentence—which, on the face of it, implies that she locked the door before she went out or while she was going out, either of which would be a neat trick. Yet "Having locked" is only a slight improvement. I think *both* sentences are bad because they emphasize a normal, "understood" action. If the idea was that she made sure to lock the door, then that's what the writer should have said; if she just locked it as usual, why bother to say so at all? Bernstein also stumbles when he O.K.'s "After having passed through customs, the travelers proceeded." "After passing through customs . . ." says the same thing (the "after" tells you which came first) and saves a word.

To sum up: the proper sequence of tenses within a sentence, or a series of sentences, naturally reflects the sequence of events being described—but the reflection sometimes resembles that in an amusement-park mirror. This isn't a very satisfactory situation, but there's nothing to be done about it.

TERRIBLE (= very bad). Bernstein lists this under "Atomic Flyswatters"—powerful words used in relatively trivial contexts. He reasons that "terrible" means "terrifying," and should therefore be reserved for really appalling things. I'm afraid, however, that nowadays there's not much that's atomic about this word; it has gone the way of "awful," "horrible," **"UNIQUE"** and many other once powerful adjectives. True, it started out meaning "terrifying," but for some four centuries has also meant merely "very bad"—and the second meaning has by now all but eclipsed the first.

For example, I have in my time suffered attacks of several extremely painful diseases, but while the attacks were certainly terrible they weren't terrifying, since I was never in any danger of checking out. Had I been unlucky enough to be in Mexico City during its 1985 earthquake, however, I'd certainly have called the experience "terrifying," but not "terrible"—unless I had been seriously injured.

TERRIBLY. *HDCU* considers this an acceptable informal synonym for "very"; I'd say it's a bit stronger than that, and should be used only when you mean "extremely." To me, at least, a "very sick" person is merely severely ill, but a "terribly sick" one is either at death's door or coming up the front steps. Likewise, "very expensive" means that I can probably afford whatever-it-is, if I want it badly enough; "terribly expensive" means I can't.

THAN HE/THAN HIM. Sentences like "Now you can be taller than her" annoy purists, who say that it should be "taller than she." Technically, they're right; the "implied" construction is

". . . taller than —— *is,*" and nobody would say "taller than her is." Usually, however, the meaning will be clear whichever form you use.

Once in a while, however, the wrong pronoun can lead to confusion, as in "She loves me better than he." Here it's impossible to be sure whether the writer meant "better than he *does*" or "better than *she loves* him." In such cases, the safest course is to "spell out" the sentence in full—that is, include the "understood" words, such as those I've italicized in these examples. Doing this not only will clarify your meaning but will, or should, make crystal clear which pronoun to use.

THANK YOU (KINDLY) (MUCH) (VERY MUCH). *HDCU* calls "Thank you kindly" a "quaint but nonsensical" phrase. Quaint it certainly is, and should be avoided unless quaintness is what you're after (" 'Thank you kindly, sir,' she said.") But since its meaning is clear, calling it "nonsensical" is— nonsense.

"Thank you very much" is, of course, perfectly acceptable to everyone; logically, "Thank you much" should be just as acceptable, but isn't. It may have started as a regionalism— at least I first heard it in Helena, Montana—but seems to be spreading. I think it carries at least the suggestion of "I'm thanking you—but not very enthusiastically," and I'd avoid it; a simple "Thanks" will do just as well. "Thanks a lot," too, should be avoided unless you're being ironic; more often than not it means "Thanks a bunch" or, as the British say, "Thanks for nothing."

THAT/WHICH. The choice between these two relative pronouns is bound up with the distinction between restrictive and nonrestrictive clauses (see **COMMAS AND RESTRICTIVE CLAUSES**). "That" goes only with restrictive ones and no commas ("the girl that I married"); "which," on the other hand, has for centuries been used with both kinds of clauses, the commas alone marking the distinction. It is *required* in restrictive clauses following an earlier "that" ("the love *that* dares not speak its name," but *"that* love *which* dares not speak its name."

Since it's the commas that really do the job, and can muddle your meaning if you misuse them, the main value of the rather nebulous that/which distinction is that it forces you to think about whether your clause is or isn't restrictive—that is, whether the commas are needed; if you get the commas right, you can use "which" (or "who," if you're talking about people) on any occasion. Note, too, that "that" can often be dropped entirely ("The girl I married")—which is one less decision (that) you'll have to make.

The "that" in a restrictive clause must, of course, refer to a specific noun or pronoun preceding it, as it does in the above examples ("the *love* that" etc.). If more than one noun or pronoun precedes it, then it must refer specifically to the last of these—not "The woman and her children that I married," but "The woman that I married, and her children."

Some people think that the same principle applies to the nonrestrictive "which." That is, it must refer to a specific noun or pronoun, meaning that you can't say "The President once again denounced the 'evil empire,' which some observers felt was inappropriate in the present situation." They reason that "which" obviously doesn't refer either to the President or the evil empire, but to his denunciation—and this word, though implied, is not actually included in the sentence.

Bernstein calls this rule "ultrafinicky," and considers the construction permissible provided it's not ambiguous—as it isn't in the preceding example. I'd still avoid which'es of this sort, since in my experience they *are* ambiguous more often than not. Avoiding the construction may not always be essential but *will* help keep you out of trouble. And these bewildering distinctions, like many others, can often be avoided by restructuring: "The President once again denounced the 'evil empire'; many observers felt his remarks were inappropriate. . . ."

THIS HERE. "This here dog" is, of course, either blue-collar or regional; "this dog here," illogically but indubitably, is neither—but *is* a redundancy, since the "here" adds nothing to the sense.

THIS/THESE (= a, some). "This" has for some decades been common shorthand for "an unidentified [person]" ("this woman came up to me"), as "these" has been for "some unidentified [people]" ("these guys started yelling"). Both are good colloquial English, but "some" will always be right, singular or plural ("some woman . . . ," "some guys . . ."").

THUS (= for example). The basic meaning of "thus" has always been "in this manner"; later its sense expanded to include "therefore" and, still later, "for example." This last usage is controversial; *RHD* says yes, *AHD* says no and the *HDCU* panel splits right up the middle. I'd say it's a matter of taste —but, as always when a word has multiple meanings, watch your context.

TOM SWIFTIES. When I was a kid, many of my contemporaries devoured the Tom Swift books (*Tom Swift and His Flying Machine, Tom Swift and His Electric Boat,* etc. etc. *and* etc.). The style of these works—if that's the right word—was notable for its compulsive avoidance of "he said." Tom and his friends (and enemies) never said anything; they grunted, laughed, growled, cried, snarled or gulped it.

The scene now shifts to the 1950s, when somebody—I suspect on Madison Avenue—invented a game called "Tom Swifties," which involved making up sentences "appropriate" to the various substitutes for "he said." Examples: " '*I* don't have a drinking problem,' Tom gulped"; " 'I'll have second helpings of everything,' Tom grunted"; " 'I love you passionately,' Tom ejaculated." A slightly less sophisticated version used adverbs: " 'This knife won't cut,' Tom said bluntly."

The point of this little tale is that there's nothing wrong with "he/she said," and straining after substitutes is the mark of an amateurish writer. Putting it another way: when you're writing dialogue, the wording of the dialogue *itself,* plus the situation, should, most of the time, tell the reader whether the person snapped it or gulped it or snarled it. Injecting unnecessary descriptive verbs or adverbs distracts attention from the dialogue—and the story.

Often enough, even "(s)he said" can be omitted; if only two people are talking, when A stops the next speaker *must* be B. But be careful: an entire page of dialogue with nothing to indicate who is speaking at any given moment may well force the reader to stop and reread the whole passage, simply to make sure who's saying what to whom (see almost any novel by George V. Higgins, who writes some of the best dialogue ever put on paper). I've even seen cases where the writer, or proofreader, has so muddled things that a remark apparently made by A *must* have been made by B.

Be super-careful if more than two people are talking: the possibility of confusion increases as the square of the number of speakers. (See Robert A. Heinlein's *The Number of the Beast,* in which most of the dialogues involve four people. His repeated failure to make clear which of them is talking weakens an otherwise fine yarn.)

So feel free to use "(s)he said" (or "John said" or "Mary said") as often as needed—but no oftener. An alternative is to drop in little bits of "business" (in the theatrical sense) that will tell the reader who's speaking, and how. Example: "The jeweler examined the diamond minutely with his lens. *'How* much did you say?' " Obviously it's the jeweler who's asking the question; equally obviously, he's asking it ironically. But this device, too, can be overdone; too much "business" slows down the action.

TRANSPIRE. As a synonym for "perspire," it's either obsolete or a Nice-Nellyism, or maybe both ("perspire" itself is a Nice-Nellyism for "sweat"). As a synonym for "happen" ("What transpired?"), it's pretentious. Leave the word to the botanists, who speak of plants "transpiring" in a very precise sense: emitting vapor (usually water vapor) through the pores of their leaves.

TRIGGER (verb). Follett calls this one of the most overused words in English, claiming that it has been used as a synonym for "set off," "produce," "initiate," "cause" and half a dozen similar expressions. I think he's overstating the case a little, but basically right. If you use it at all, use it precisely, of a small-scale, often unobtrusive action that produces conspicuous consequences, as pulling the trigger of a gun produces a shot.

For example, the continuing buildup of nuclear arms will not *trigger* a nuclear war—though it might well help cause one. On the other hand, the famous assassination at Sarajevo in 1914 didn't *cause* World War I (the causes were much bigger and more complicated), but it certainly triggered it.

TROOP(S)/TROUPE/TROOPER/TROUPER. A troop is a group of people—usually a relatively small military or paramilitary unit; sometimes, it's a group of animals (zoologists speak of "a troop of baboons"). And you can speak of several "troops of baboons" or "troops of cavalry," though the latter phrase, like cavalry itself, is all but obsolete. Normally, however, "troops" doesn't mean units of soldiers but soldiers (any number) collectively. And a company of actors, dancers, etc. is a troupe; more than one company, troupes.

All clear? Now take a deep breath. A trooper is a member of a military troop, or of the paratroops, or a state cop—but *not* a member of a baboon troop. A trouper is a member of a theatrical troupe—and to call somebody "a real trouper" is high praise: it means somebody you can rely on when the show must go on.

TURNPIKE, THRUWAY, PARKWAY, SUPERHIGHWAY, FREEWAY, EXPRESSWAY. I began this entry with "turnpike" for reasons of seniority; the word, in its "modern" sense, dates from the eighteenth century, when it referred to English highways equipped with "pikes" (poles) that forced travelers to stop and pay a toll, after which the pike was turned to let them proceed. It still means that sort of highway, though nowadays the "pikes" are raised and lowered electrically. A thruway is the same thing as a turnpike—though the only example I know of is the New York State Thruway.

Modern turnpikes are, of course, also superhighways (divided highways with limited access), but not all superhighways are turnpikes: some are "freeways" (on the West Coast and some other places) or "expressways" (in New York and Boston). A parkway is a street, highway or superhighway whose siting or decorative plantings emphasize aesthetics rather than speed. Some parkways charge tolls, some don't, and many of them exclude trucks. Finally we have the strange case of the Connecticut Turnpike, which has quit collecting tolls and turning pikes along a good part of its length—but is still "the turnpike."

-TYPE. Immediately after World War II, Britain's whisky industry, like the rest of its civilian economy, was a shambles—meaning that real Scotch whisky was hard to get. Some enterprising Japanese distiller thereupon began producing imitation Scotch, but called it "Scotch-type" whisky (those who tasted it called it other things). This is the first example I can recall of the now common usage—or overusage—of "type" as a suffix-adjective.

Bernstein cites such examples as "V-type engine," "a New Deal–type candidate," "O-type blood" and "cantilever-type bridge," all of which he seems to approve at least tentatively. The first two are passable—though "New Deal–type candidate" is politically obsolete. But "type O blood" rolls as easily off the tongue as "O-type blood," and "cantilever-type bridge" is ridiculous: it's a "cantilever bridge," just as the Brooklyn Bridge is a suspension bridge—not a suspension-type bridge.

The noun "type," used to modify another noun, needs "of" in between, as in "that type *of* guy." "That type guy" is regional—probably a **YIDDISHISM**.

U–V

UNALIENABLE/INALIENABLE. The first of this pair is a word that every American should know, since it's used in one of the greatest documents in American—or human—history. "We hold these truths to be self-evident: that all men are created equal; that they are endowed by their Creator with certain unalienable rights; that among these are Life, Liberty and the Pursuit of Happiness." (If you don't know the rest of this magnificent paragraph by heart, then shame on you! See any encyclopedia, or the *World Almanac,* under "Declaration of Independence.") But though the words ring out as they did two centuries ago, "unalienable" is obsolete; today the rights are "*in*alienable," in theory—and sometimes in practice.

UNCOMPARABLE/INCOMPARABLE. The first appeared in the fourteenth century, meaning "with which there is no comparison, matchless, peerless." The second arrived in the following century, with the identical meaning. Gradually, "uncomparable" dropped out of use, but has been revived with the special grammarians' sense of "not capable of being compared" (see **ADJECTIVES, UNCOMPARABLE**).

If, then, you want to say that something is in a class by itself or, as the French say, *hors concours,* use "incomparable"; if you're talking about grammar, "uncomparable." If, however, you're dealing with two things that can't properly be compared—that is, that are too different for any comparison to be meaningful—say "not comparable." Stars and planets are comparable (both celestial bodies), so are horses and mules (both draft animals) and so, if you stretch a point, are horses and people (both mammals). But horses and planets are simply not comparable.

UNDERWHELMING. The first writer who described a second-rate theatrical performance or a dull speech as "underwhelming" got a well-deserved chuckle; so, probably, did the second. By now, however, this **BACK FORMATION** (from "overwhelming," of course) is pretty tired, and its use is almost guaranteed to underwhelm the reader.

UNIQUE. Do you now or have you ever used such expressions as "very unique," "the most unique" and so on? If so, you are "illiterate" (Fowler), "dumb" (an *HDCU* panelist) and various other unpleasant things according to other experts. You are also thumbing your nose at 94 percent of the *AHD* usage panel and almost as large a proportion of the *HDCU* panel.

All these harsh words stem from the delusion that "unique" means "that is one of its kind" *and only that*—a view supported by some dictionaries and most usage experts. Thus Fowler describes the word as "applicable only to what is in some respects the sole existing specimen." If this were true, expressions such as "more unique" would indeed be logically absurd, since a thing obviously can't be more or less one of a kind: either it is or it isn't.

But though logic is on the side of the experts, history is against them. The English career of "unique" (barring a brief, temporary appearance in the seventeenth century) dates from the late eighteenth century, when it was (re)borrowed from French. At that time, its unique meaning was indeed "that is one of its kind." However, within a few decades it began to be used in the weakened sense of "remarkable, unusual."

Thus as early as 1808 we find a historian describing the sixteenth century statesman Sir Thomas More as "so unique . . . that"—which clearly implies that other statesmen must have been *less* unique than the sainted Sir Thomas. Similar usages—all of them, according to the *OED*, "objected to" by grammarians—include "thoroughly unique" (1813), "absolutely unique" (1866) "totally unique" (1871) and even "uniquest" (1885); "very unique" itself showed up soon afterward in one of Conan Doyle's tales.

There is nothing unique—in either sense—about this shift in meaning: a dozen other once powerful English adjectives have similarly shrunk into near–triviality. Thus "awful" (as in "He's an awful jerk") once meant "awe-inspiring," and "horrible" (as in "He's a horrible bore") meant "horrifying"; see also **TERRIBLE**. We find an even more exact parallel in "singular," which (as you might guess from its resemblance to "single") originally, like "unique," meant "that is [the single] one of its kind." Today, it's used by even the purest purists to mean merely "remarkable" or "unusual."

"Unique," in short, no longer has an absolutely unique meaning, and has therefore become a "watch your context" word. If you really mean to say that something is one of a kind, call it "absolutely unique" or "literally unique." If you're merely talking about something unusual, then a simple "unique" will be understood in that sense by almost anybody. However, you'll save yourself a lot of flak from the purists by using a synonym; if you have trouble finding one, then you are indeed a remarkable, unusual, singular, even extraordinary individual.

UNLESS AND UNTIL. A redundancy—and a clichéd one at that: the phrase says nothing that "unless" or "until" can't say alone. Even worse, it's confusing, since the words have somewhat different connotations. For example, a parent might say "You can't go to the movies until you clean up your room," implying that the room will get cleaned up, though probably under protest. "You can't go *unless* you clean up your room," however, implies some doubt as to whether the room will ever get cleaned—a not unusual feeling among parents of teenagers. "Unless and until," then, implies that the outcome both is and isn't in doubt—which is obviously impossible.

Much the same objections apply to "if and when." Saying "If I go to Europe . . ." clearly implies that you're not sure you're going; "When I go to Europe . . . ," that you *are* sure. Clearly you can be either sure or not sure, or sometimes one and sometimes the other—but not both at once. Adding "as," to make it "if, as and when" (or sometimes "when, as and if"), compounds the felony.

UP. A very frequently used—and occasionally overused—word. As *HDCU* points out, it adds nothing to such phrases as "wash up the dishes" and "make up the bed."

But the editors go too far when they reject "clean up the house": to me, "clean the house" implies merely sweeping, dusting, mopping, etc., while "clean up the house" involves the much more burdensome business of straightening, putting things away and throwing out junk, *plus* cleaning. Likewise, "fix the car" implies some specific defect that needs fixing, while "fix up the car" suggests a general retuning and refurbishing. See also **STUDY UP ON**.

VERBAL LITTERING. For at least twenty years, American and, y'know, Canadian speech has been sort of polluted with various, like, meaningless interjections. For many people—some of them well educated—these expressions have become sort of the equivalent of, y'know, a tic; any sentence of more than six words will be kind of disfigured by one or more bits of, like, verbal litter. Occasionally, I even find myself, like, doing it.

A neat and incisive dissection of this depressing habit was performed by my friend Professor F. Clark Fraser, of McGill University:

> *Are you ever afraid of appearing absurd*
> *For not being able to think of a word?*
> *There's a ruse you can use when your speech is abortive:*
> *Just fill in with "basically," "you know," "like sort of."*

Dr. Fraser's verses, which I unfortunately haven't the space to quote in full, continue with the problem of a physician whose patient has expired and is searching "For a word that means basically, you know, like—dead," and ends by reassuring the reader that "You'll never be struck, like—you know—sort of dumb/With these useful non-words to, like, sort of chose from!"

Don't be a verbal litterbug!

VERY (MUCH) PLEASED OR INTERESTED. "Very," like a few other adverbs, cannot modify verbs, but only adjectives. From this fact some grammarians have leaped to the conclusion that you can't say that someone was "very pleased," or "very interested," since the words in question aren't adjectives but participles, which are a sort of verb. Properly, therefore, one must say "very *much* pleased."

This is an outstanding example of how some people—not all of them grammarians—can so befuddle themselves with theory that they trip over the facts. The fact is that when participles like "pleased" and "interested" function as adjectives, as they constantly do (see **PARTICIPLES, a.k.a. GERUNDS**), they can be modified by "very" like any other adjective. Would anyone say "He's a very much loving husband"?

What you can't say is "His performance very pleased the audience," since here "pleased" functions as a verb and using "very" to modify it isn't idiomatic English: the sentence should read ". . . very much pleased the audience" or ". . . pleased the audience very much." Yet, illogically, you can't idiomatically say "pleased the audience much," though you can say "much pleased the audience."

VIABLE. "Viable" originally meant something capable of living or surviving—for example, a healthy newborn baby. Soon it acquired a figurative meaning, but one still close to the original: ". . . no race [apparently] more viable, yet death reaps them with both hands" or ". . . a romance in embryo; one, moreover, that never attained a viable stature and constitution" *(OED)*.

Since World War II, the word has been taken into **BUREAUCRATESE,** as in "I don't think the proposal is viable," meaning that it isn't practical, or practicable (see **PRACTICAL/PRACTICABLE**), or, perhaps, that it's just plain dumb. A usage with this much ambiguity is intolerable—though I fear it remains all too viable among bureaucrats.

VICIOUS CIRCLE/VICIOUS CYCLE. The first of these phrases means a situation in which one problem, or an attempt to solve it, creates another problem, which intensifies the first problem, which intensifies the second problem, and so on. (I speak of two problems merely for simplicity; in fact, any number can play.) Personally, I think "vicious spiral" is even more graphic, since it implies ascending (or descending) viciousness, but very few people use it.

Since a "cycle" normally refers to something that repeats itself *without* change ("the cycle of the seasons"), "vicious cycle" seems to me a metaphor that doesn't quite come off. However, I *was* almost hit by a vicious cycle on the street recently.

W-Z

WANT OUT. *HDCU* describes this as a "regionalism," most common in the Midwest. I'm not sure this was true in 1975, and I'm damn sure it's not true now. The phrase is in general use as a stronger version of "I want to go out" (of an actual place) or, more often, "I want to get out" (of a situation, business deal, etc.): in the famous words of Sam Goldwyn, "Include me out!" That is, it doesn't say merely that the speaker wants to leave, or withdraw, but that (s)he is eager, nay determined, to do so.

For example, my wife and I, whenever our cat stands at one of the doors of our summer home and complains, say that she wants out. If you know cats, you know that when they want out they are indeed determined to leave—and the same goes, of course, when they're out and want in.

WATERGATE ENGLISH. The Watergate revelations, culminating in two historic "firsts" (the resignation, and subsequent pardon, of an American President) shocked nearly all Americans. Some usage experts were doubly shocked—not just by the misdeeds of leading federal officials but also by the way the perpetrators expressed themselves, both in public and in private.

The experts' reactions demonstrated once again that indignation, however justified, is no substitute for thought. Enraged at Nixon, Mitchell, Haldeman, Erlichman et al., these experts (notably, *HDCU*'s editors and contributors) succumbed to the fallacy I have discussed in the Introduction: English spoken by bastards must be bastard English. More particularly, they managed to muddle together several categories of bad, or allegedly bad, usage: **BUREAUCRATESE, EUPHEMISMS, CLICHÉS** and—in a quite different category—certain novel or seemingly novel expressions that not only didn't hurt the American language but enriched it.

Bureaucratese was particularly favored by John Mitchell, then U.S. attorney general, of whom it was later said: "Was he a criminal lawyer?" "Yes, very." Mitchell's contributions to the Watergate dialogue included "subject matter" (= subject), "in the area of" (= about) and "in that time frame" (= then; around that time). (Whether he actually originated these phrases I don't know, but he certainly made good—or bad—use of them.) Another bit of bureaucratese was common coin among the miscreants: "at this point in time" (= now).

Clichés, frequently muddled into mixed metaphors, included Nixon's discussion of the possible advantages of throwing Mitchell to the wolves: ". . . if they [the grand jury] get a hell of a big fish, that is going to take a lot of the fire out of this thing." Euphemisms—for which the need was certainly pressing—included the memorable "is inoperative" (= was false).

So far, so good—or so bad. But when it comes to "caper," which the *HDCU* editors apparently considered a coined euphemism for "crime," political outrage has warped stylistic judgment: the word has had that meaning since the 1860s, according to Eric Partridge's *Dictionary of Slang and Unconventional English.* It originated as criminal slang (and has been a cliché of American crime writers since the 1930s) and was therefore peculiarly appropriate in the Watergate context.

Three other expressions deplored by *HDCU* are "stroke" (= soothe or cajole), **LAUNDER (money)** and **PLUMBER**.

As I've indicated earlier, the last two were needed as concise descriptions of certain activities or people—and, unfortunately, still are. As for "stroke," I personally find it an excellent metaphor—maybe because I've been soothing and cajoling cats that way for years.

Thus *HDCU*'s verdict on Watergate English ("horrible examples of language gone astray or, more aptly, torn asunder") must be classed as, at best, overkill and, at worst, nonsense. Even the Nixons of this world are entitled to be judged on their merits, or demerits—and so is the language they use.

WE (= everybody). A favorite ploy among laborers in the lush vineyards of pop sociology and pop anthropology is what I've elsewhere christened the evasive "we" (the term includes the evasive "us" and "our"). It shows up in such statements as *"We* [human beings] are naturally aggressive" (Lionel Tiger and Robin Fox), *"We* [Americans] are forcing people to adapt to a new life pace" (Alvin Toffler) and *"Our* [American male] sexuality is so confused, *our* masculinity is so uncertain . . ." (George Gilder).

As these examples suggest, the evasive "we" can serve either of two rhetorical functions: (1) turning a personal opinion into a general "truth" (Gilder); (2) shifting the responsibility for a problem from somebody to everybody—and therefore, of course, to nobody (Toffler). The author of *Future Shock* may have had a point when he ascribed it to people being forced to adapt to a faster life pace. But if "we" Americans are forcing it on *ourselves,* nobody is really to blame—and little if anything can be done about it.

Sometimes, indeed, an evasive "we" can serve both functions simultaneously, as in the Tiger/Fox example above. The question of whether human beings are "naturally aggressive" —not to mention how and when they're aggressive—is very much a matter of personal opinion. And—if they are indeed naturally aggressive, then nobody is really responsible for such manifestations of aggression as violent crime and war.

The quickest way of detecting an evasive "we" is to substitute "I/me and my friends": if the result is nonsense, then the writer is conning you—or himself/herself. "I and my friends are forcing people to adapt to a new life pace?" Not I—and not my friends either. "My masculinity and that of my friends is uncertain?" Not that we, or our women friends, have noticed. And if you and all your friends are indeed "naturally aggressive"—maybe you should find some new friends.

It's rather like the tale of the Lone Ranger and Tonto, surrounded on all sides by Indians. Says the Ranger, sadly, "Looks like we've had it, old pal!" Tonto: "What you mean 'we,' white man?" What you mean "we," Gilder?

If you find yourself using "we" to characterize some large group of which you're a member, ask yourself: Is what I'm saying really true of the group—or only of me and my friends? If the latter, then "we" is bad usage—unless, that is, you're engaged in a rhetorical con game of your own.

WELSH (verb). Bookies and others have been "welshing" on bets for well over a century. The word has no traceable connection with the natives of Wales, except—just possibly—through the old nursery rhyme "Taffy was a Welshman, Taffy was a thief." I doubt that anyone nowadays imagines that it reflects in any way on the Welsh people, but—I wouldn't use it in Wales.

WHETHER (OR NOT). Some writers claim the "or not" is always redundant, others, that it's always necessary; both are wrong. The confusion arises because "whether" is commonly used in two different contexts. In the first it means **"IF"** ("I don't know whether he's telling the truth"); in the second, its precise sense is hard to define: it is a way of introducing two alternatives, either of which applies, or may apply, to the statement in question ("I'm going whether it's rainy or sunny"; "Whether I am elected or defeated, I still hope to continue serving the people of this state"). In such constructions, *both* alternatives must be stated—or "or not" added (". . . whether it's sunny or not"; "Whether I am elected or not").

Bernstein suggests a useful test, which I find almost always works: substitute "if" for whether; if the meaning of the sentence changes, you need "or not." Thus "If I'm elected" obviously means something quite different from "Whether I'm elected"—that is, it should be "Whether or not I'm elected." Likewise, "If it's raining, I'm going" doesn't mean the same thing as "Whether it's raining"; make it "Whether or not it's raining"—or "Even if it's raining."

WHO(EVER)/WHOM(EVER). "Whom" is another of the vanishing **INFLECTIONS** in our language. As far back as the early 1800s, Noah Webster took a dim view of it, and by 1928 the *OED* could write that the word "is no longer current in natural colloquial speech." Today, few people use it except in very special circumstances; some people never do.

One reason "whom" has virtually disappeared from English is that even professional writers get confused about where to use it. A typical example comes from E. M. Forster's *A Room with a View,* published more than sixty years ago: "There was an old man . . . whom he said had murdered his wife." Forster evidently thought that "whom" was the object of "he said"; in fact, if you drop those two words the sentence reads "whom . . . had murdered his wife," which is obviously wrong; that is, "who(m)" is the subject of "had murdered."

About the only place where "whom" sounds natural is directly following a preposition. "To whom are you referring?" sounds "righter" than "To who are . . ."—but also sounds pretty pompous; most of us would say "Who are you referring to?" But there's nothing wrong with "He's a man for whom

I have the greatest respect"—though ". . . a man I have the greatest respect for" says it quicker.

"Whomever" is a still rarer bird: even following a preposition it sounds somewhat self-conscious ("I'll give it to whomever I choose").

If you use "who" and "whoever" consistently, the worst that can happen is a sneer or two from some purists; your meaning will always be clear. So never send to see for whom the bell tolls: it tolls for "whom."

WHOSE. Everyone agrees that "who" (and, if you absolutely insist, "whom") applies only to persons; "which," to things: "The diplomat *who* was kidnapped" but "The car *which* was stolen." The problem comes with possessive relationships: you can certainly say "The diplomat whose car was stolen"— but what about "The car whose owner was kidnapped"?

"Whose" was, in fact, used of both persons and things from the fourteenth century until nearly the end of the nineteenth. Shakespeare had no problems with it ("I could a tale unfold whose lightest word/Would harry up they soul") and neither did the poets Milton and Southey or the novelist Charles Reade.

Then, someone—I suspect a schoolteacher or academician —decided, for reasons best known to himself, that the impersonal "whose" was wrong, and should be replaced with "of which." I think it was a dumb idea then and still is. Are we going to start singing about the flag "The broad stripes and bright stars of which, thro' the perilous fight . . ."?

-WISE. As a suffix meaning "in the manner or way of [a noun]," it has a long history in English ("clockwise," "sidewise," etc.). For some generations, however, it ceased to be linguistically "productive"—meaning that it was no longer incorporated into new words. Around 1950, it was rather suddenly revived —probably on Madison Avenue—with the sense of "in relation to," and hip young men and women began using such coinages as "budgetwise" and "mediawise." The **FAD WORD**—or fad suffix—spread, producing "saleswise," "newswise" and even "votewise."

The fad had a rather longer run than such things usually do, but today "-wise" is used, if at all, only with a figurative snicker—by -wise-guys, so to speak. Clichéwise, or even joke-wise, we can well do without it.

WRACK/WREAK/WRECK. The first, meaning roughly "wreckage," is obsolete or obsolescent except in the expression "wrack and ruin" (a cliché) and in the rare sense of "sea vegetation driven ashore or growing at the water's edge." Occasionally it's used as a misspelling for the verb "rack," meaning to stretch or twist painfully, as if on the Inquisitors' rack ("Body all achin' and racked with pain"); even less frequently, of the noun "rack" (= mass of wind-driven clouds).

"Wreak" is equally obsolescent or, at best, archaic, as in "wreak vengeance" or "wreak havoc"—the latter a cliché. Which is to say that the simplest rule for using either "wrack" or "wreak" is—don't. If you're destroying or ruining or totaling something, say "wreck."

YIDDISHISMS. No language save those of the Native Americans and, perhaps, Mexican Spanish has contributed more to American English than Yiddish; indeed none of the other foreign tongues brought to American (e.g., German, Italian, Polish) have contributed anything like as much. How this came about requires a bit of thought. Jews have never amounted to more than a small fraction of our population—and a fraction, moreover, that until the end of World War II endured dislike, distrust and discrimination from a great many other Americans.

Nor, despite the paranoid fantasies of a few 110 percent patriots, do Jews "control" America. We've never had a Jewish President or Vice-President, the number of large corporations owned by Jews is far outnumbered by those controlled by WASPs and other ethnics, and most Jews, like most of the rest of us, don't own corporations of any sort.

The Jewish influence on the American language came about in two ways. First, for rather complicated historical reasons, a large proportion of our Jewish immigrants settled in large cities, especially New York, Chicago and Los Angeles. And in any country, it's the big cities that set the "tone" of national life and language.

Second, New York was and is the center of American theater and vaudeville, while Los Angeles was almost from the beginning the center of the motion picture industry; inevitably, the two metropolises came to dominate American television. And the Jews of those cities—partly because of the barriers against them in most other well-paid jobs—got into show business in disproportionate numbers, sometimes as writers, sometimes as performers. They brought with them their peculiarly ironic humor, and bits and pieces of their native tongue—a dialect of medieval German with heavy borrowings from Russian and Hebrew.

It was largely through Jews in show business, then, that the American language acquired such now widely understood Yiddish words as "kibitzer," "kosher," "schlemiel" and "schlock." Of more restricted, but growing, currency are "chutzpah," "klutz," "nosh," "maven," "schlimazl," "schmuck," "schlep," "schmotta" and, most recently, "schlong." (There must be something about the SH sound that appeals to the American ear.)

Some of these terms are already widely known, and I expect most or all of the rest to become so before very long. I have therefore defined them, and added a few thoughts on when and when not to use them; starred (*) terms are likely to bewilder a sizable number of readers (including even a few Jews) and should be used with caution, if at all. Finally, all these words are at least mildly slangy, and are subject to the same cautions on overuse as are other **SLANG** terms.

chutzpah. Almost unbelievable gall; effrontery, squared. The "classic" case is that of the (fictitious) man who killed his parents, then asked the judge for mercy on the ground that he was an orphan. A real example occurred during the gasoline shortages of the 1973 Arab oil boycott, when the ambassador of one of the oil states complained that his chauffeur had to wait in line for gas. (The CH is pronounced as in Scottish "loCH" or, if you have trouble with this sound, as H.)

kibitzer. This noun, perhaps the most widely used Yiddish term, originally meant an onlooker at a card game—usually, one who comments on the play. The meaning has broadened to include any giver of unwanted advice, or even any onlooker whose actions distract others from what they are doing—though I think this last sense is confusingly broad. The verb that describes what a kibitzer does is "kibitz."

*klutz. A clumsy, often stupid person. The derived adjective, "klutzy," is more often applied to things (e.g., a piece of furniture, a theatrical performance) than to people.

kosher. Originally, conforming to Jewish dietary laws (as, food or cooking utensils), but now widely used in the sense of legitimate, on the up-and-up (e.g., a business deal).

*maven. Literally, a scholar, hence an expert, but often used with an ironic twist suggesting that the expert's expertise may be mainly in his or her own mind.

*nebbish. An insignificant, ineffectual person.

nosh. Related to "gnash," it originally meant to nibble, but now, to eat a snack. As a noun, it's the snack itself; if you give a cocktail party, you serve noshes with the drinks.

schlemiel. A fool or incompetent person.

*schlep. Literally, to drag; hence, to transport or travel laboriously ("I had to schlep my kids to Macy's to see Santa Claus"). As a noun, a difficult or laborious journey ("With the Christ-

mas traffic, it was a hell of a schlep to Macy's").

schlock. Junk, goods of very low quality; hence, as an adjective, junky, tawdry. Many years ago I reviewed a best-selling book of pop sociology; my article was titled "Future Schlock."

*schlong. A rude term ultimately derived from the German *Schlange,* snake, and meaning precisely the organ you would expect.

*schlimazl. A luckless person, loser. If a waiter spills hot soup down a customer's neck, the waiter is a schlemiel or, perhaps, a klutz; the customer is a schlimazl.

*schmotta. Literally, a rag, hence a worn garment, or, humorously, women's garments generally (it is the ultimate source of the British slang term for the garment industry, "the rag trade"). A Jewish lady, complimented on her dress, might say deprecatingly "Oh, *this* old schmotta!"

schmuck. Ultimately, from a German word meaning "jewel, adornment"; in Yiddish, originally a man's most precious adornment, then an unpleasant male epithet (as its English equivalent still is). Today, most people use it to mean merely an unpleasant schlemiel, but some elderly Jews still consider it a vulgar expression.

zaftig. (Of a woman): well endowed; pleasingly plump.

Quite apart from its noticeable impact on the American vocabulary, Yiddish has influenced American syntax—something that, as far as I know, can't be said of any other language. As any linguistician will tell you, languages don't, strictly speaking, "borrow" syntactic constructions from other tongues. However, foreign-born speakers of a language often translate phrases or sentences of their native tongue literally into their adopted one, and the resulting constructions are occasionally adopted by native speakers.

Certain types of **INVERSION**, as "This I've got to see" and "With friends like him, you don't need enemies" are very likely translations of Yiddish sentences, and the phrase "by me" (as in "O.K. by me") is unquestionably a literal translation of the Yiddish phrase *bei mir.*

YOURS (VERY) TRULY/(VERY) TRULY YOURS. "Yours truly," "Yours very truly" and "Very truly yours" are all acceptable closings for a business letter; "Truly yours," for some curious reason, is considered substandard. Nor can you say just "Truly," though you *can* say "Sincerely," along with "Yours sincerely" and "Sincerely yours." The simplest and safest course is to always start with "Yours," followed by anything you please. So I will conclude this Guide by signing myself

Yours very truly,

Robert Claiborne

SELECTED BIBLIOGRAPHY

DICTIONARIES
American Heritage Dictionary (1973)
Random House Dictionary (1966)
Funk and Wagnalls New Standard Dictionary (1959)
Webster's Third International Dictionary (1964)

Both of the first two employed usage panels to guide them on disputed questions, and either one will give you a pretty good idea of how most respectable people feel about these matters. So far as the *facts* of usage are concerned, they seem equally reliable—or unreliable.

Funk and Wagnalls ignores many usage questions (e.g., **hopefully**) and is sometimes inaccurate or confusing on others. For instance, it describes **aggravate** (to annoy) as "erroneous"—but now established. I'd say that no usage established for over three centuries can properly be called erroneous—although it might be undesirable for other reasons.

Webster's Third gives *no* guidance on usage, for which it was widely and, I think, justly criticized. However one views a particular usage controversy, such controversies exist, and a dictionary that pretends they don't isn't doing its job. The volume also contains some odd recent coinages —e.g., "funeralize" (to hold a funeral or memorial service for). These inclusions are unimportant, except insofar as they might mislead people into thinking that the words in question are or were in general use— which "funeralize" certainly never was.

OTHER WORKS

Since writing books about words is a minor industry in this country, it would be pointless to try and list all those now in print. The following titles include books referred to in the text, and some others that are sufficiently well known to be worth mentioning, if sometimes only by way of warning. Starred (*) titles are available in paperback.

Bernstein, Theodore M.

> *The Careful Writer: A Modern Guide to English Usage.* New York: Atheneum, 1965, (paper) 1983.

> *Dos, Don'ts and Maybes of English Usage.* New York: Times Books, 1977.

Curiously, the earlier of these is the more useful; *Dos and Don'ts* is less comprehensive, and includes a good deal of extraneous material. Indeed, I'd call *TCW* the single most useful guide to "respectable" usage you can get—though I wish the publisher would hire someone to update it. As my own text makes clear, I don't always agree with Bernstein, and sometimes he's simply wrong on the facts (as who isn't). But if *he* approves a particular usage, not even the stodgiest academic can reasonably criticize *you* for adopting it. A further plus is his style, which is invariably courteous and almost invariably clear.

Bryant, Margaret M.

> *Current American Usage.* New York: Funk and Wagnalls, 1962.

Now out of print, but obtainable in large urban libraries. Though inevitably somewhat dated, it's worth checking out because it is one of the few usage guides solidly based on scholarly studies of how the language is actually used, rather than how the author thinks it should be used.

Claiborne, Robert

> *Our Marvelous Native Tongue: The Life and Times of the English Language.* New York: Times Books, 1983.

As its title indicates, this book is not mainly about usage. But if you're interested in the history of our language, and especially in how its extraordinarily rich and diversified vocabulary got that way, then this— though I say it as shouldn't—is the book for you. The paperback edition is currently available only through the Quality Paperback Book Club, but a regular, trade paperback is scheduled for late 1986.

Follett, Wilson

Modern American Usage: A Guide. New York: Hill and Wang, 1966.

Follett died in 1963; his book was completed and edited by Jacques Barzun. If you know anything about Barzun, you can guess that the book is somewhat old-fashioned: I'd call it the last word on American usage circa 1950. It also tells you a lot more than you probably want to know about many subjects, and not always in the clearest language.

Fowler, H. W.

A Dictionary of Modern English Usage. 2d ed. New York: Oxford University Press, 1965, (paper) 1983.

Fowler was the Grand Old Man of English usage (he died in 1933). Even the revised edition of his book is now somewhat dated; more to the point, it reflects primarily British rather than American usage.

Morris, William and Mary

Harper Dictionary of Contemporary Usage. New York: Harper and Row, 1975; 2d ed., 1985.

Unfortunately, the second edition of this guide appeared when my own manuscript was in its final stages, so that the quotations I have used are all from the first edition. I have, however, checked out the revised version, and have to report that it isn't much of an improvement on the original: it contains the same loaded questions (e.g., under "hopefully") and the same misinformation (e.g., under "aggravate")—sometimes word for word. Nominally, it's more up to date than Bernstein's *The Careful Writer;* practically, I think you'll find the latter more useful.

Newman, Edwin R.

Strictly Speaking. Indianapolis: Bobbs-Merrill, 1974; New York: Warner Books, 1975.

A Civil Tongue. Indianapolis: Bobbs-Merrill, 1976; New York: Warner Books, 1977.

Newman, as a TV newsman, is one of the better-known usage experts, and one of the least reliable: he simply doesn't bother with the facts.

Even worse—and despite the title of his second book—his own tongue is often far from civil, since he habitually snarls at those who don't use English as he thinks they should. Finally, a good part of both books doesn't deal with usage at all, but rather with Newman's views on the state of the nation. I share those views more often than not, but don't find them notably original or well expressed—not sufficiently so, at least, to have encouraged me to finish either work.

Safire, William

   On Language. New York: Times Books, 1980; Avon, 1981.

   What's the Good Word? New York: Times Books, 1982; Avon, 1983.

Since both books are collections of newspaper columns, they can't (and weren't intended to) serve as guides. However, Safire is often fun to read, and his approach is far less dogmatic than you might expect from his political columns. (My private theory is that Safire is really nonidentical twins, both named William: one writes on politics, the other on language.) He makes mistakes, of course—occasionally silly ones—but is perfectly willing to admit it when they're pointed out. Nobody who does that can be all bad.

Simon, John

   Paradigms Lost: Reflections on Literacy and Its Decline. New York: C. N. Potter, 1980; Penguin, 1981.

If you think English usage should have been put into a permanent deep freeze in 1940 and despise anyone who thinks otherwise, Simon's your man. He's not mine: as my references to him in the text indicate, I find him both unreliable and dogmatic. And in a badmouthing contest, he'd probably nose out even Newman.

(Anonymous)

   "Punctuation" and Style. San Diego: Oasis Systems, 1982.

Since this is the first book I've written on a computer, it occurred to me to check out software dealing with usage. This is the best-known (for all I know the only) program on the subject—and it's not very good. Some of its judgments I disagree with, and some, I think, almost any usage expert would reject. In particular, the substitutes it proposes for "questionable" usages are often not really synonyms; that is, using them will change your meaning. Worst of all (and in contrast with available spelling-checker programs), it is completely inflexible: there is no way you can revise or expand it to reflect your own needs and judgment. I still think a usage program could be valuable, but writing it will require far more expertise than went into this one.

INDEX